SOUTH BRIDGE
CATALOGUED
RCommonism
Bouscaren
47085

TO BE
DISPOSED
BY
AUTHORITY

A Guide to Anti-Communist Action

by

Anthony Trawick Bouscaren
Associate Professor of Political Science
at Marquette University

with Chapters by

David Sarnoff

"Ferreus"

Geoffrey F. Hudson

John Foster Dulles

Hanson Baldwin

Captain W. D. Puleston, U.S.N.

Herbert R. O'Conor

and an Introduction by

Mark Graubard

HENRY REGNERY COMPANY

Chicago: 1958

© 1958
HENRY REGNERY COMPANY
CHICAGO 4, ILLINOIS

LIBRARY OF CONGRESS CATALOG INFORMATION

Bouscaren, Anthony Trawick.

A guide to anti-communist action. With chapters by David Sarnoff [and others] and an introd. by Mark Graubard. Chicago, H. Regnery Co., 1958. 244 p. 22 cm. Includes bibliography. 1. Communism–Hist. 2. World politics–1945– 1. Title. HX40.B64. 335.4. 58–12406 ‡

Manufactured in the United States of America

To Harry Lynde Bradley, Patriot; to the Freedom Fighters of Hungary and to those in the other nations enslaved, in whole or in part: May your courage be matched in the nations still free, so that our inevitable victory over Communism will be hastened.

Contents

Preface

FBI Director J. Edgar Hoover wrote in 1956: "We are not entering an 'era of peace.' Contrary to the opinion of wishful thinkers, the threat of Communist tyranny has not been lessened. The unaltering Communist goal of world domination has not been rejected in favor of 'peaceful coexistence,' nor has the recent 'desanctification' of Stalin severed the umbilical cord which binds the Communist Party, U.S.A., to that of the Soviet Union."[1] Since the Twentieth Congress of the Communist party of the U.S.S.R., convened in February, 1956, international Communism has stressed what it calls "the return to Leninism."

The essence of Lenin's philosophy is found in Volume 10 of his *Collected Works*: "As long as capitalism and socialism exist, we cannot live in peace; in the end, one or the other will triumph. This is a respite in war. . . . From the point of view of the danger of a collision between capitalism and Bolshevism, it must be said that concessions are a continuation of the war, but in a different sphere."

On June 30, 1956, the Central Committee of the Communist party of the U.S.S.R. issued a resolution designed to answer Marxist criticism of the Twentieth Congress. This resolution asserted that Stalin had made many contributions to the advance of Communism, and it also reiterated the doctrine of force and violence as basic to bringing about the transition from Socialism to Communism and the withering away of the state.[2]

The Communist *Daily Worker*, in its issue of September 30, 1956, urged all Communist-front organizations to dissolve and instructed their members to penetrate non-Communist groups. To avoid becoming isolated, and thus neutralized, Communist leaders told their followers to revive the Popular Front strategem of the 1930's, when friends of the Soviet Union reached the top echelons in writing, education, entertainment, industry, and government. This was the heyday of Alger Hiss, Harry Dexter White, Henry Collins, Nathan Witt, John Abt, Nathan Gregory Silvermaster, Frank Coe, and Harold Glasser, and of the Institute of Pacific Relations, which influenced persons in government, the universities, and the publishing industry toward a pro-Chinese Communist point of view. This issue of the *Daily Worker* declared: "The possibility of labor and popular forces gaining decisive influence in a number of key Democratic Party state organizations, coupled with a growing collaboration of independent and liberal Republican political movements, may determine the form in which a new anti-monopoly party emerges." It went on to urge all "liberals and progressives" to stand together to fight for peace, weaken the security program, and destroy the last vestiges of "McCarthyism." In short, if the Communists can convince Americans that Paul Hoffman of the Fund for the Republic is right when he says, "The greatest danger comes not from Communism, but from anti-Communism," they will have gone a long way toward achieving their objective of a Soviet America.

Most Americans realize that the international Communist movement has done great damage to the United States in the past, through espionage, infiltration, and aggression. The memory of 150,000 American casualties in Korea and the 10,000 American prisoners of war who were murdered by the Communists in Korea is still fresh in the minds of many. The continued maltreatment of American citizens behind the Iron and Bamboo curtains and the shooting down of American patrol planes over international waters by Chinese Communist and Soviet pilots are facts which cannot be ignored; nor can the brutal repression of freedom in Hungary at the end of 1956 be forgotten. The fantastic courage of the Hungarian patriots is a reminder to America that the freedom forces behind the Iron Curtain reject "coexistence" because it is incompatible with liberty.

The great majority of Americans are non-Communists (neither

pro-Communist nor anti-Communist). The minority consists of smaller groups in the population: (1) those who are Communists or who follow the lead of the Communists (as, for instance, the one million Americans who voted for the Progressive party in 1948) and (2) those Americans who are sufficiently concerned about Communist gains on a global basis since 1944 to do something about the situation. Unfortunately, however, whereas the Communists in the United States have trained young Americans at such schools as the Jefferson School in New York and the California Labor School in San Francisco, the anti-Communists have no such schools. Indeed, the overwhelming majority of students in the United States never learn anything about the reality of Communism in the classroom. This, together with a general lack of knowledge about United States government and history, led many American prisoners of war in Korea to collaborate with their Communist captors. These were the so-called "progressives." The "reactionaries" were those soldiers who remained loyal to the United States and their comrades-in-arms and refused to collaborate with the Communist enemy to any degree.[3]

There is a need for anti-Communist leadership training in the United States, and there is a demand for such training. Many Americans not only want to know the basic facts about Communist subversion and aggression, but they also want to know what they and their country can do to counteract subversion and aggression. As long as Communists throughout the world continue to consider themselves at war with the United States and insist on the establishment of a Soviet Republic in the United States as a necessary prerequisite to achieving the transition from Socialism to Communism and the withering away of the state, realistic Americans have little choice but to prepare themselves for the counterattack, the objective of which must inescapably be the permanent defeat of Communism at home and abroad.

"What can I do about it?" That is the question that always arises after a lecture or discussion about Communism. How can the

United States—and its individual citizens—most effectively block Communist aggression and subversion and ultimately defeat Communism? This book is an attempt to answer that question.

First, it is necessary to review the theory and practice of Communism and the history of Communist expansion in Europe and Asia. The second step is to recognize and evaluate the failures of Western diplomacy in its attempts to cope with Communist expansionism. The third step is to consider alternative courses of action which may succeed in securing American and Free World objectives in areas where the techniques now in use have already failed or seem likely to fail. Finally, we should consider how individuals can contribute to the defeat of Communism.

In the pages that follow, then, the reader will review the external and internal workings of Communism, and in each instance he will have offered for his consideration positive and constructive programs for combating it. Know the enemy, then attack him; this is the scheme of this book.

Seven of the eighteen chapters in this book are the contributions of others. The authors of these chapters, specialists in their fields, have described, better than I could possibly have done, how we can best act where these fields of action are involved. I am therefore indebted to David Sarnoff, "Ferreus," Professor Geoffrey F. Hudson, John Foster Dulles, Hanson Baldwin, Captain W. D. Puleston, and Herbert R. O'Conor for their incisive analyses and constructive suggestions. To Mark Graubard goes credit for the Introduction.

This book was inspired by members of my adult anti-Communist leadership training course, who urged me to prepare a short basic text on Communism and how to fight it. I am obliged to them for their inspiration, their suggestions, and their loyalty. My thanks also to David Keyser for his helpful suggestions.

ANTHONY TRAWICK BOUSCAREN

Milwaukee, Wisconsin
September 16, 1958

Introduction

What ever happened to the American sense of proportion, not to mention the American conscience? At a time when millions of people in Europe and Asia live under a communist terror, denied the elemental freedoms of action and thought which we take for granted, leading writers and intellectuals in the free United States spread abroad the falsehood that oppression and book-burning prevail in the United States, that terror stalks our universities, school boards, libraries and even haunts the average citizen.

What a contrast to the situation in the U.S.A. when another totalitarian tyrant, Adolf Hitler, rose to power! Even before the Aryan laws, the pogroms and the incineration chambers darkened the German horizon, the reaction of the American public, its Government and the college campus was prompt and unequivocal.

Opposition to Nazism in the United States was nationwide. In colleges committees were formed to aid refugees from Nazi persecution; student newspapers protested the exclusion of Jews from German universities, the burning of books and the race laws. Some Americans even suggested intervention; others demanded a boycott of German goods.

How different the scene today! For the past ten years, communism has shouted to the world that America must be destroyed; that America is the chief warmonger, the cause of world poverty and the mainspring of tyranny and oppression. Its first task was to obliterate America's good name among the peoples of the world. For this enterprise the Soviet propaganda machine has received

The introduction to this volume is reprinted from Mark Graubard, "Where Are Yesterday's Foes of Dictatorship?" *The Saturday Evening Post* (July 2, 1955). Copyright 1955 by The Curtis Publishing Company. Reprinted by permission of Mark Graubard and *The Saturday Evening Post.*

aid from the writers of hysterical books and articles deriding America as a tyrant.

Soviet propaganda has encountered no opposition of the kind that made Nazi propaganda futile in the United States. There is hardly a single campus committee to aid refugees from the sovietized universities in Europe and Asia; no student anticommunist congresses; no Women's Leagues against Concentration Camps. The eloquent voices of our liberal leaders are raised more passionately against alleged American misdeeds and tyranny than against the darkness behind the Iron Curtain. One receives no telegrams urging one's signature under a manifesto pledging the signers' "lives, fortunes, and sacred honor" to the downfall of the Red tyranny. There are no placards reading "Stop Khrushchev!" attached to the front bumpers of motorcars. There were some silly aspects of the anti-Nazi campaign in the late 1930's, but at any rate few of us confused slavery with "human engineering," or tyranny with progress.

Had American liberalism displayed the same moral vigor against communist fanaticism that it did against Hitlerism, the world might be a safer place; and our moral leadership, established by our stand against oppression in the 1930's and our unstinted effort in World War II, would be unquestioned. We are now paying dearly in taxes, confusion and fear for maintaining a double standard of political morality.

PART I

The External Communist Threat and How to Combat It

CHAPTER 1

Communist Theory and Socialism in the Soviet Union

MARXISM-LENINISM

The story of Communism properly begins with Karl Marx. It is true, of course, that "communism" with a small "c" had been advocated and practiced many years previously, but this form of "communism" is not identical with the Soviet type of Communism.

During the second quarter of the nineteenth century, Marx moved away from his native Germany, first to France and then to England. As a philosopher, he had been much impressed with the dialectical method of Hegel—a method that he grafted onto his own materialism. He borrowed not only from Hegel, but also from Feuerbach and other contemporary political thinkers. Indeed, the philosophy of Karl Marx was in large part a combination of the ideas of other men.

Marx was not a very practical man, and thus it was that his friendship with Friedrich Engels proved to be a profitable one. A partnership developed in which Marx did the thinking and writing and Engels picked up the bills. With the assistance of Engels, Marx influenced certain people who were attracted to the doctrines of "dialectical materialism" and formed the First International—a Marxist coalition bent on achieving political and economic control, first on a national and then on an international scale. Marx's two most important works were the *Communist Manifesto,* and *Das Kapital.* Here he expounded his theories about capitalism, the proletariat, imperialism, and the ultimate withering away of the state.

Marx held that historical development depends to a large extent upon economic factors. According to Marx, the mode of production and distribution of a given era determines all the manifestations of that era—politics, religion, art, social structure, and so forth. He insisted that the capitalist mode of the nineteenth century would lead to inevitable class struggle; Marxism as embellished by Lenin held that the great world powers would clash with each other over world markets and that they would be internally plagued by proletarian revolutions. The proletarians would overthrow the capitalists by sheer force of numbers and with the aid of imperialistic wars; these proletarians would then establish, first in one country and then in all countries, the "dictatorship of the proletariat." However, this could not be successfully accomplished unless the proletariat were led by a "class-conscious vanguard." This vanguard was the Communist party—itself not necessarily proletarian in character. Marx, like Lenin and Stalin after him, had nothing but contempt for romantically minded revolutionaries who wished to man the barricades upon the least whim or fancy. These three also frowned upon humanitarian-minded reformers who would not go all the way into revolution. They insisted that the proletariat be led by a professional, well-disciplined elite, which would make the decisions and call the tune. In effect, therefore, the result would be not a dictatorship of the proletariat, but rather a dictatorship of the Communist party.

According to Marxism-Leninism, the establishment of a dictatorship in the country which was most advanced industrially (probably Germany) would be followed by the establishment of similar dictatorships in other countries and ultimately throughout the world. Then a miraculous event would take place: *the state would wither away.* Following the creation of a world proletarian dictatorship, the state—police, army, tax collectors, the bureaucracy—would wither away, and the "government of persons would be replaced by the administration of things." Socialism would then be replaced by true Communism, and all would live in proletarian bliss.

Marx's end might have been no different from that of other lunatic-fringe philosophers except for the fact that his ideas were carried by his followers to Russia, where they actually came to power. Ironically, the Marxian doctrine first achieved success in Russia—a relatively backward agrarian country—and not in Germany or any industrially advanced country. Marxian Communism became important, not so much because of its quite unscientific ideology, but mainly because its proponents gained control of a territorial state, raw materials, a promising economy, and a military force. If the Communists had not gained control of a state, Communism would simply have remained one of many exotic political theories. We are today little concerned about Trotskyites, Kautskyites, and similar Marxist dissidents. Since they control no governments, military forces, or atom bombs, they do not immediately threaten America. Marxian Communism, however—Soviet version—is vitally important to all Americans because it controls a vast Soviet empire which has killed American soldiers with its T-34 tanks and MIG-15 planes. The soldiers in Korea were not afraid of Communism the idea but of Communism the military force. During World War II, we feared the ideology of National Socialism less than the power of the *Wehrmacht* and the *Luftwaffe*. Communism has gained control of eastern and central China, North Korea, and North Viet-Nam by military power and diplomacy, bolstered by the activity of Soviet fifth columns called Communist parties. Communism, then, is basically Soviet power: military, diplomatic, psychological, and economic.

Marx's death was followed by a large number of quarrels among his followers, who frequently disagreed on their interpretation of the master's teachings. A Second International was formed by Marxian Socialists, but Socialists in France, Germany, Russia, and elsewhere gradually became divided into two camps: those who believed that Marx meant what he said about the need for wars and revolutions to create proletarian dictatorships and those who wished to strive for the realization of Marxian ideals within the framework of parliamentary government. These two Socialist factions occasionally attempted "unity" meetings to try to come to some sort of agreement on doctrine. At one such meeting held in London in 1903, the Russian Socialists met to seek harmony. The leader of the moderates was Martov, and the leader of the extremists was Lenin. The meeting ended in a complete break between the two factions. From that day until January, 1918, Russian Socialists were classified as either Martov-Mensheviks or Lenin-Bolsheviks. The term "Bolshevik" means majority; it so happened that at the London meeting, Lenin's group was in the majority. In Russia and western Europe, however, the evolutionary, or moderate, Socialists (Mensheviks) predominated.

RUSSIA IN 1917

The story of Communism (Bolshevik Socialism) now turns to Russia itself. March, 1917, saw increasing internal discontent with the Russian participation in World War I on the side of the Allies. The czarist government of Nicholas II had proved inefficient and, in some cases, corrupt. Distribution of food in the cities was poorly handled, and soldiers were sometimes ordered to attack without guns. The slow-but-sure development of constitutional government and national reform which had characterized Russia from 1850 to 1914 had ended abruptly with the advent of war. As the war went more and more against Russia, the leading political groups pressed for a more honest and vigorous government. These leading political groups were the Social Revolutionaries (agrarian radicals), Menshevik Socialists (evolutionary Marxists), and the Conservatives. The Bolsheviks were not at that time an important political faction.

Political leadership of the Parliament (Duma) was in the hands of Aleksandr Kerenski and Prince Lvov. These men finally prevailed upon Nicholas II to abdicate in favor of his brother, Grand Duke Mikhail. The latter indicated that he was willing to await the decision of a constituent assembly on whether Russia would remain a monarchy or become a republic. Pending this decision, Kerenski and Lvov established a provisional republic. This regime controlled Russia from March, 1917, to November of the same year. The constituent assembly never had a chance to make a decision on the future of Russia, for it was destroyed by Bolshevist bayonets in January, 1918, following the election of an anti-Bolshevist majority.

The March "revolution," by which the Kerenski provisional government came into existence, was, comparatively speaking, a minor uprising in which most of the people seemed to acquiesce. Discouraged with the czarist war effort, the people seemed willing to let Kerenski and Lvov try to improve matters. The three parties supporting this revolution had a majority in the Duma, which was now granted wider powers. The party leaders promised to bring reforms to Russia while staying in the war as loyal allies of Britain and France.

Kerenski soon gained the upper hand in the provisional government and promised to bring "democracy" to Russia overnight, even during a war and regardless of whether or not the Russian people were ready for it. This misguided idealism was to be Kerenski's undoing. Soldiers in the front lines were told that they could elect their officers and vote on whether to attack the Germans or go back to their farms. The result of this misguided application of "democracy" was chaos and anarchy—which the Bolsheviks and the Germans were quick to take advantage of.

At this time (the spring of 1917), the German general staff sought ways and means of liquidating the eastern (Russian) front so that the entire German war effort could be directed against France and the western front. The Germans were therefore interested in any Russian political faction which might be persuaded to collaborate with them on the basis of a mutual aim: overthrow of the Kerenski regime in Russia and its replacement by a new Russian government which would make a deal with Germany and pull out of the war. Only one such political faction existed—the Bolsheviks of Lenin.

German emissaries met with Lenin, who was in exile in Switzerland, and discussed with him the possibilities of co-operation against the Russian government. Both would benefit by such a collaboration; Germany would be able to liquidate the eastern front, and the Bolsheviks would gain control of Russia. Lenin agreed to the German plan, and the German government transported the leading Bolsheviks to Petrograd (formerly St. Petersburg, now Leningrad). Germany promised Lenin financial support and the full assistance of German agents.

Shortly after Lenin's arrival in Petrograd in the spring of 1917, Trotsky arrived from New York, and Stalin, who had recently escaped from jail, joined his superiors. These three and their associates determined on a course of action to win control of Russia: They would conceal their real motives and utilize slogans designed to deceive the people with respect to their ultimate intentions. The Bolsheviks proceeded to infiltrate and control political organizations known as the "Soviets," or Councils, which were intended to represent the workers and soldiers. Operating under the banner of the Soviets, the Bolsheviks were able to command the loyalty of many persons who might otherwise not have helped them. A good many Russians continued to support the Soviets without realizing that they had fallen under the control of the Bolsheviks. The Bolsheviks camouflaged their basically antireligious doctrines and paraded under the popular slogans of "bread, land, and peace."

Meanwhile, the Kerenski government continued its foolhardy attempt to make Russia a democracy overnight. The ensuing breakdown of authority was duly noted by the Bolsheviks. They encouraged defeatism, fraternization, and desertions in the army, and the Soviets gradually evolved into a shadow government which challenged the authority of the Kerenski regime. Some persons joined them solely through disgust with the antics of the provisional government. In July, the Bolsheviks tested their strength in an abortive revolt. It failed, and they decided to pull in their horns and await a more auspicious moment.

This moment was forthcoming in November, 1917. By this time, Kerenski's intervention in military affairs had progressed to the point where the Russian chief of staff, General Kornilov, felt that it was time to protest. He told Kerenski that he could no longer permit "democracy" in the army and that further attempts to bring politics into the war effort would not be tolerated. Kerenski was enraged and accused Kornilov of planning a *coup d'état*. To defend himself against the army chief, Kerenski accepted allies wherever he could find them—including the Bolsheviks, who were hiding under the banner of the Soviets. This was Kerenski's great error. Actually, the Kornilov "threat" was nothing compared to that of the Soviets. Kerenski, however, insisted on soliciting Bolshevik support in a program to undermine the authority of Russian army officers. With Kerenski's attention riveted on Kornilov, the "Red Guards" of Trotsky suddenly seized the public buildings in Petrograd and Moscow, paralyzed the public utilities, and proclaimed a new Soviet regime. From early November until the end of 1921, Russia was submerged in a blood bath, with the Bolshevik Soviet fighting to retain its bridgeheads of power in the cities. By the early part of 1918, the Soviet regime had shown itself to be ruthless and cunning enough to gain a stronghold in the Russian heartland, a strangle hold which the Whites (anti-Bolsheviks) were never quite able to break.

EVOLUTION OF THE SOVIET REGIME

Upon coming to power in November, 1917, Lenin and his colleagues proclaimed the three basic features of the new Soviet government, features which have been retained to the present day through Lenin, Stalin, and Khrushchev: (1) political dictatorship; (2) state economy; (3) the doctrine of inevitability of conflict with the outside world until a world Soviet government has been established. The new Soviet regime quickly abolished the Constituent Assembly, which had been elected by an anti-Bolshevik majority; and concluded a treaty with Germany (the Treaty of Brest Litovsk) to carry out its bargain with the German general staff. And it changed the name of the only political party from "Bolshevik" to "Communist."

The Soviet leaders expected spontaneous Communist revolutions to break out all over the world, but these did not materialize. Only in Hungary was there anything like a success. The hoped-for German revolt quickly failed when most German Socialists turned against the German Communists. By 1921, Lenin could only conclude that Communist revolutions could not be spontaneous but had to be carefully planned and executed under Soviet leadership. From that day to this, no local Communist party has staged a successful revolution giving it governmental control without the diplomatic and/or military support of the Soviet government. Lenin decided that the best course of action was to forego, for the moment, the creation of a world Soviet government and concentrate on building up Soviet Russia so that it could become a pattern for world revolution. Increasingly, then, the Soviet army and Soviet diplomacy were substituted for Communist revolution, which nowhere materialized.

Within Russia, the Bolsheviks (now called Communists) attempted to carry out Marxian doctrine as it related to state economy, but the project met with considerable resistance, especially from the peasants, who opposed collectivization. By 1921, Lenin and his lieutenants decided that concessions would have to be made to the peasants and, to a lesser degree, to the city merchants in order to gain at least passive obedience from these factions. This was called the New Economic Policy. It lasted until 1928. The adoption of this policy coincided with the victory of the Red Army over the scattered White forces and the end of the war with Poland, which was marked by the Treaty of Riga.

During the middle of the New Economic Policy (1924), Lenin died. He was succeeded by a triumvirate of Stalin, Kamenev, and Zinoviev, with Trotsky still present as a threat to their power. Stalin used Kamenev and Zinoviev as tools against Trotsky, forcing the latter out of the party in 1927. Trotsky was first sent to Siberia, then exiled. However, he refused to remain silent, and in 1940, Stalin dispatched an agent to Mexico City, where he promptly sank a pickax into Trotsky's skull. After Stalin had exiled Trotsky, he proceeded to pit Kamenev and Zinoviev against each other and finally executed both of them in the purge trials of the 1930's.

In 1928, the end of the New Economic Policy, Stalin abandoned the concessions to free enterprise and launched the first Five-Year Plan, which was aimed at industrializing Russia, with emphasis on electrification. In order to achieve many economic projects in remote areas of the Soviet Union, Stalin began to utilize that characteristic Soviet contribution to modern civilization—slave labor. Compulsory labor camps were built, first in the Arkhangelsk-Murmansk area and then in Siberia. Today the Soviet population includes an estimated fifteen million slave laborers.

In 1934, Stalin's ostensible protégé, Kirov, was assassinated in Leningrad. Stalin used his death as a pretext to launch the infamous purges, which lasted until early 1939. Stalin called this the "cleansing process." Among those brought to the bar of "justice" by Chief Prosecutor Andrei Vishinski were Zinoviev, Kamenev, Rykov, and many other former Bolshevik heroes. One leading authority described the parade of persons purged during these fateful years as constituting a "who's who of the Communist party in the 'twenties." At the end of 1938 and the beginning of 1939, the purges carried over into the army. The famous Marshal Tukhachevski and most of his chief lieutenants died violent deaths. By the spring of 1939, Stalin proudly announced that the cleansing process had been accomplished; he stated that Soviet Russia was at long last a one-class state. Someone then asked him if this meant that the state would then wither away. Stalin replied that this would not occur until "capitalist encirclement" had been eliminated and a world Soviet government established through wars and revolutions.

In 1936, the famous "Stalin Constitution" was proclaimed. This "constitution" purported to grant certain rights and liberties to the people of the Union of Soviet Socialist Republics. Actually, it did nothing of the sort. Indeed Stalin admitted that the leading position of the Communist party in Soviet life remained unimpaired. The Stalin Constitution, on paper, created a Council of Ministers (cabinet), a Presidium (legislative committee), a Supreme Soviet (bicameral legislature), and sixteen state governments. Theoretically, the people elected the lower house of the Supreme Soviet directly, with the upper house representing the states. The line of command then allegedly went through the Presidium to the Council of Ministers and the Premier. Actually, the Stalin Constitution did nothing to change the real power of the Soviet Union, the Communist party. The party organization was still the real source of power. The governmental organization was simply the façade, or screen. At the top of the party structure stood the Politburo, followed by the Organization Buro, the Secretariat, the party's Central Committee, and finally the regional and local party groupings. In theory, six million party members elected a party Congress, which in turn elected the Central Committee and the buro. Actually, power in the party (as in the government) ran from top to bottom. Stalin, the dictator, dominated both the party and governmental structures. He was Premier, Secretary of the Communist party, and Generalissimo of the Army. The Politburo members were, for the most part, also the members of the Council of Ministers (cabinet). The party Congress corresponded to the governmental Supreme Soviet (legislature).

The Soviet state is like a coin—the government is one side, the party on the other. Six million party members control 215,000,000 non-party Soviet citizens, and among the 6,000,000 party members, only the inner clique actually has any power. This clique is the general staff of the party organization—the Central Committee and its immediate creations. Only in theory do the people elect their government. In fact, there is only one choice. Stalin never lost an election, and Khrushchev doesn't propose to.

WORLD WAR II AND AFTER

The Hitler-Stalin pact caught the Soviet people unawares. For several years they had been warned about the Fascist threat. Now, said Stalin, Fascism was but a matter of taste. The Russians were told that England and France were the real enemies and that Hitler was not such a villain after all. Hitler gave Stalin a sphere of influence in eastern Poland, Finland, the Baltic States, and portions of Romania.

In January, 1941, however, Hitler decided that Stalin's application for membership in the Axis carried too many provisos.[1] Hitler therefore launched "Operation Barbarossa." On June 22, German armies began to cut through western Russia like a hot knife slicing through butter. Stalin, who had sent military aid to Germany during the Nazi-Soviet honeymoon, found it difficult to explain the new situation to his people. With the Communist party already long discredited in the eyes of the people, Stalin begged the Russians to defend Mother Russia, the Orthodox church, and the Slavic race. It was only through these elemental appeals that Stalin was able to get even passive support from many Soviet citizens. Nonetheless, many Soviet soldiers surrendered to the onrushing German forces, regarding them as their liberators from the hated Communist oppressors.

Only the tactics described above, together with all-out aid from America and Britain, saved Russia. In addition, Stalin's alliance with Japan permitted him to concentrate all his forces on the German front. Hitler, meanwhile, sought to fight in North Africa and man Fortress Europe in addition to conquering Russia. The wonder is that he succeeded as long as he did.

The end of World War II saw no relaxation in Soviet Russia. The military establishment remained intact, and German scientists were put to work on nuclear weapons and missiles programs. Appeals to the people stressed adulation for the old czarist military and political heroes. The Soviet government proclaimed that the Russians had discovered television, the "coke" machine, the jet engine, the atomic bomb, the skyscraper, and most of the other paraphernalia of modern life. It was even claimed that the game of baseball was a Russian invention! At the same time, however, all elements of the population were reminded that Communist doctrine remained supreme. Purges were carried out in the arts and sciences. Soviet scientists were told what to think about heredity and environment. Soviet musicians were warned to be on the lookout for insidious capitalistic influences in their music. Soviet athletes were instructed to win or suffer the consequences.

The death of Stalin in early March, 1953, brought Georgi Malenkov to power, supported by Beria, Molotov, Bulganin, and Khrushchev. However, Malenkov's power did not last, and party boss Khrushchev became dictator. Beria was purged, and in February, 1955, Malenkov was ousted as Premier, to be succeeded by Bulganin; Khrushchev, however, retained real power.[2] Two years later, Malenkov and Molotov were ousted from the party Presidium; in 1957, Marshal Zhukov was purged, and in 1958, Bulganin was downgraded. Khrushchev reigned supreme.

SOVIET SOCIAL STRUCTURE

Soviet society remains rigidly stratified. It is more class conscious than any other society. Each class has its own shops, seats in theatres, sections in trains and stations, and sometimes even uniforms. Generally speaking, there exist four main classes: the "intelligentsia" (state employees of top rank), the rural and urban workers, the peasants, and the slave-labor class. The intelligentsia includes the party leadership and dominates Soviet life in every sector. Most of the intelligentsia come from the ranks of the seventeen million members of the Comsomol (Young Communists). One

Comsomol in three joins the Communist party at the age of twenty-six. The rest take key positions in government, education, the mass media, and industry. The rural and urban workers are mobilized in a government-operated union which rules them in military fashion. Strikes are not permitted, and tardiness at work is severely punished. The peasants are mobilized in huge collective farms; they must deliver grain quotas to the state, retaining only what they can produce above and beyond the high quotas. In agriculture, as in industry, work norms are determined by the Stakhanovites—the pacemakers—whose output serves as a goal to all workers. If a worker cannot keep pace with the Stakhanovite, his pay is reduced. The sick and the aged do not survive long under this sweatshop system. Finally, there are the slave laborers—more numerous than the "free" laborers. The slave-labor class is, economically, the most productive. It has built many of the gigantic dams, canals, military installations, and mines of the Soviet empire.

In its essentials, the Soviet Union of today differs little, if at all, from the regimes of Lenin and Stalin.[3] The basic doctrines of the Soviet government remain: political dictatorship, state economy, and inevitability of conflict with the outside world.[4] Khrushchev proclaims himself to be a faithful disciple of Lenin—the architect of world revolution.

CHAPTER 2

Soviet Foreign Policy and International Communism

THEORETICAL FOUNDATIONS

The basis of Soviet foreign policy is found in the Marxian doctrine of class conflict and revolutionary war. Thus within each state, the "proletarian class," led by the "class-conscious vanguard" (Communist party), will overthrow the "capitalist class" to create the dictatorship of the proletariat or, more exactly, the dictatorship of the Communist party. Simultaneously, industrially advanced "capitalist" states will turn to "imperialism" and find themselves at war, not only with "backward colonial areas," but with each other. The existing "dictatorship of the proletariat" (Communist party) and its allies will proceed to transform these wars into revolutionary struggles and, by military force and cold war techniques, ultimately establish Communist dictatorships throughout the world. It is in this way that the Soviet leadership proposes to destroy the non-Soviet realm by force and violence and create a world Soviet government. At this stage of history the state (Soviet) "withers away," and Socialism is replaced by Communism; the millenium has arrived.

This is the strategy of Soviet foreign policy: to build a Soviet world through wars, revolutions, and diplomacy. Soviet strategy has remained constant from Lenin through Stalin to Khrushchev. It is based on the fundamental proposition that peaceful coexistence between the Soviet and non-Soviet realms is impossible. As Lenin once said: "One or the other must conquer; a number of terrible clashes is inevitable." Accordingly, no matter how much the non-Soviet realm may wish to coexist with the Soviet empire, there can be no such coexistence, inasmuch as Soviet leadership has ruled out its long-range possibility. This fundamental proposition can be proved from two sources: first, the writings of the Soviet leadership and secondly, the behavior of the Soviet government in world affairs.

Lenin, Stalin, and their successors have written a number of books and articles, have delivered countless speeches, and have otherwise indicated what their intentions are toward the Free (non-Soviet) World. The basic documents are Lenin's *State and Revolution* and *Imperialism,* and Stalin's *Problems of Leninism.* These emphasize the long-range possibility of peaceful coexistence between the Soviet and non-Soviet realms. These basic texts, reissued each year for the guidance of the Communist elite, are to be taken more seriously than occasional statements by Soviet leaders to the effect that the Soviets want peace. Indeed, if one understands what the Soviets mean by "peace," one can see that fundamentally, there is no contradiction between the basic documents and the peaceful-sounding statements which are issued at various times to lull the outside world into a false sense of security. Lenin and his successors have repeatedly pointed out that "peace" can only be achieved under the conditions of a world Soviet government. Until this end is achieved, wars and revolutions are necessary to destroy the non-Soviet states. When the Soviet leadership says it wants peace, it actually means that it wants war, so that the last remaining obstacles to a Soviet "peace" can be eliminated. This long-range Soviet strategy is in no way changed by tactical applications of the Soviet "peace policy" or the united-front ruse. The two latter techniques are employed to confuse non-Soviet states and to encourage them to make concessions to the Soviets at the conference table in the name of "peace."[1]

STRATEGY CONSTANT, TACTICS CHANGING

The essentially warlike Soviet strategy, as evidenced by the writings of the Soviet leaders, is confirmed by the behavior of the Soviet Union in international politics. Ten important conflicts have been instigated by the international Communist movement: (1) those with the Baltic States, Poland, and the Transcaucasian Federation during the years 1919–1921; (2) the attack in Manchuria in 1929; (3) the intervention in Spain in 1934 and, more successfully, between 1936 and 1939; (4) the invasion of Poland, the Baltic States, and Romania between 1939 and 1941; (5) the invasion ("liberation") of formerly independent states in eastern and central Europe between 1944–1947; (6) the intervention in Greece, first in 1944 and then in 1947; (7) the Chinese "civil war" from 1945 to 1949; (8) the instigation of civil wars and guerrilla activity in Viet-Nam and southeastern Asia after World War II; (9) the invasion of the Republic of Korea on June 25, 1950; (10) the Soviet invasion of Hungary in 1956. Soviet and Communist "conflict management" in Indonesia and in the United Arab Republic during 1957 and 1958 could also be added to the list.

How much has been gained in the expansion of the international Communist movement through wars, fifth columns, and diplomacy can readily be seen by comparing the Soviet Union in 1939 with the Soviet empire of today. In 1939, the U.S.S.R. comprised 8,000,000 square miles of territory, with a population of 170,000,000; today the empire extends to 16,000,000 square miles of territory and a population of 970,000,000.[2] Continued Communist aggressiveness in the Middle East and Far East makes it clear that Moscow has not abandoned its long-term goal of conquering the world. Aggressive and warlike Soviet behavior confirms the Soviet *Mein Kampf*: As far as the Kremlin is concerned, peaceful coexistence between the international Communist movement and the non-Soviet realm is impossible; wars and revolutions instigated by the Soviet leaders will continue until the Communist version of "peace" (a world Soviet Union) is achieved. As Khrushchev once told a Western leader: "We will bury you."

So much for Soviet strategy. What confuses many persons is the fact that from time to time the U.S.S.R. adopts tactical changes which appear to wishful thinkers as changes in strategy. For example, some people claimed in 1941, when Russia became our ally in Europe, that Stalin had changed into an "old-fashioned Russian nationalist"; Malenkov's accession to power in 1953 caused certain "experts" to believe that the subsequent tactical changes in Soviet policy really meant a change in strategy—that world revolution had been abandoned as a goal. Zhukov's prominence in 1955 led others to believe that his old "friendship" with Eisenhower might lead to a "reduction of tensions." Khrushchev's speech to the Twentieth Congress of the Russian Communist party on February 14, 1956, caused many to conclude that the Soviets had given up their insistence on force and violence as a methodology.[3]

Lenin and Stalin reiterated many times that whatever advances the cause of world revolution is good. Tactical changes take place with the "ebb" and "flow" of the revolutionary tide. Lenin laid down the principle that Communist policy must "zig" and "zag" in order to reach the ultimate goal; he described this procedure as "taking one step backwards in order to take two steps forward." Thus Moscow exploits areas of weakness and advances until it meets stiff opposition, at which time it halts temporarily to disclaim hostile intentions and lull the opposition by talk of "peace."

The two most frequently employed Communist tactics are the frontal attack and the united-front or "peace" tactic. These two and their variations have been utilized at least eight times. The first tactical period started in 1918 with a drive toward world revolution and ended in disillusionment in 1921. Lenin, far from realizing his fond dream of immediately successful "spontaneous" Communist revolutions in other countries, found himself fighting for his very life at home—against the "White" armies, the Poles, and for what at one time looked like effective foreign intervention. He and his associates then realized that Communism could be exported successfully only after the consolidation of power in Russia and the establishment of a sturdy base of operations at home. This meant industrializing Russia, building an effective military force, training fifth columns, and purging the weak and the suspect. In the future, the power of the Soviet Union was to be substituted for Communist revolutions that had nowhere permanently succeeded. Meanwhile, the Communist International was created to implement the subjection of Communist parties abroad to Moscow.

The second tactical period began in 1921 and ended with the abolition of the "New Economic Policy" (appeasement of the peasants) in 1928. This period was marked by consolidation of power in Russia and relative calm abroad. Stalin's doctrine of "Socialism in one country"—widely misinterpreted abroad—held that world revolution would have to wait until Soviet power had been sufficiently developed in the U.S.S.R.

The third period began in 1929 and closed in 1934. Stalin tried to take advantage of a world depression to foment civil strife and bring about the collapse of capitalism. The Communist International was more active than ever before. Soviet forces invaded Manchuria in 1929 and captured the key railroads (later sold to Japan and regained at Yalta). Communist-supported revolutionaries created a Soviet republic in Spain in 1934 during a revolt which was crushed by the Spanish army.

The fourth period lasted from 1935 to 1939. Georgi Dimitrov of the Comintern, acting under instructions from the Soviet government, ordered foreign Communists to transform themselves from wild-eyed revolutionaries into respectable "liberals" ostensibly interested in social reform and the ultimate defeat of Fascism. This was the era of the "united front," during which Communists utilized the Trojan horse technique to bore from within. They infiltrated labor unions, university faculties, editorial boards, and governmental bureaus. Communists were instructed to enter into coalitions with "liberals" and reformers until they had acquired enough power and prestige to cast aside their pretense of co-operation; they were then to liquidate those foolish enough to collaborate with them. In its ultimate form, this stratagem aimed at obtaining the key posts of government: the ministries of Justice and the Interior (police). From these posts, the rest of the government could, in time, be Communized. Communists in Spain gained control of the government through this method of the united front. Spanish Communist leader Andres Nin declared in November, 1936: "The Government no longer exists; we are the government." From the summer of 1936 until the early spring of 1939, Spanish collaborationists Juan Negrin and Alvarez del Vayo allowed Soviet General Goriev to direct the war effort of the International Brigades against Franco's Spanish army. In France, the Communists gained considerable influence in the Popular Front government of Socialist Léon Blum; in China, the Communists of Mao Tse-tung wormed their way into the Nationalist government, ostensibly to help the latter fight Japan. In the United States, Harold Ware, John Abt, Nathan Witt, Henry Collins, Victor Perlo, Harry D. White, and Alger Hiss began to penetrate key agencies of the American government.

The Hitler-Stalin pact launched the fifth tactical period of Soviet foreign policy. On August 23, 1939, Stalin and Hitler decided to start World War II with the attack on Poland. Recognizing their common interest in totalitarianism and realizing that by working together they might eject American, British, and French influence from the Eurasian continent, the two dictators took the military step which dragged the rest of the world into conflict. Stalin's armies invaded eastern Poland, Lithuania, Latvia, Estonia, Finland, and two provinces of Romania: Bessarabia and Bucovina. Through this alliance with Germany and subsequent treaties with

Fascist Italy and Tojo's Japan, Soviet Russia became a *de facto* member of the Axis. Stalin sent telegrams of congratulations to Hitler upon learning of German victories in Norway, Denmark, the Low Countries, and France. Stalin also sent Hitler grain, petroleum, and winter clothing for the German army. Refusing to heed British and American warnings that Germany was going to attack him, Stalin was completely taken by surprise when the *Wehrmacht* drove deep into Russia, beginning June 22, 1941.

From the date of the German invasion of Soviet Russia until the end of World War II, Stalin's primary effort was to save the Soviet base of operations from destruction; for without this base of operations, the world revolution could never succeed. His alliance with Japan in the Far East allowed him to defend western Russia with all his available military forces; this, in conjunction with all-out American and British aid and the fact that Hitler was simultaneously fighting on several other fronts, saved world Communism. This sixth tactical period can be divided into two phases: that which was essentially defensive, until Stalingrad, and the offensive phase during the years 1943–1945. In the offensive phase, Soviet armies invaded ("liberated") formerly independent east-central European countries, bringing with them Communist *émigrés* who had been trained in Moscow to administer the new order in central Europe. This Soviet military advance was paralleled by Soviet diplomatic successes at Teheran (1943), Yalta (1945), and Potsdam (1945). At these conferences, the United States and Britain abandoned their traditional Yugoslav, Polish, and Chinese allies in favor of made-in-Moscow ersatz national groups.

The seventh Soviet tactical period began with the conclusion of World War II; it not only consolidated the gains of the Soviet empire, but extended these gains in the opening campaigns of what might be called World War III (beginning in December, 1944, when the Communists attacked in Greece). Combining cold- and hot-war techniques, Communist armies, diplomats, and fifth columnists advanced the cause of Communism in Greece, Czechoslovakia, Germany, Colombia, Guatemala, Iran, China, Korea, Tibet, and southeastern Asia. By alternating and combining military and psychological pressures with the "peace" campaign, the Kremlin was able to keep the non-Soviet realm confused and divided. While the Communists talked peace at Panmunjom, they practiced war in Indochina and subversion elsewhere. In the meantime, pro-Soviet and neutralist pressures in the United Nations transformed that body into an ineffectual debating society.

The eighth period began with the end of the fighting in Korea. After intervening in June, 1951, the Soviets enabled the Chinese Communists to escape military defeat through diplomatic victory, extracting major concessions from the Free World at the Panmunjom and Geneva conferences which permitted them to retain control of North Korea and gain control of North Viet-Nam. In February, 1955, a further gain was made when the United States forced Chiang Kai-shek to relinquish the Tachen Islands to the Chinese Communists. The "Summit" conference at Geneva in 1955 was designed to raise false hopes of peace in the non-Communist world. This was the beginning of the "peace offensive," which was formalized at the Twentieth Congress of the Communist party of the U.S.S.R. But so-called "relaxation of tensions" and "national Communism" were shown to be utter shams by the Soviet repression of the Freedom Fighters in Hungary in November, 1956. Since then, Soviet diplomacy and fifth columnists have gained footholds in Egypt, Syria, the Indian State of Kerala, British Guiana, Indonesia, and Laos. The Communist threat in the Middle East—especially the threat to Jordan and Lebanon—appeared to be the most dangerous in late 1958, particularly after the pro-Nasser take-over in Iraq.

The most important gains of the Soviet empire were made after 1939. Soviet military, diplomatic, and fifth-column activity achieved incredible successes in both Europe and Asia. Knowledge of these successes, together with the accompanying Western blunders, is basic to an understanding of the world situation today.

COMMUNIST EXPANSION IN EUROPE

Hitler and Stalin, looking at a map of the Eurasian continent in 1939, agreed to divide most of that great land expanse, with certain crumbs going to Italy and Japan.[4] In addition to his gains in Poland, the Baltic States, Finland, and Romania, Stalin was given a sphere of influence south from the Transcaucasian area to the Indian Ocean. But then he and Hitler quarreled over Bulgaria, and Hitler secretly decided on Operation Barbarossa—the invasion of Russia. This invasion ended Soviet control of northern and eastern Europe, but only temporarily. After Stalingrad, and with the acquiescence of the United States and Britain, Soviet power not only re-entered the former areas of Soviet control, but spread into vast reaches of land never previously under Soviet domination.

At the Teheran Conference, Stalin met Churchill and Roosevelt for the first time. It proved to be a fruitful friendship for him. This conference, held in the fall of 1943, resulted in the Western democracies abandoning their Yugoslav ally, Mihajlović, and supporting the veteran Communist agent, Josip Broz (Tito). In February, 1945, Stalin insisted that an ailing President Roosevelt join Winston Churchill again and travel halfway around the world to meet him in the Crimea, at Yalta. Here Stalin was to gain his most dramatic diplomatic success: carte blanche in eastern Poland, Manchuria, and other territories. The Polish agreement was divided into two parts: (1) a grant by the Western powers to the Soviet Union of substantially the same Polish territory that it had received under the terms of the Hitler-Stalin pact and (2) a promise by the Western powers to recognize the made-in-Moscow Lublin Committee as the Polish government when this committee had been broadened to include non-Communist Poles and had agreed to hold free elections. Communist control of the Lublin Committee was never relinquished, free elections were never held, and yet the Western powers proceeded to recognize the Lublin Committee and admit it to the United Nations.[5] The Polish exile government of Stanislaus Mikolajczyk, one of the first members of the Allied forces in World War II—the Poland that Britain had gone to war to defend—was abandoned in this Machiavellian scheme. At Yalta,[6] the Soviets also obtained Western acquiescence and assistance in their seizure of Japanese and Chinese territory and bases at a time when Soviet Russia was still Japan's *de jure* ally, primarily at the expense of the Republic of China, which was America's faithful and long-term ally in Asia. We agreed to recognize Communist control over Outer Mongolia, and pre-eminent Soviet interests in Manchuria and Dairen, and the Soviets were given a fifty-year lease on Port Arthur as a naval base. The United States also agreed to give the U.S.S.R. the southern half of Sakhalin Island and the Kuril Islands, which extend from the Bering Strait to Hokkaido, the northernmost Japanese island. In return for all these, Stalin promised to enter into the Pacific war after the defeat of Germany. Actually, Stalin's military assistance was not needed in the Far East, and his intrusion into Far Eastern affairs had the same disastrous results that it had in Europe. The United States subsequently forced President Chiang Kai-shek of the Republic of China to agree to this territorial blackmail, to the detriment of Chinese and American national interests and to the benefit of the Soviet empire.[7] The Yalta concessions to Stalin in the Far East radically changed the balance of power in that area in favor of Communism. The dividends of the Yalta investment were to be paid off with the blood of American fighting men in Korea. Soviet power thus augmented in Asia spread into all of China, parts of southeastern Asia, and Korea. Also in 1945, the United States told the Soviet Union that the Soviet army (once Russia had entered the Pacific war) could accept Japanese surrenders north of the thirty-eighth parallel in Korea. This gave the Soviets a pretext to transform North Korea into a Soviet satellite.

The next Soviet diplomatic victory came at the Potsdam Conference in June, 1945. Roosevelt's death brought to the presidency and to the State Department two men totally inexperienced in world affairs: Harry S. Truman and James Brynes. Poorly advised by Charles Bohlen and the pro-Soviet millionaire turned diplomat, Joseph L. Davies, they made incredible concessions to Stalin in Germany and Austria, concessions which were to compound the errors of Yalta and bring Soviet power into its areas of deepest penetration in Europe. The great crime of Potsdam was to bring suffering and death to millions of Germans and Austrians, who, like their Yugoslav, Polish, and Chinese predecessors, were mere pawns in the great game of power politics.

As the result of the Potsdam agreement with Soviet Russia, the following situation was brought about: Northern East Prussia, including the key port of Königsberg, was given to the Soviet Union and southern East Prussia to Communist Poland. Eastern Germany and eastern Austria were assigned to the Soviets as zones of occupation. One-third of the current production of West Germany was to go to the Soviet zone, as were its dismantled factories. All former German external assets along the Danube River were handed over to the Soviets. Berlin and Vienna, both inside Soviet zones of occupation, were put under four-power (American, British, French, and Soviet) administrations. Both Germany and Austria were to be treated as economic units and were ultimately to be given independence. But refusal of the Soviets to co-operate in this regard ultimately forced the Western powers to grant economic unity and political independence to West Germany and West Austria under adverse economic conditions.[8] Thus the end of World War II, far from bringing new hope to the peoples of Germany, Austria, and Korea, forced many of them into Soviet tyranny and brought war, both cold and hot, to their unhappy lands.

The Soviets achieved two other victories in 1945 and 1946. These were the San Francisco UN Conference and the Paris "peace" Conference. Alger Hiss was the Secretary General of the UN Conference which was characterized by a diplomatic climate uniformly favorable to the Soviets. Any and every concession was made by the non-Soviet participants to accommodate the Soviets: exclusion of Spain, the Polish government in exile, and every country displeasing to Stalin; veto power over substantive questions and new members; three votes in the General Assembly for Communism (the U.S.S.R., White Russia, and the Ukraine). The San Francisco Conference succeeded in creating an international organization in which the Soviets and their satellites had wonderful opportunities for propaganda and in which action to check and punish Communist aggression was discouraged and even blocked by the Security Council system of minority rule.

The Paris "peace" Conference of 1946 facilitated Soviet control of Finland, Hungary, Romania, Bulgaria, Albania, and central Europe generally.[6] These unhappy countries, and Italy as well, were forced to pay Soviet Russia an average of $300,000,000 each in reparations. Additionally, Italy had to turn over to Soviet Russia (which had had no hand in the liberation of Italy) part of its modern fleet.

At the same time that these diplomatic victories facilitated the spread of Soviet power in Europe and Asia, Soviet and satellite military power forced Communism down the throats of millions of persons who had been led to believe that World War II would bring them freedom. As was the case in the diplomatic settlements, these people found the Western democracies unwilling to save them from Communistic military invasion and subversion.

From January, 1944, until the summer of 1945, Soviet armies rolled into east-central Europe and conquered ("liberated") formerly independent countries. These armies brought with them *émigré* Communist leaders to establish the future "people's democracies." Anti-Communists were rounded up and deported as "collaborators," were denied food cards, and were in other ways discouraged or prevented from taking part in political activity. Communists seized control of the key ministries of Justice and the Interior and forced other political factions to agree to single-state elections. Cabinet posts were allocated in advance, regardless of the election results. Working first within a political "front," the Communists, with the aid of the Soviet occupation armies, weeded out the remaining non-Communists and consolidated control. The United States and Great Britain stood by while freedom was destroyed in central Europe. Little men like Gomulka in Poland, Tito in Yugoslavia, Gottwald in Czechoslovakia, Rakosi in Hungary, Bodnares in Romania, and Chervenkov in Bulgaria repeatedly and successfully defied the United States and Britain. Courageous men like Petkov, Mihajlović, Stepinac, Mindszenty, Mikolaczyk, and Ferenc Nagy were purged, and the Western powers did not lift a finger to save them. By 1947, the Baltic States, Poland, Hungary, Romania, Yugoslavia, Bulgaria, and Albania had been drawn into the Soviet Empire. Stalin then instructed Yugoslavia, Bulgaria, and Albania to attack Greece. This attack finally forced the United States to act, by applying the defensive-containment doctrine in Greece and Turkey. In 1949, the Communists temporarily gave up the struggle for Greece, partly because of the defection of Tito the previous year. But Stalin had by no means ended his expansion. Sensing that the Truman Doctrine was merely an *ad hoc* defensive measure without general application, he ordered Soviet Ambassador Zorin in Prague to mobilize the Communist "action committee" of Gottwald and Zápotocký and overthrow the limited democracy of Beneš and Masaryk. The *coup d'état* of March, 1948, erased Czechoslovakia as a free country.

COMMUNIST EXPANSION IN THE FAR EAST

It was in Asia, however, that the Soviets achieved their greatest military triumphs. Hot war, waged by Communist forces, swept southeastern Asia, China, and then Korea. Neither appeasement nor containment was able to check the onslaught, any more than the French Maginot Line psychology was able to stop German expansion in 1940. All this during a period when the United States enjoyed a monopoly in nuclear weapons.

The most spectacular Soviet success came in China. During the war against Japan, the Communist leaders instructed their forces in China to conserve their energy for the greater fight that was to come—the attack on the Nationalist government. Mao Tse-tung declared: "Our policy is seventy per cent expansion, twenty per cent dealing with the Kuomintang, and ten per cent fighting Japan." The fall of 1945 found the Nationalist government in control of southern and central China, with Soviet Russia and the Chinese Communists in northern China and Manchuria. The Communist forces soon made it clear that they would prevent the Nationalist government from restoring its authority in these areas. Unfortunately for the Nationalist government, it failed to receive the same support from the United States against Communism that it had received against Japan. In fact, through the instrumentality of the ill-famed Marshall mission to China, the United States government proceeded to treat the Chinese government and the Chinese rebels as equals. Marshall told Chiang Kai-shek to take Communists into the government or all American military aid would be cut off. This contrasted with Marshall's later ultimatum to the Greek government to throw out the Communists as a precondition of American aid. Naturally, Chiang refused to take traitors into his government, whereupon the United States imposed an arms embargo on Nationalist China from July, 1946, to June, 1947. At the same time, the Soviets fed a constant stream of military aid to the Chinese Communists. The result was the military conquest of the Chinese mainland by the Communists, followed by the transfer of Chinese governmental authority to the island of Formosa in the summer of 1949. The United States had gone to war in the Pacific in 1941 in large part to maintain a free and independent China. Eight years later, it stood by, hat in hand, while free China was destroyed.

Diplomats John Stewart Service, John P. Davies, Jr., and John Carter Vincent influenced United States policy against support of Nationalist China and leaned strongly toward the Communists. The Civil Service Loyalty Review Board subsequently concluded that both Service and Vincent were of doubtful loyalty; Service was fired, and Vincent was allowed to resign.[10] Davies, after going from China to Germany, and later to Latin America in a diplomatic capacity, was finally fired for "bad judgment." Owen Lattimore, whose governmental service during World War II and subsequent influence was exerted along pro-Chinese Communist lines, was indicted on seven counts of perjury in 1952 as the result of evidence unearthed by the Senate Internal Security Subcommittee in 1951 and 1952,[11] but a friendly judge (Luther Youngdahl) threw out the two key counts as "too vague."[12]

During the entire period of Communist aggression in China, the United Nations, far from applying sanctions against the Communists, failed even to consider the problem. Nationalist China, a permanent member of the UN Security Council, was left to its own devices. To add insult to injury, some UN members, including Britain and India, recognized Red China.

Communistic military activity was by no means confined to China. Shortly after the end of World War II, Communist groups became active in Indochina, Malaya, Thailand, Burma, Indonesia, and the Philippines. Open warfare spread to most of these countries, with most of the fighting taking place in Indochina. North Viet-Nam was handed over to the Communists at the Geneva Conference (July, 1954), and Cambodia and Laos were neutralized. Burma and Indonesia, with strong Communist parties, are openly pro-Chinese Communist. Chinese Communist elements are also dominant in Malaya.

A further discouraging sequel to the Communist military victory in China was the war in Korea. The establishment of Soviet power in Manchuria and North Korea in 1945, compounded by the military invasion of China between 1946 and 1949, endangered the position of the newly created Republic of Korea. In the summer of 1949, Owen Lattimore advised the State Department to "let South Korea fall, but don't make it look as though we'd pushed it." On January 12, 1950, Secretary of State Acheson informed the world that we did not consider Korea to be within our Pacific security line. Despite pleas from President Rhee of the Republic of Korea for guns, tanks, and planes, no real military aid was given to Korea until the attack of June 25, 1950.

On June 27, 1950, the UN labeled North Korea the aggressor and asked UN members to support the Republic of Korea and to refrain from aiding the enemy. However, only fourteen UN members gave any aid, while several others helped the Communist enemy. The United States and the Republic of Korea sustained 97 per cent of the casualties; the United Nations, apart from the United States and South Korea furnished 3 per cent. The containment policy of the United States and the UN granted the Chinese Communists a gigantic sanctuary in Manchuria, even after the massive intervention of the forces of Mao Tse-tung in Korea in November, 1950. In the meantime, the United States and Great Britain prevented Nationalist China (a UN member) from sending 33,000 troops (equal to the contributions of all our UN allies combined) against the common enemy. The U.S. Seventh Fleet was sent to the Straits of Formosa to "neutralize" the Nationalists. This meant that Red China did not have to worry about the United Nations opening a second front.

Various proposals, submitted by General MacArthur to Washington, to win the war were rejected, including a four-point program approved by the Joint Chiefs of Staff: economic sanctions against Red China, naval blockade, air reconnaissance over Manchuria, and use of Nationalist forces against the common enemy. In April, 1951, MacArthur was removed from his command by President Truman after issuing an ultimatum to the enemy commander to sue for peace or suffer the consequences (air strikes against Manchurian bases). General James Van Fleet took command of the UN forces in Korea and had victory in his grasp in June, 1951, when the Soviet Union intervened to salvage the situation for Red China by proposing truce negotiations. The United States halted its advancing armies, and the Communists were permitted to keep most of North Korea. The UN resolution[13] calling for the establishment of a free, united, and independent Korea and the military liberation of North Korea remained unfulfilled.

Admiral C. Turner Joy was the chief UN truce negotiator in Korea at Kaesong and Panmunjom. Time after time, he was instructed to give in to the Communist demands in order to get peace at any price. The important concessions were: permitting the Communists to build airfields in North Korea, permitting the Communists to remain in North Korea in violation of two UN resolutions, agreeing to use "neutral" nations (including Czechoslovakia and Poland) for truce supervision rather than the UN, and causing the anti-Communist Chinese and Korean war prisoners (80 per cent of our captives were anti-Communist) to be forcibly detained, after the truce settlement, for four months, during three of which they were forcibly "interrogated" by Communist brain-washers from eastern Europe. The Republic of Korea refused to sign the Panmunjom agreement, considering it to be appeasement. Most American commanders who had served in Korea agreed with this estimate of the situation. Generals Van Fleet, Stratemeyer, Almond, and Clark, as well as Admiral Joy and General MacArthur, unanimously concurred that we had allowed the Chinese Communists to escape military defeat through a diplomatic victory.[14] The Panmunjom agreement (July, 1953) left the Chinese Communists in control of North Korea and freed their armies for action in southeastern Asia and the Straits of Formosa.

A year later, after months of Communist demands for a conference on Indochina, the Western powers agreed to meet with the U.S.S.R., Red China, and Communist leaders from Indochina at Geneva. French Premier Mendes-France made it clear to the Communists that he badly wanted peace. The French and the British proceeded to buy peace by selling twelve million Viet-Namese (north of the seventeenth parallel) into Communist slavery. As a sop to their consciences, they managed to extract a Communist promise to permit some of the people in North Viet-Nam to migrate south—a promise immediately violated with impunity. The United States did not sign the agreement, but Undersecretary of State Walter Bedell Smith was there to give his "moral approval." The Viet-Namese government naturally refused to sign, but its refusal did not deter France and Britain. Viet-Namese Foreign Minister Tran Van Do pathetically declared: "We have been betrayed by those who call themselves our friends."

The Chinese Communists now turned their attention to the Chinese Nationalist offshore islands. Capture of a small island adjacent to the Tachens induced President Eisenhower to force Chiang Kai-shek to evacuate these islands, even though Admiral Radford, head of the U.S. Joint Chiefs of Staff, had stated that they were vital not only to the defense of Formosa, but also to the defense of American bases on Okinawa. The Chinese Communists followed this up with intense propaganda and military demonstrations aimed at the conquest of the offshore islands of Quemoy and Matsu, where Nationalist forces bottled up the invasion ports of Amoy and Foochow.[15]

THE "SPIRIT OF GENEVA"

The advent of Khrushchev to power in Russia accelerated the Soviet "peace" campaign. The Soviets persuaded President Eisenhower and the French and British premiers to meet with the dictator of the U.S.S.R. in Geneva in 1955. Although the Soviets made no concessions and no agreements were arrived at, many people were led to believe that the Communists had now become peaceful because Khrushchev had smiled and exchanged toasts with the three Western statesmen. Yet even Khrushchev admitted that Soviet policy had not wavered from its long-term objective of world conquest. He told a visiting East German delegation in mid-1955: "If anyone thinks that our smiles mean that we have abandoned our belief in the doctrines of Marx, Engels, and Lenin, he might as well wait for a shrimp to learn how to whistle."

The Communists look upon the "spirit of Geneva" as a means by which to extract further concessions from the Free World at the conference table, such as recognition of Communist China by the United States, a UN seat for Red China, control of the offshore islands in the Straits of Formosa, neutralization of Germany, and a recognition of Soviet interests in the Middle East. Anyone who does not take the Soviets at their word is an enemy of the "spirit of Geneva." President Eisenhower became so alarmed at the success of the Communist "peace" campaign that he warned Americans: "There can be no true peace which involves acceptance of a *status quo* in which we find injustice to many nations. . . . Eagerness to avoid war—if we think no deeper than this single desire—can produce outright or implicit agreement that injustices of the present shall be perpetuated in the future. We must not participate in any such false agreement. In the eyes of those who suffer injustice, we would become partners with their oppressors. In the judgment of history we would have sold out the freedom of men for the pottage of a false peace. Moreover, we would assure future conflict."

But these strong words were not matched with strong deeds. In October, 1956, Hungarian patriots rebelled against their Communist government. For six days the patriots managed to control Budapest and most of the rest of Hungary. Little Austria sent medical supplies, food, and clothing to patriotic groups, but the United States did nothing to assist the Hungarian bid for freedom or to capitalize on this tremendous opportunity to breach the Iron Curtain and roll back the Red power. Soviet forces, after waiting a week (apparently to see what we would do), entered Hungary in strength and, following a horrifying bloodbath, put down the uprising. The United States even refused to recognize the Freedom Fighters' Committee and opposed the sending of a UN delegation to investigate the Hungarian situation. Whereas the West had been willing to go to great lengths to liberate Europe from Fascism, it was afraid of doing anything to liberate the Continent from Communism.

The international Communist movement registered further gains in 1957, most importantly through the establishment of a semi-satellite in Syria and the development of an intercontinental-ballistic-missile capability. Using a position of strength in Syria and exploiting their strength in Egypt, the Soviets, in 1957, carried out intensive cold-war activities aimed at weakening the Baghdad Pact (Britain, Turkey, Iran, Iraq, Pakistan) and transforming Iraq, Lebanon, and Jordan into satellites of the Soviet Union. In July, 1958, a pro-Nasser group in Iraq, with Communist support, overthrew the existing anti-Communist government, and assassinated King Faisal and Premier Nuri es-Said. Beginning in August, 1958, Communist China bombarded the Chinese Nationalist offshore islands of Quemoy and Matsu as a possible prelude to invasion.

CHAPTER 3

Coexistence with, or Freedom from, Communism?

THE MEANING OF COEXISTENCE

Some influential Americans seem to think that the only alternative to "peaceful coexistence" is "war."[1] This has become such a fixation with these persons that they quickly dismiss any and all plans for aid and encouragement to oppressed peoples behind the Iron Curtain as "leading to war." When Senators Knowland and Jenner made public the almost unanimous testimony of former Far Eastern military commanders that the containment policy in Korea frustrated their desires for victory and led to needless casualties in the retreat from the Yalu, they were denounced as "warhawks" (to use a phrase of the *Daily Worker* subsequently repeated in many non-Communist publications).

When a blockade and diplomatic sanctions were suggested as effective means of freeing hundreds of Americans held prisoner by the Chinese Communists, the "let's coexist" fraternity denounced the idea as a "war action." The same answer greeted those who suggested that we might do something beyond sending a note of protest when the forty-sixth American airman was shot down without provocation by Communist pilots and plunged to his death in a burning B-29 reconnaissance bomber. In North Viet-Nam, thousands of refugees on the coast were prevented from going south, in violation of the Geneva agreement. Yet proposals to free these unfortunate people by ship were rejected as "endangering the peace."

There was a similar reaction to anti-Communist suggestions that the United States or the United Nations actively assist the East German patriots in 1953 and their Hungarian counterparts in 1956.

Few people are aware of the fact that the term "peaceful coexistence" was coined by Stalin in 1927 to describe a manouvor designed to lull non-Communist nations into a false sense of security. Stalin made it clear that coexistence would be utilized by the Soviet Union to stay the hand of non-Communist nations when the Kremlin needed a breathing spell. Stalin stressed that coexistence was a mighty weapon in the Soviet arsenal which would achieve at least the minimum goal of freezing the *status quo* and prevent any penetration of the Soviet slave empire by the forces of freedom. Coexistence, said Stalin, was to be encouraged only until such time as the Soviet power had sufficiently renewed itself to take the offensive against an enemy paralyzed by a defensive psychosis. "We are speaking," he said, "of temporary agreements with the capitalist governments in the sphere of industry, trade, and perhaps diplomatic relations."[2] But coexistence is ruled out by the Soviet leadership as a fixed policy capable of offering hope to the non-Soviet realm. Stalin, quoting Lenin, writes: "We are not living merely in a state, but in a system of states, and the existence of the Soviet Republic side by side with imperial states for a longer time is unthinkable. One or the other must triumph. . . . A series of frightful clashes between the Soviet Republic and the bourgeois is inevitable."[3] Coexistence is also a stratagem employed by the Soviets to obtain at the conference table something they would otherwise have to obtain by force of arms.[4]

It is manifest that, from the Soviet point of view, periods of coexistence (usually associated with peace slogans and united-front activity) benefit the international Communist movement and enervate non-Communists and anti-Communists. Generals MacArthur, Van Fleet, Stratemeyer, Clark, and Almond, together with Admiral Joy, were unanimous in their testimony that the American policy of containment-coexistence denied them victory in Korea and saved the Chinese Communist armies. In 1956, acceptance of coexistence by the United States precluded aid to the Hungarian patriots, and in 1958 it led us to refuse succor to the anti-Communist rebels in Indonesia.

In the final analysis, coexistence means that the United States and its allies, both nominal and real, will refrain from any *effective* countermeasures when provoked by the international Communist movement. It is no longer fashionable to give American citizens abroad the same protection they received in the days of Theodore Roosevelt. Coexistence means that we accept as final the Chinese Communist conquest of North Korea (in violation of UN resolutions in October, 1950, and February, 1951), Communist control of North Viet-Nam, and Soviet occupation of East Germany and central Europe. Because of coexistence, the people in the eastern European satellites are destined to remain slaves. For a time there was speculation about what might happen in the event of a serious uprising in the Soviet empire. The answer came in June, 1953, when the United States refused to help the East German workers as they pitifully threw rocks at Soviet tanks, and in October, 1956, when Russian divisions cut down the Hungarian patriots in a veritable sea of blood. Few Americans recognize the magnitude of these missed opportunities.

If it is our objective to coexist with the Soviet empire, we must, of necessity, retreat every time the Soviets move forward. Otherwise we would "antagonize" the U.S.S.R., "bypass" the United Nations, and be guilty of a "war action." The Soviets, recognizing our desire for peace at any price, fully appreciate the vulnerability of our position. A review of the "compromises" at Panmunjom and Geneva makes this clear. The Communists got their way on the forcible detention of anti-Communist war prisoners for four months, the minimum designated ports of entry in North Korea, a "neutral" commission rather than a UN committee to supervise the troops, and permission to stay in North Korea and build airfields there. In Viet-Nam, the communists won out again on the issues of a "neutral" commission, *de facto* control of North Viet-Nam, and control of the key cities of Hanoi and Haiphong. For the sake of "peaceful coexistence," we acquiesced in the abandonment of twelve million North Viet-Namese to Communist slavery. This is the true measure of the morality of our policy. George Kennan, creator of the containment doctrine, no doubt rejoices that his book urging the exclusion of morality from international politics has not only been widely read, but also put into practice. Mr. Kennan must have been disturbed by the Hungarian uprising of 1956, for he had said previously that the United States must recognize that "there is a certain finality" about the Communist *status quo* in central Europe.

Coexistence has a long history, one which has invariably promoted aggression and weakened free nations. In order to coexist with Fascism, Britain and France acquiesced in the conquest of Ethiopia. To "keep the peace," no effective action was taken to break Hitler's conquest of Austria. When the Japanese invaded Manchuria, the League of Nations chose to debate with the enemy rather than defeat him. At Munich, Chamberlain and Daladier sold out Czechoslovakia for the sake of "peace in our time."

Coexistence, as conceived by aggressor states to prevent effective counteraction by its proposed victims, not only insists that the victim remain peaceful should "limited war" commence, but also insists that he not "extend the war." The "don't extend the war" doctrine really means "don't win the war." Few people realize that this slogan, used so effectively by the Communists and their allies during the Korean War[5] to enable them to escape military defeat through diplomatic victory, actually originated during the Hitler-Stalin pact. On September 25, 1940, Nazi Foreign Minister von Ribbentrop wired his ambassador in Moscow, Count Schulenburg, complaining that the "war-mongering agitation in America . . . is seeking a last outlet in the extension and prolongation of the war." Von Ribbentrop instructed Schulenburg on October 18, 1939, to tell Stalin that "the responsibility of England and France for the continuation of the war would be established" if they persisted in fighting on after the partition of Poland. Both Hitler and Stalin several times warned France, Britain, and the United States against "extending the war"; that is to say, they insisted that the Western powers remain on the defensive and refrain from effective counter-offensive action. The similarity between these strictures to the victims not to "extend the war" and the admonitions of Red China, India, and Britain during the Korean War (directed at the United States and the Republic of Korea) is striking. So long as the victims of aggression can be persuaded to coexist or merely to contain the aggressor, but nothing more, the psychological and military advantage lies with the aggressor—a very dangerous situation in the age of nuclear weapons. As James Burnham so succinctly puts it, "containment is but a pause, a stopping-off place, beyond which there must be a further move: backward to appeasement or forward to offensive and victory." Coexistence (or containment) is a policy of drift, of indecision, which usually follows on the heels of appeasement but which has largely the same result. Appeasement, after all, is based on coexistence, and this is manifestly better appreciated by the unfortunate millions sacrificed on the altar of coexistence than by the fear-ridden diplomats of the Western World.

Coexistence, the Soviet victory weapon, has caused one disaster after another for free peoples. From Munich to Geneva, coexistence with aggression has meant diminution of the free world. The time is long past for the statesmen of the great powers to continue to hand over small nations to the U.S.S.R. for the sake of "peaceful coexistence." This is but surrender on the installment plan.

WHAT CAN BE DONE?

We are faced with the necessity of action to end the retreat. Territories and populations continue to be seized militarily or bargained away at the conference table; war prisoners and citizens of the Free World continue to be shot down with impunity; Communist subversion eats away at our free institutions while some "intellectuals" continue to look upon Communism as purely an ideology or a political party. Germans, Poles, Hungarians, and other enslaved peoples rise up to regain their liberty, only to be beaten down by Soviet power. Freedom must be served.

What, then, is to be done? Appeasement and coexistence having been rejected, what alternatives remain to be considered in order to halt the inexorable advance of Communism? Here are some suggestions for the United States and the Free World:

1. The United States and its allies must reject "peace at any price" and coexistence and accept the risks that this implies.

2. We must adopt liberation from Communism as our long-range objective and convince the enslaved that we mean it.

3. We should cease all aid to *any* Communist state anywhere and end any trade with Communist countries that could even indirectly strengthen their economies. Because of Red China's violation of the Panmunjom agreement, we should consider naval blockade of the Chinese mainland.

4. We should re-evaluate aid programs to countries such as India, Burma, and Indonesia, which constantly side with Communist China and look at the Soviet Union through rose-colored glasses; and we should consider whether this aid might not more profitably be extended to countries which recognize what Communist colonialism is and are willing to combat Communist subversion and aggression.

5. We must resolutely determine to defend such exposed areas as South Korea, Formosa, Quemoy, Matsu, South Viet-Nam, West Germany, Lebanon, and Jordan from Communist aggression and subversion and make it unmistakably clear that *any* further Communist attempt to expand will be answered by appropriate diplomatic, economic, and military action.

6. In the cases of the East German revolt of 1953 and the Polish and Hungarian revolts of 1956, the West missed unique opportunities to aid patriot forces in the liberation of their homelands. Plans must be readied to help freedom-loving peoples who seek to throw off their shackles.

7. The United States government should base its internal security on the proposition that Communists owe their first allegiance to the Soviet Union; it should also recognize that the suspect who refuses to deny Communist affiliations under oath or to co-operate with his government against tyranny has *ipso facto* established the presumption of guilt and should be so regarded.[6] Legislation (like the Butler bill) is needed to offset the Supreme Court decisions of 1957 and 1958, which all but dismantled internal security.

8. The United States government should energetically sell anti-Communism to its own people and to its allies. Governmental leaders, educators, and those who have suffered at the hands of Communists should use all possible media to tell the people the facts about Communist slave labor camps, the secret police, aggression, and subversion. The motivating philosophy should be comparable to that finally adopted toward Hitler, Mussolini, and Tojo: the moral degradation of the enemy and the impossibility of coexistence with that enemy.

9. Refugees and exiles from Communism of military age and fitness should be permitted to join together in "Liberation Battalions" to be trained and supported by Western military organizations such as the North Atlantic Treaty Organization and its counterparts in the Far East. The Kersten Amendment to the Mutual Security Act should be implemented.

10. Refugees and exiles from Communism not of military age and fitness should be fed, clothed, and, wherever possible, employed by the West for intelligence, educational, or other work appropriate to their backgrounds. Not only should this be governmental policy, but private foundations and organizations should also be encouraged so to act.

11. The United States should advance vigorously to the offensive in the matter of psychological warfare in all the mass media, especially beamed to lands abroad, and should strengthen and extend anti-Communist sentiment and solidarity both inside and outside existing international organizations, such as the United Nations.

12. The United States should seek maximum international cooperation in demanding a redress of grievances from the Soviet Union and Communist China with respect to violation of international agreements and human rights and should warn that failure to redress will result in progressive diplomatic, economic, and other suitable sanctions. A concrete example: a request for sanctions in connection with Soviet military intervention in Hungary to crush the patriot uprising in 1956 or the sending of a UN commission to Budapest when the Patriots were in control, or recognition of the Nagy regime.

13. We should strengthen our military position and that of our allies and reject suggestions of unilateral disarmament and cessation of nuclear testing. This involves gearing Free World defenses against missile attacks; rapidly establishing intermediate range ballistic missile bases on the periphery of the Soviet empire with minimum Allied restrictions; speeding up our intercontinental ballistic missile and anti-missile missile program; increasing our naval missile capability; and, above all, willingly using our power when necessary.

14. We should end a Middle East policy which is based to a considerable degree on domestic political considerations and develop countersubversion programs to check Communist subversion in that area.

15. The United States should not allow a few timid allies to block effective anti-Communist action when it is in our interest and that of threatened allies.

Such a program might lead to the weakening of the Communist regimes in central Europe, the Far East, and southeastern Asia, to a lessening of Communist influence in the Middle East, and perhaps, ultimately, to liberation. This policy will serve to weaken and even penetrate the Soviet realm, making us stronger than we are now and the Soviets weaker. Such a policy might conceivably (although less probably) so weaken the Soviet empire from within that revolts, economic ruin, and continued and increased jealousy among the Soviet leadership would lead to a successful internal upheaval. Above all, such a policy would free us from the fear-ridden Maginot Line straitjacket which now stifles us.

This policy involves risks, but these risks have been thrust upon us against our will by Soviet aggression and Communist subversion. Furthermore, unless we take these risks, we will continue to move inexorably toward certain defeat. As things stand now, the Soviets are doing quite well through small wars and subversion and at the conference table. Michael Karpovich recently wrote: "From time to time we hear it said that this course would provoke the Soviet Union to resort to arms. Past experience, as well as everything we know about the psychology of the Soviet leaders, indicates the exact opposite."[7]

Ours is the choice, then: to continue to lose "World War III," in which we have lost 8,000,000 square miles of territory and 800,000,000 people to Soviet expansion, not to mention the 150,000 American casualties in Korea, through the defeatist coexistence policy; or to stir ourselves out of our lethargy immediately and take these effective steps, which alone can lead to ultimate victory and genuine peace.

Above all, let our policy be guided by a constant reminder of Soviet intentions toward us, as stated by Dimitry Manuilsky at the Lenin School of Political Warfare in 1931:

"War to the hilt between Communism and Capitalism is inevitable. Today, of course, we are not strong enough to attack. Our time will come in twenty or thirty years. To win we shall need the element of surprise. The *bourgeoisie* will have to be put to sleep. So we shall begin by launching the most spectacular peace movement on record. There will be electrifying overtures and unheard-of concessions. The capitalistic countries, stupid and decadent, will rejoice to co-operate in their own destruction. They will leap at another chance to be friends. As soon as their guard is down, we shall smash them with our clenched fists."

CHAPTER 4

U.S. Counterattack: The Sarnoff Plan

[In April, 1955, Brigadier General David Sarnoff of the Radio Corporation of America suggested to President Eisenhower a course of action which would involve minimum risks and yet advance the cause of freedom. Although little or nothing has been done to implement the Sarnoff plan, it is herewith presented, in abbreviated form, in the belief that it constitutes a practical program in cold warfare which free people everywhere should seriously consider.]

TAKING THE COLD WAR OFFENSIVE

The democracies are familiar with war-making in the normal military sense and hence do not hesitate to make huge investments and sacrifices in its name. They do not shrink from the prospect of casualties. All of that seems "natural." But they are startled by proposals for effort and risk of such dimensions in the life-and-death struggle with non-military means.

Under these circumstances it has become incumbent upon our leadership to make the country aware that non-military or Cold War is also terribly "real"—that the penalty for losing it will be enslavement. . . .

The material in this chapter first appeared in a memorandum which David Sarnoff sent to the White House on April 5, 1955, and it is reprinted here by permission of Gen. Sarnoff. Subheads have been supplied by Mr. Bouscaren.

The primary threat today is political and psychological. That is the active front on which we are losing and on which, unless we reverse the trend, we shall be defeated. . . .

Unless we meet this cumulative Communist threat with all the brains and weapons we can mobilize for the purpose, the United States at some point in the future will face the terrifying implications of Cold War defeat. . . .

Logically we have no true alternative but to acknowledge the reality of the Cold War and proceed *to turn Moscow's favorite weapons against world Communism.* We have only a choice between fighting the Cold War with maximum concentration of energy, or waiting supinely until we are overwhelmed. Our political counter-strategy has to be as massive, as intensive, as flexible as the enemy's. . . .

The question, in truth, is no longer *whether* we should engage in the Cold War. The Soviet drive is forcing us to take counter-measures in any case. The question, rather, is whether we should undertake it with a clear-headed determination to use all means deemed essential—by governments and by private groups—to win the contest.

Our counter-measures and methods must be novel, unconventional, daring and flexible. They must, moreover, be released from the inhibitions of peace-time, since it is peace only in outer forms. . . .

Our current posture shares the weakness inherent in all defensive strategy. The hope of a real compromise is a dangerous self-delusion. It assumes that Soviet Russia is a conventional country interested in stabilizing the world, when in fact it is the powerhouse of a dynamic world movement which thrives on instability and chaos.

Our duty and our best chance for salvation, in the final analysis, is to prosecute the Cold War—to the point of victory. To survive in freedom we must win.

The free world, under the impact of Moscow's Cold War victories, has tended to fix attention on Soviet strengths while overlooking or discounting Soviet weaknesses.

The Communists expertly exploit all our internal tensions, injustices and discontents. Yet within the Soviet empire the tensions are incomparably greater, the injustices and discontents more vast. Our opportunity, which we have failed to use so far, is to exploit these in order to undermine the Kremlin, exacerbate its domestic problems, weaken its sense of destiny. . . .

Our potential fifth columns are greater by millions than the enemy's. But they have yet to be given cohesion, direction and the inner motive power of hope and expectation of victory.

No one knows whether, let alone when, the internal Soviet stresses can reach a climax in insurrectionary breaks. It would be frivolous to count on such a climax. But we have everything to gain by promoting a spirit of mutiny, to keep the Kremlin off balance, to deepen existing rifts, to sharpen economic and empire problems for them.

For the purposes of our Cold War strategy it suffices that the potential for uprisings exists. . . .

COLD WAR OBJECTIVES

Our guiding objectives in an all-out political offensive are fairly obvious. They must include the following:

1. To keep alive throughout the Soviet empire the spirit of resistance and the hope of eventual freedom and sovereignty. If we allow that hope to expire, the Kremlin will have perpetuated its dominion over its victims.

2. To break the awful sense of isolation in which the internal enemies of the Kremlin live—by making them aware that, like the revolutionists in Tsarist times, they have devoted friends and powerful allies beyond their frontiers.

3. To sharpen by every device we can develop the fear of their own people that is already chronic in the Kremlin. The less certain the Soviets are of the allegiance of their people, the more they will

hesitate to provoke adventures involving the risks of a major showdown.

4. To provide moral and material aid, including trained leadership, to oppositions, undergrounds, resistance movements in satellite nations and China and Russia proper.

5. To make maximum use of the fugitives from the Soviet sphere, millions in the aggregate, now living in free parts of the world.

6. To appeal to the simple personal yearnings of those under the Communist yoke: release from police terror, ownership of small farms and homes, free trade unions to defend their rights at the job, the right to worship as they please, the right to change residence and to travel, etc.

7. To shatter the "wave of the future" aura around Communism, displacing the assumption that "Communism is inevitable" with a deepening certainty that "the end of Communism is inevitable."

8. To inspire millions in the free countries with a feeling of moral dedication to the enlargement of the area of freedom, based on repugnance to slave labor, coerced atheism, purges and the rest of the Soviet horrors.

This inventory of objectives is necessarily sketchy and incomplete. But it indicates the indispensable direction of the Cold War effort.

We must be quite certain of our destination before we can begin to figure out means of transportation. There is little point in discussing the *how* of it until a firm decision for an all-out political-psychological counter-offensive is reached.

In Hot War, you need a *weapon* and means of *delivering* it to the target. The same is true in Cold War. The weapon is the *message;* after it has been worked out, we can develop the facilities for *delivering* it to the world at large and to the Communist-captive nations in particular.

The essence of that message (and its formulation is the critical first step) is that America has decided, irrevocably, to win the Cold

War; that its ultimate aim is, in concert with all peoples, to cancel out the destructive power of Soviet-based Communism. . . .

Adjustment of our thinking in accord with such a decision to win the Cold War demands clarity on at least the following points:

1. The struggle by means short of general war is not a preliminary bout but the decisive contest, in which the loser may not have a second chance.

2. It must therefore be carried on with the same focused effort, the same resolute spirit, the same willingness to accept costs and casualties, that a Hot War would involve.

3. In order to establish credence and inspire confidence, our conduct must be consistent. Our philosophy of freedom must embrace the whole of mankind; it must not stop short at the frontiers of the Soviet sphere. Only this can give our side a moral grandeur, a revolutionary *élan,* a crusading spirit not only equal to but superior to the other side's.

4. We must learn to regard the Soviet countries as *enemy-occupied* territory, with the lifting of the occupation as the over-all purpose of freedom-loving men everywhere. This applies not only to areas captured since the war, but includes Russia itself. Any other policy would turn what should be an anti-Communist alliance into an *anti-Russian* alliance, forcing the Russians (as Hitler forced them during the war) to rally around the regime they hate.

5. The fact that the challenge is global must be kept clearly in view. Red guerrillas in Burma, Communists in France or the U.S., the Huks in the Philippines, Red agents in Central America—these are as much "the enemy" as the Kremlin itself.

6. We must realize that world Communism is *not* a tool in the hands of Russia—Russia is a tool in the hands of world Communism. Repeatedly Moscow has sacrificed national interests in deference to world-revolutionary needs. This provides opportunities for appeals to Russian patriotism.

7. Though the Soviets want a nuclear war no more than we do,

they accept the risk of it in pushing their political offensive. We, too, cannot avoid risks. (It might become necessary, Mr. Dulles said recently, "to forego peace in order to secure the blessings of liberty.") The greatest risk of all, for us, is to do less than is needed to win the Cold War. At worst that would mean defeat by default; and at best, a situation so menacing to the survival of freedom that a Hot War may become inevitable.

Our present lead in the possession of nuclear weapons and the ability to use them may be matched by the Communists in the next few years. This is the view expressed by competent statesmen, scientists and military experts. If and when nuclear parity is reached, the enemy's fanatics (and there may be a powerful madman—a Hitler—among them) might be tempted to use them against us by throwing a sneak punch. Since our policy is not to throw the first nuclear punch but only to retaliate if it is thrown against us, we may find, as more horror-weapons are unfolded, that to yield to the enemy the initiative of the first offensive punch is tantamount to national suicide.[1] . . .

ORGANIZING THE OFFENSIVE

An organizational framework for fighting the Cold War already exists. It needs to be adjusted and strengthened in line with the expanded scale and intensity of operations.

A Strategy Board for Political Defense, the Cold War equivalent of the Joint Chiefs of Staff on the military side, is suggested. It should function directly under the President, with Cabinet status for its Head. Top representatives of the State Department, the Defense Department, the Central Intelligence Agency, the U.S. Information Agency, should sit on this Board. Liaison on a continuous basis should be maintained with all other agencies which can play a role in the over-all effort. . . .

We must go from defense to attack in meeting the political, ideological, subversive challenge. The implementation of the attack would devolve upon specialists and technicians. In gearing to fight a Hot War, we call in military strategists and tacticians. Likewise, we must have specialists to fight a Cold War.

This implies in the first place the mobilization of hard, knowledgeable anti-Communists who understand the issues and for whom it is not merely a job but a dedication. *The specialist in communications is important; but the message to be communicated is even more important.*

The main weakness of our efforts to date to talk to the masses—and even more so to the elite groups (Army, intelligentsia, etc.)—in the Soviet camp is that we have not always been *consistent* in what we had to say to them. Our message has been vague and subject to change without notice. As long as we regard Communist rule as permanent, we can have no strong psychological bridges to those who are under its yoke. The only free-world goal that is relevant to them is one that envisages their eventual emancipation.

With the formulation of a message, we will at last have something to say that interests *them,* not only *us,* and can devote ourselves to perfecting the means of delivering the message. . . .

In all categories the arena of action is the whole globe. Our Cold War targets are not only behind the Iron and Bamboo Curtains, but in every nation, the United States included. *In the battle for the minds of men, we must reach the Soviet peoples, our allies, and the uncommitted peoples.*

The agencies involved will be both official and private. The objectives must aim to *achieve dramatic victories* as swiftly as possible, as a token of the changed state of affairs. While the Kremlin has suffered some setbacks and defeats, its record in the Cold War has been strikingly one of success piled on success. This trend must be reversed to hearten our friends, dismay the enemy, and confirm the fact that Communist Power is a transient and declining phenomenon. . . .

Propaganda, for maximum effect, must not be an end in itself. It is a preparation for action. Words that are not backed up by deeds, that do not generate deeds, lose their impact. The test is whether they build the morale of friends and undermine the morale of foes.

No means of communication should be ignored: the spoken word and the written word; radio and television; films; balloons and missiles to distribute leaflets; secret printing and mimeographing presses on Soviet controlled soil; scrawls on walls to give isolated friends a sense of community.

The Communist sphere must be ringed with both fixed and mobile broadcasting facilities, of a massiveness to overcome jamming. The Voice of America will acquire larger audiences and more concentrated impact under the new approach. . . .

Besides the official voice, we have other voices, such as Radio Free Europe and Radio Liberation. There are other popular democratic voices that should make themselves heard: those of our free labor movement, American war veterans, the churches, youth and women's organizations.

Already there is a minor flow of printed matter across the Iron Curtain, especially aimed at the Red occupation forces. The volume and effectiveness of this effort can be enormously enlarged. Magazines and newspapers which outwardly look like standard Communist matter, but actually are filled with anti-Communist propaganda, have brought results.

A greater hunger for spiritual comfort, for religion, is reported from Soviet Russia and its satellites. Programs of a spiritual and religious character are indicated. They should preach faith in the Divine, abhorrence of Communist godlessness, resistance to atheism. But in addition they can offer practical advice to the spiritually stranded—for instance, how to observe religious occasions where there are no ordained ministers or priests to officiate.

The enslaved peoples do not have to be sold the idea of freedom; they are already sold on it. The propaganda should wherever possible get down to specifics. It should expose the weaknesses, failures, follies, hypocrisies and internal tensions of the Red masters; provide proof of the existence of friends and allies both at home and abroad; offer guidance on types of resistance open even to the individual. It should appeal to universal emotions, to love of family, of country, of God, of humanity. . . .

We need in every country, newspapers; magazines; radio and TV stations, consciously and effectively supporting our side. Those that exist should be aided materially to increase their range and vitality; others should be started with our help. The strongest individual anti-Communist voices must be provided with better facilities for making themselves heard in their own countries.

Mobile film units are already penetrating backward areas. The operation should be enlarged, its message and appeal perfected. In addition, mobile big-screen television units in black-and-white and in color can carry our message. Their very novelty will guarantee large and attentive audiences. Vast regions in Asia and elsewhere, where illiteracy bars the written word and lack of radios bars the spoken word, could thus be reached. To quote the Chinese saying: "One picture is worth ten thousand words." . . .

Mass production of cheap and light-weight receivers tuned to pick up American signals is now feasible. They should be made available by the million at cost or gratis, as expedient, to listeners in critical areas and behind the Iron Curtain. . . .

Pockets of guerrilla forces remain in Poland, Hungary, the Baltic states, China, Albania and other areas. There is always the danger of activating them prematurely. But their existence must be taken into the calculations and, in concert with exiles who know the facts, they must be kept supplied with information, slogans and new leadership where needed and prudent.

Many of these resistance groups are so isolated that they do not know of each other's existence. The simple realization that they are not alone but part of a scattered network will be invaluable; methods for establishing liaison, for conveying directions, can be developed.

The uprisings in East Germany, the strikes and riots in Pilsen, Czechoslovakia, the dramatic mutinies inside the concentration camps of Vorkuta in the Soviet Arctic, are examples of revolutionary actions that failed. But they attest that insurrection is possible.

We must seek out the weakest links in the Kremlin's chain of power. The country adjudged ripe for a break-away should receive concentrated study and planning. A successful uprising in Albania, for instance, would be a body blow to Soviet prestige and a fateful stimulus to resistance elsewhere. (That little country is geographically isolated, ruled by a handful of puppets; able leadership is available in the Albanian emigration.)

Eastern Germany is among the weakest links. Its revolt would ignite neighboring Czechoslovakia and Poland. The time to prepare for such actions is now—whether the time to carry them out be in the near or distant future. Meanwhile we must not allow the Soviet propaganda to make unification appear as the Communists' gift to the Germans. It is a natural asset that belongs to West Germany and her allies.

Tens of thousands of self-exiled fugitives from Communist oppression emerge eager to plunge into movements for the freeing of their homelands. When they fail to find outlets for their zeal, disillusionment and defeatism set in.

Maximum exploitation of this manpower and moral passion is indicated. They must be drawn into specific, well-organized, well-financed anti-Communist organizations and activities; utilized for propaganda and other operations; enabled, in some cases, to return to their native lands as "sleeper" leaders for future crises.

Officers' corps of emigres can be formed; perhaps groups of only a score to a hundred, but available for emergency and opportune occasions. The existence of such nuclei of military power—a fact that will be widely known—should help generate hope and faith among their countrymen back home.

Escapees have come, and will continue to come, spontaneously, now in trickles, other times in rivers. Beyond that the need is to stimulate defection on a selective basis. Individual "prospects" in Soviet missions and legations, in Red cultural and sports delegations, can be carefully contacted and developed. Types of individuals needed to man Cold War undertakings will be invited to escape, assured of important work. Special approaches can be worked out to encourage defection of border guards, Army officers, secret-police personnel disgusted by their bloody chores, scientists, important writers, etc.

Escapees today are often disheartened by their initial experience. They are taken into custody by some foreign Intelligence Service, pumped for information, and sometimes then left to shift for themselves. Their honest patriotism is offended by the need to cooperate with foreigners before they are psychologically ready for it.

It is suggested that emigre commissions be set up, composed of trusted nationals of the various countries. The fugitive would first be received by the commission of his own countrymen. Only when found desirable and prepared for the step, would he be brought into contact with American or British agencies.

The immediate and prospective activities of the Cold War offensive will require ever larger contingents of specialized personnel for the many tasks: to provide leadership for resistance operations; to engage in propaganda, subversion, infiltration of the enemy; even to carry on administrative and civic work *after* the collapse of Communist regimes in various countries, in order to stave off chaos.

Already, limited as our political efforts are, there is a shortage of competent personnel. Meanwhile thousands of younger men and women among the emigres are being lost to factories, farms, menial jobs. This amounts to squandering of potentially important human resources.

We need a network of schools and universities devoted to training *cadres* for the Cold War. The objective is not education in a generic sense, but specific preparation for the intellectual, technical, intelligence and similar requirements of the ideological-psychological war.

This training, of course, should not be limited to people from the Soviet areas. A sort of "West Point" of political warfare—analagous to the Lenin School of Political Warfare in Moscow—might be established. Staffed by the ablest specialists obtainable, it would seek out likely young people willing to make the struggle against Communism their main or sole career. . . .

The Kremlin treats foreign affairs as a primary arena of ideological and psychological effort. It makes moves on the diplomatic chessboard for their propaganda impact: to rally its friends in the outside world, to win over a particular element in some country, to embarrass its opponents. In the measure that democratic diplomacy fails to do likewise, it is defaulting in a vital area of the Cold War. Let us bear in mind:

1. Day to day conduct of foreign affairs is pertinent to the struggle for men's minds. The rigid observance of protocol, in dealing with an enemy who recognizes none of the traditional rules, can be self-defeating. We must make proposals, demands, exposés, publications of official documents, etc., that are carefully calculated to show up the true motives of the Kremlin, to put a crimp in Moscow political campaigns, to mobilize world opinion against Soviet crimes and duplicities.

For ten years we have made one-shot protests against Soviet election frauds in satellite countries, against violations of treaties and agreements, against shocking crimes in areas of Human Rights as defined by the U.N. Charter. The archives are packed with these documents. These should be followed up through consistent publicity, renewed protests, etc.

Even when nothing practical can be immediately accomplished, the facts of slave labor, genocide, aggressions, violations of Yalta, Potsdam and other agreements must be kept continually before the world. Diplomacy must champion the victims of Red totalitarianism without let-up. At every opportunity the spokesmen of free nations should address themselves to the people in the Soviet empire over the heads of their masters; to the people of free countries in terms of universal principles of morality and decency.

2. The measures of reciprocity should be strictly applied to Soviet diplomats, trade, and other representatives. These should enjoy no more privileges, immunities, access to information than is accorded to free-world representatives in Communist lands. Even socially they should be made aware of their status as symbols of a barbarous plexus of power. The desire to belong, to be respectable, is by no means alien to Red officialdom.

3. Economic leverages, too, must be applied. Trade can be turned into a powerful political weapon. The stakes are too high to permit business-as-usual concepts to outweigh the imperatives of the Cold War. Where acute distress develops in a Communist country, our readiness to help must be brought to the attention of the people as well as their bosses. If and when food and other relief is offered, it must be under conditions consistent with our objectives—to help the victims, not their rulers.

4. In virtually all countries outside the Communist sphere there are large or small organizations devoted to combating Communism, at home or abroad or both. There is little or no contact among such groups—no common currency of basic ideas and slogans, no exchange of experience. Without at this stage attempting to set up a world-wide anti-Communist coalition, or Freedom International, we should at least facilitate closer liaison and mutual support among anti-Soviet groupings already in existence.

CHAPTER 5

The Fourteen Fundamental Facts of the Nuclear Age

[Many people argue that the compelling facts of the nuclear age make risky, if not impossible, effective anti-Communist action by the makers of foreign policy in the Free World. Because much nonsense has been written on this point, the following analysis by a distinguished political scientist is presented for the consideration of those who feel that the cause of freedom can well be served in the nuclear age as it has been in the past.]

THE FIRST THIRTEEN FACTS

1. The inevitability of the nucleonic age and the emergence of nuclear industrial potentials is the first fundamental fact which we must grasp firmly.

2. International control would be possible only as a sham and, if adopted, would constitute an extreme and unacceptable security hazard. This is the second fundamental fact which we must understand.

3. Soviet talk about control is designed to disarm the United States and enhance the nuclear posture of world communism. This is the third fact which we must always keep in mind.

This discussion by "Ferreus" first appeared in the October 1954 issue of *The Review of Politics* under the title "Courage or Perdition? The Fourteen Facts of the Nuclear Age." Copyright 1954 by *The Review of Politics*. Reprinted by permission of the editor.

4. The atomically armed future aggressor may be the greatest military realist of all times, and hence end up as the first true world conqueror in history. This possibility is the fourth fact of the nuclear era.

5. Nuclear weapons are the key of modern military power, and hence, the irreplaceable key to American security. This is the fifth fundamental fact of the nuclear problem.

6. The nuclear problem is not susceptible to solutions by legal agreement, nor by any other trick aiming at the evanescence of nuclear weapons. This is the sixth fact with which we must come to grips.

7. In a modern war the first battle may decide the outcome of the entire conflict. This is the seventh fact which we never should allow to be forgotten.

8. Hence, war potentials have lost much of their significance, while forces in being and weapons stockpiles have become of crucial importance.

9. Phony security is the excessive hazard in the present phase of the nuclear age. This ninth fact of the period often has been wilfully and perilously overlooked.

10. Our tenth fundamental fact is that the industrial application of nuclear energy offers an excellent chance for the social strengthening of the free world.

11. American technological and industrial time lags are too long. This is the eleventh fact to which we must pay attention.

12. Shall we consider the need to weaken, modify, or replace the Soviet government to be the twelfth basic fact of the nuclear age?

An effective liberation policy appears as one of the few alternatives to continued life in the shadow of nuclear death, with its expensive and growing demands for constant military readiness. It is true that a policy of liberation in and by itself poses the threat of atomic conflict, the important difference being, however, that an initiative policy by the free world would make it impossible for the aggressor to rig the game entirely in his favor and to create situations which would be most favorable to his plans of attack. If the would-be aggressor were kept off balance and forced to busy himself with his own defenses rather than with offensive plans, the threat of atomic devastation might be diminished.

In the nuclear age, political and military *initiative* is an indispensable prerequisite of security, while loss of initiative poses insoluble problems. The term "initiative" is not used here as a circumlocution for preventive war. Hundreds of initiatives are possible without resort to military conflict. As an example of a successful American initiative, we may recall the decision to acquire the hydrogen bomb before the Soviet Union. However, the time may come when a dispassionate survey of the security problems of the free world would indicate that these problems cannot be solved except through the deliberate resort to force. We should hope that such a moment never will come. But we must remember that in order to secure our safety without an offensive strategy, our military posture would have to be strengthened considerably and that, conversely, if no such strengthening occurs, the fateful decision may become inevitable. It is easy to pronounce cliché opinions about this grave problem and to take pleasure in pointing out that "preventive war" is logical nonsense: War cannot be fought to prevent war. True; but war can, and occasionally *must* be fought to prevent disaster and perdition. *Only one thing is worse than nuclear war: defeat in such a war. And this is the thirteenth fact to which I wish to call attention.*

THE FOURTEENTH FACT

Article I, section 10, paragraph 3 of the Constitution of the United States anticipated the need of initiative and offensive security actions in case of "imminent danger as will not admit of delay"; if such dangers occur, the States may "engage in war . . . without the consent of Congress." So long as the United States clings to the concept that under no possible circumstances will it initiate war, not even while the opponent is preparing to strike, so long the initiative will remain in Soviet hands. In the seven generations of its existence, the United States has waged quite a number of wars and in every one of them—this possibly includes World War II—the United States faced up to the ineluctable decision and initiated hostilities on its own volition. There is absolutely no factual basis for the contention that democracy abhors war. The very nature of democracy demands that it accept its responsibilities and that, while it should not seek war lightly and do everything to avoid conflict, it must fight if and when there is no other choice but the destruction of the democratic system. Has it not become apparent now that the world would be a better place—and that many millions of innocent human beings still would be alive—if Hitler had been stopped between 1933 and 1936? The concept of peace *à outrance* has proved to be unmanageable, excessively costly, and utterly destructive.

No doubt, in the nuclear era, a war decision is of far graver import than a similar decision before 1945. Personally, I never would favor a war decision unless there is a clear, urgent, and immediate need to anticipate and forestall attack, with no other solution being available, and unless there is no other way to avoid a clearly inevitable war at a later date and under significantly more unfavorable circumstances.

However, looking back at my own reactions of twenty years ago, I remember arguing, too, that war should be waged against Hitler only under conditions of extreme necessity. But was that policy so wise? Was it not based on the invalid assumption that the Nazi regime was unstable? Did this policy not provide Hitler with many trumps and allow him to out-arm his opponents? Maybe the ideals of pacifism are so lofty that the price which we had to pay—and which in the end possibly will have included a future World War III—was not too high. But again, was it such a good idea to refuse paying the relatively small price required to hold China during

1947 and 1949, seize North Korea in 1950, and liquidate Communist China after it actually had attacked United States forces? Far from embracing preventive war, the United States adopted a strategy of not fighting back and of deliberately averting its own victory. What did this new departure in militant peacefulness save for us in Southeast Asia? What will it have saved for us after Communist China and Russia will have developed modern industries and combined their military resources? Clearly, do we not have a policy of avoiding the smaller and easier wars to make the big and costly wars ever more inevitable? In any event, in proclaiming good intentions of peacefulness with respect to future wars we are forced to look hard at the *fourteenth fact of the atomic age which, perhaps, is the most ominous of all: that in an atomic conflict the force which plans to strike second never may be in a position to strike at all.*

In the discharge of its security duties toward itself, its allies and toward the free world, the United States must seize the political initiative. Yet this initiative cannot be seized so long as the opponent *knows* that the United States does not mean it seriously and will shrink away from the ultimate consequence. The United States also may have to seize the military initiative, but nothing effective can be done in either field so long as the opponent is allowed to count upon his double ability to determine the timing of the war and to strike the first blow. No sustained and successful American initiative is possible while the by far most important decision is left in Soviet hands.

Without vigorous initiative, there can be no liberation, nor can the Soviets be dissuaded from their clearly avowed aggressive intentions. Yet unless this Soviet objective of world domination is eliminated, there is no real chance of avoiding war; and, naturally, unless the basic military initiatives are in free world hands, there will be no protection against devastation, loss of life and defeat, nor preservation of free institutions and democracy. We may get away with a policy of the least effort, but only if our opponent is thoroughly frightened by what we can do to him after we received his first blows. It is in the nature of atomic war that he has no overwhelming reason to be excessively frightened.

To sum it all up: We have a policy of avoiding war, but we have achieved only this—the danger of war is becoming ever more unmanageable. To keep the military situation under control and to preserve our democratic institutions, we shall have to make a stand at some time. On the basis of the record of the years 1933 to 1954, we can say confidently that the sooner and the firmer the United States will make this stand, the easier the task will be and the greater the chance of forestalling atomic warfare.

The world is full of unprecedented dangers. We may argue about the means by which the dangers *could* be overcome, if such means were utilized. But we should realize that, in all probability, the dangers will persist. It is easy to predict the doom of our civilization and quite unrewarding to propose concrete—and costly and unpopular—military and political measures aiming to insure the survival of that civilization. I cannot help feeling, however, that this civilization is a spiritual force and, therefore, not susceptible to physical destruction. In any event, it cannot survive if the people who live under its blessings display a deplorable weakness of conviction and lack the ethos of courage. Nor can this civilization survive if its intellectual elites, fearful of risk, effort, and self-assertion, advise collective political suicide. This is a statement which can be supported with historical evidence and which I intend to be an objective proposition. I realize that the advocacy of suicide is not always intentional and that praiseworthy desires often are the midwives of deadly proposals.

I would like to add, and say it clearly, that I have nothing but contempt for those who are willing to surrender to Communism in order to avoid nuclear war and thus to assure the physical survival and the enslavement of the maximum number. If such a spirit were typical of the free society, our civilization would be dead now. I do not believe that doom is near, let alone that it has come. But I am worried that the voices of cowardice are heard far more often than the voices of determination. I, too, want my family and my friends to survive, and I do want to live to the end of my natural days. Everyone has the instinctive animal fear of death. But it hardly pays to survive for the blessings of a slave existence, and it will be intolerable to purchase survival through the betrayal of value and conscience. Policies cannot be based just on the instinct of self-preservation. Do intellectuals and politicians have a lesser moral obligation than the simple private of whom they expect that he sacrifice himself when ordered into battle? Our entire society has been pushed into mortal conflict. In some way, most of us are now manning a battle station. Must we not be true to our duties?

The issue of the present world conflict is whether communism will be victorious or be destroyed. The hydrogen bomb has not changed this issue, not by one iota. If the desire for freedom were a variable dependent on the expected rate of casualties, we should not even attempt to fight. If, however, national and individual freedom is our highest political value, then we should do our best to keep casualties to a minimum—even in the country of our opponent—but we should not be deterred by the cost of the conflict; the cost of defeat and of loss of principle would be still higher.

We are living today twice as long as the generations who conquered freedom for us and established the foundations of good government. Our task is to preserve and improve freedom for ourselves and for our descendants, and to bring freedom to those who still are enslaved. The way to solve a serious problem is not to distort or ignore it, but to handle it; to take all precautions which prudence imposes, to accept the irreducible risks, to bear the required responsibilities, and to follow the dictates of one's conscience. To cringe before the enemy, to bewail fate even before it is known, to become paralyzed from fear and pessimism, and to abandon oneself to the visions of apocalyptic horror is despicable. It is moral self-destruction to which atomic devastation would add little but physical confirmation and merited punishment.

CHAPTER 6

The Fallacies of Disarmament

[Wishful thinkers and pacifists within free nations have from time to time urged that the best way to deal with aggressive dictators is to reduce armaments, end our weapons testing, and even disarm. Most such proposals do not require foolproof inspection techniques to insure that *all* parties involved comply with the clauses of disarmament agreements. The West was almost destroyed in 1939 because it reduced its armaments unilaterally; in 1945 the West repeated its error. Yet today great pressure continues to be exerted on the United States to come to some sort of a disarmament agreement with the Communist bloc. The analysis of the fallacies of disarmament, made by Professor Geoffrey F. Hudson of Oxford University in 1957, deserves careful study.]

DO THE RUSSIANS REALLY WANT DISARMAMENT?

Since the beginning of this year there has been a perceptible shift of emphasis in Western-Soviet relations away from questions of political dispute into the field of disarmament. The hopes of the West, frustrated by the apparently insuperable roadblock in the way of any progress toward a political settlement in Europe, have been diverted into speculations on demilitarized zones, "open skies" and bans on nuclear tests. The idea behind the current trend is that, even if the West cannot reach agreement with Russia on

The material in this chapter first appeared in an address delivered by Geoffrey F. Hudson at St. Antony's College, Oxford, in June, 1957, and is reprinted here by permission.

any major political issue, it can at least reduce the danger of war by making it a little less easy for belligerents to grapple with each other in the first few hours of an armed conflict.

Unfortunately it is extremely difficult, because of the actual circumstances of the strategic situation in Europe, to imagine any agreement on limitation of arms which, however fair it might seem on the surface, would not in practice work out to the disadvantage of the West.

The North Atlantic Treaty Organization forces in Germany are not only gravely inferior to the Soviet power facing them—the Soviet superiority in armored units is estimated at 3 to 1—but they are reckoned to be too thin on the ground to be sure of dealing decisively even with a raid across the border by an Pankow *Freikorps* [East German armed force]; any further restriction on them would render them virtually incapable of acting in Germany at all.

Any "open skies" agreement of considerable depth equal on both sides would cover Western Europe, while leaving the interior of the Soviet Union untouched, and would thus affect Western defense far more than the highly mobile offensive power of the Soviet Union. Further, any practical agreement for limiting forces in particular parts of Europe must necessarily accept their existing geographical distribution as its starting point, and by thus giving a formal recognition to the line through Germany as something more than a mere boundary between zones of Allied postwar military occupation—which is all that it has ever been acknowledged to be so far—it must have an extremely damaging effect on West German morale and confidence in the NATO coalition.

It would not be surprising if the rulers of Russia were to be attracted by the idea of gaining such strategic and political advantages by an agreement for nominally equal sacrifices by the two blocs.

According to reports from Washington, President Eisenhower has been persuaded by Bohlen [former U.S. Ambassador to Russia] and Stassen [Special Assistant to the President for Disarmament] that the Russians really want a disarmament agreement and that the time has come to break the deadlock by an offer of acceptable terms. The proposals put forward are said to have been unanimously opposed by the American service chiefs, but a new flame of optimism appears to have been kindled somewhere between the White House and the Augusta golf course.

Despite the assurance given to Adenauer [West German Chancellor] and the President's insistence that only an "initial" and not a "comprehensive" agreement is envisaged, Western policy seems now to be gliding gently on a very slippery slope. Both the American and British governments have made public statements encouraging their peoples to expect a disarmament pact of some kind in the near future, and it will be very difficult for them now to draw back if the Russians begin raising their price, as it will be natural for them to do.

The background to this move for "initial" disarmament is the great debate in the West over the "nuclear deterrent."

On the one hand, there are those who pin their faith to the threat of massive retaliation with strategic bombing in the event of any Soviet aggression in Europe, and are prepared to reduce the role of NATO ground forces to that of a "trip wire."

On the other hand, there is the widespread intense aversion to the idea of nuclear warfare, which finds expression in the declaration of the Bishop of Manchester that it would be better to be defeated than to use the hydrogen bomb.

Inevitably the introduction of the nuclear arm into war has caused not only the darkest forebodings and searchings of heart on moral grounds, but also intense controversy among military experts as regards the technical possibilities of its use. Yet the basic conditions of strategy as modified by nuclear weapons should not be quite so much obscured by the smoke of mental confusion as they are today.

The trouble is that measures dictated by considerations of budget economy or domestic politics are being presented as illuminations of up-to-date strategic wisdom, with the result that the public, instead of being enlightened by official explanations, is merely being led further and further away from the realities of the situation.

There is no good reason to believe that, in a war in which both sides were well equipped with nuclear and thermonuclear weapons, the issue would be decided simply by strategic bombardment. However vast the devastation that might be inflicted by such means, the decision would be reached by the capacity to destroy the enemy's armed forces and to seize and control his territory.

The instrument of battle would be the army, no longer composed of masses of infantry, but of fast-moving and widely dispersed armored and mechanized units supported by tactical atomic weapons and tactical air forces. With such armies depending for their supplies entirely on tracked vehicles and air transport, the power of the overland offensive becomes greater than ever before.

Tactical atomic weapons can be used defensively also, but if the covering armored troops are insufficient, they can quickly be overrun; it has always been recognized in military theory that an army which relies on artillery and has not enough infantry merely has its guns captured, and the same principle holds good if tanks are substituted for infantry and Corporals [atomic missiles] for howitzers.

There is every prospect, therefore, that a future war will still be won or lost by the army in the field, while the strategic bombing, though far more terrible, will have essentially the same function as in the last war. But it is quite likely that the most feared form of strategic bombing, the attack on the enemy's homeland with hydrogen bombs, may not occur at all.

It is clearly to the interest of the belligerent who is stronger on the ground to avoid the mutual carnage of hydrogen warfare, since he can be confident of winning without it; the losing side, on the other hand, may well shrink from invoking it—or may be prevented by popular panic from doing so—if the enemy declares that he will not use it first.

WHO IS DETERRING WHOM?

It is all very well to pin one's faith in the deterrent power of the hydrogen bomb, but if the other side does in fact take the risk, then the deterrent as such has failed, and the deterrent begins to work the other way, for the decision to use it must at once bring retaliation in kind.

Psychologically, the theory of the nuclear deterrent has never been adequately thought out, and this is in no way surprising, for it is essentially a piece of humbug designed to cover up the fact that the Western nations are unwilling to make the effort needed to provide themselves with adequate military defense.

The greatest danger of war in the near future lies in the great military superiority which the NATO powers have allowed Russia to obtain and keep in Central Europe. There is a standing temptation to Russia to make use of it in a crisis to overrun the residue of the Continent and throw the Americans back across the Atlantic. But there is no reason as regards total manpower and resources why the NATO nations should not be able to maintain military forces sufficient to engage the Russians on the Elbe on equal terms.

That they cannot do so, and are reduced to talking about their armies in Germany as a "trip wire," is because they are unwilling to make the sacrifices required to meet the Soviet challenge. Therefore they take refuge in the nuclear deterrent, and deceive themselves with the idea that it will be enough to avert the possibility of war; thus their leaders can provide defense on the cheap, can abolish conscription, and need not lose a single by-election through having to bring unpleasant facts to the notice of the electorate. As for General Norstad, who cares about the opinion of NATO's Supreme Commander?

It is indeed extraordinary that it is the British government which should be leading this rout of the Gadarene swine, for Britain is the last country which should invoke hydrogen strategy if it can possibly be avoided. While it may be a good thing to keep a few hydrogen bombs in the locker if the worst should come to the worst, the energies of Britain should be devoted to the joint building of such a military defense for NATO that the temptation for the enemy to attack in Europe would be removed.

For Britain to concentrate on the type of warfare by use of which she would suffer most is a perversity only too reminiscent of the follies of the Baldwin-Chamberlain era. The vulnerability of Britain to thermonuclear strategic bombing is many times greater than that of the Soviet Union or North America, with their vast areas and the great distances of at least large parts of their territories from hostile bases.

What is now happening in Western Europe is not an increase of the deterrent to an aggressive Russia, but a diminution of the only real deterrent, which is that provided by an army ready to give battle.

The present trend is also morally and politically to the advantage of Russia. The more the Western powers rely on nuclear weapons, and particularly strategic nuclear weapons, for the defense which they shirk providing by proper means, the more they incur responsibility in the eyes of neutrals, of the peoples behind the Iron Curtain, and of their own peoples, for putting their stake on the most frightful of all forms of warfare when Russia is constantly appealing for its abolition.

Even though the West has a sound case in refusing to abolish nuclear weapons without a knaveproof system of inspection and control, it is becoming more and more obvious that it cannot in any case agree to a prohibition of these weapons, because renunciation of them would leave Russia with an overwhelming preponderance of power.

This is a situation which Soviet propaganda may be expected to exploit relentlessly. It can tell the peoples of the Soviet bloc that the warmongering imperialists of Washington and London are not merely instigating war against the peace-loving nations of the socialist camp, but are seeking to wage it by means of mass destruction of civilian populations, contrary to the will of the Soviet Union, which would prefer to limit fighting to soldiers in the field. And if in an armed conflict the West were to resort to this kind of warfare after the Soviet Government had declared its intention of not being the first to use it, it would, like the Nazi atrocities in Russia in the last war, enable the Communist authorities to arouse furious hatred against the West even in quarters deeply disaffected toward Communist rule.

The effect on the Afro-Asian neutrals would also be profound. Nor would the solidarity of the Western democracies themselves be likely to stand up to the disruption and demoralization caused by such a situation.

The peoples of Western Europe who might be overrun by Soviet forces would hardly appreciate a conduct of war by their friends which consisted in obliterating their cities as soon as a few Russian tanks entered them, and, even in the countries which were hitting back effectively, qualms of conscience added to fear might induce waves of hysterical defeatism which no government could ignore. The Bishop of Manchester might soon multiply himself many million times.

The development of a situation which is thus strategically and politically so favorable to the Soviet Union does not necessarily mean that the Soviet leaders would lightly start a major war in pursuit of their policies in Europe or elsewhere. At best, it would in present circumstances involve serious risks for them. But they can hope, with a continuation of present trends, to increase their advantage and disintegrate the coalition opposed to them to a point at which decisive gains could be made by pressure without having to fight at all—or at least with the risk greatly reduced. The disarmament project promoted by Stassen can, as already mentioned, take effect in this direction, and now we have Khrushchev [head of the Soviet Communist party] by courtesy of an American television company addressing the American people in their homes as the embodiment of sweetness and light.

All the signs point to a new era of appeasement, which the Soviet Government will foster by all means. What the collective leaders in Moscow now most need is to be trusted. They would like nothing better than to get back to the good old times of Joseph Davies [U.S. Ambassador to Russia, 1936–38; adviser to President Truman at Potsdam Conference, 1945].

It is true that the reign of that oracular authority did not last forever, and when President Truman finally saw that the Russians had in fact set up Communist regimes in all the occupied territories of Eastern Europe, which was what Joseph Davies had said they would never do, he began to lose faith in his infallible expert. But by that time it was too late to take steps which might have at least reduced the extent of the Soviet triumph in Europe.

The confidence trickster can never, of course, count on his victim retaining confidence in him after the trick has been played; all that is necessary is that the faith should last until the spoil has been collected. The question is whether the Soviet leaders can refrain for long enough from clearly hostile and provocative actions to build up the degree of confidence required.

They quickly spoiled the effect of the Summit Conference of 1955 by a series of such actions during the next few months, and the hopes aroused by "de-Stalinization" in the following year were soon dashed by the slaughter in Budapest—though it should be noted that there were not a few people in the West who were disposed to put the blame on the Hungarians for having set back Russia's gradual self-reform by their reckless impatience.

So it may be that Russia will once again thwart her own quest of confidence by actions too plainly in contradiction of her professions of good will. But if these mistakes can be avoided for a sufficient period of time, we can expect a revival on a large scale in the West of the state of mind which appeased Hitler before 1939 and Stalin from 1943 to 1946.

HAVE THE SOVIETS BECOME MORE REASONABLE?

It may be objected, however, that at the Twentieth Congress of the Soviet Communist Party last year there was an official revision of the old dogmas of the inevitability of war between the imperialists and the Soviet bloc, and of the necessity of civil war for the attainment of power in any country. These revisions were certainly intended to create the impression of a new peacefulness and mildness in the regime, but close attention to the contexts of the declarations deprives them of the significance which optimists in the West would like them to have had.

The reference to Poland and Czechoslovakia [at the Twentieth Congress] as countries where the Communists obtained power "peacefully" showed that there was no acceptance of democratic process as understood in the West, while the concession that war was not inevitable if the "peace fighters" in the imperialist countries were to become strong enough to stop it was only another way of saying that it remained inevitable unless all important countries submitted to control of their policies by Communist-directed organizations.

There was nothing, indeed, in these speeches incompatible with the classic formulations of the concept of world revolution. Nor was there any promise for world peace in the turn against Stalin and the return to Lenin. This may have been comforting for party functionaries and civil servants who had lived in fear of the caprices of the MVD [Secret Police], but it did not affect the violent purposes to which the regime is dedicated.

From the point of view of the West, what is wrong with the Soviet Union is not Stalinism, but Marxism-Leninism, and as long as this doctrine with its catastrophic implications remains the orthodoxy of the Soviet state, the only safety for the West lies in armed strength and close alliances.

If the above interpretation of the political needs of the Soviet regime is correct, it follows that one should expect a new Soviet forward move whenever a weakening of Western strength and locally disturbed conditions provide a suitable opportunity. Looking at Europe today, an observer can hardly fail to see in Germany the area where the signals are most clearly indicating danger. . . .

Many Germans are deeply disillusioned about a NATO coalition which can neither induce the Russians to give up East Germany nor provide more than a trip wire for the protection of West Germany. With a large part of the French Army diverted to Algeria and Britain determined to cut its forces on the Rhine as soon as possible, the military position of NATO in Germany is becoming farcical.

It is true that the Germans themselves must bear a large share of the responsibility for this by their delays in their own rearmament and their obduracy about the costs of Allied forces on their soil. But, wherever the blame may be laid, a sudden German yielding to seductive Russian approaches and a breakaway from NATO are possibilities to be taken seriously, and their implications are of the greatest import for the other countries of Western Europe.

Western forces could not stay in Germany if Germany repudiated them; the Soviet Union would piously champion the Germans' right to self-determination, and it is not to be imagined that Britain or America would be willing to take measures to keep Germany in NATO similar to those which Russia used last November to retain Hungary in the Warsaw Pact.

The danger from a German crisis would not simply be that of the loss of Germany as an ally and as a strategic territory; it would lie even more in a loss of nerve by the Western nations, which are in no way prepared psychologically for such a reverse, and might be drawn into a desperate effort to preserve peace by a capitulatory settlement with Russia, especially if "initial" disarmament had in the meantime gathered a certain momentum. Not that such a settlement would avert war. War comes a year after Munich.

CHAPTER 7

The Consequences of Recognizing Red China

[Not only friends of Red China, but some sincere but misguided Americans as well, have worked themselves into such an emotional state over Chiang Kai-shek that they have actually convinced themselves of the logic of recognizing Communist China. One of the best refutations of such "logic" was made by Secretary of State John Foster Dulles in an address in San Francisco on June 28, 1957. Excerpts from this address are presented here because they strengthen the position of the friends of free China and give extra ammunition to proponents of a liberation policy.]

THE CONSEQUENCES FOR FREE CHINA

United States diplomatic recognition of Communist China would have the following consequences:

(1) The many mainland Chinese, who by Mao Tse-tung's [Chinese Communist Chief of State] own recent admission seek to change the nature of their government, would be immensely discouraged.

(2) The millions of overseas Chinese would feel that they had no free China to look to. Today, increasing numbers of these overseas Chinese go to free China to study. Six years ago there were

This chapter originated as an address delivered by Secretary of State John Foster Dulles to the International Convention of Lions International at San Francisco, California, on June 28, 1957. Subheads have been supplied by the author.

less than 100 Chinese students from Southeast Asia and Hong Kong studying in Taiwan. Today there are nearly 5,000.

The number of Chinese students from overseas communities going to free China has increased year by year; the number going to Communist China has declined, and hundreds of disillusioned students have made their way out of the mainland in the last two years.

If the United States recognized the Chinese Communist regime, millions of overseas Chinese in free Asian countries would, reluctantly, turn to acceptance of the guiding direction of the Communist regime. That would be a tragedy for them; and it would imperil friendly governments already menaced by Chinese Communist subversion.

(3) The Republic of China, now on Taiwan, would feel betrayed by its friend. That government was our ally in the Second World War and for long bore alone the main burden of the Far Eastern War. It had many tempting opportunities to compromise with the Japanese on terms which would have been gravely detrimental to the United States. It never did so.

We condemn the Soviets for having dishonored their twenty-year treaty pledge of 1945 to support the Chinese Nationalist Government as the central government of China. We are honor-bound to give to our ally, to whom we are pledged by a mutual defense treaty, a full measure of loyalty.

(4) The free Asian governments of the Pacific and Southeast Asia would be gravely perplexed. They are not only close to the vast Chinese land mass, but they are geographically and, to some extent, politically, divided among themselves. The unifying and fortifying influence is above all the spirit and resolution of the United States. If we seemed to waver and to compromise with communism in China, that would in turn weaken free Asia resistance to the Chinese Communist regime and assist international communism to score a great success in its program to encircle us.

United States recognition of Communist China would make it

probable that the Communist regime would obtain the seat of China in the United Nations. That would not be in the interest either of the United States or of the United Nations.

The United Nations is not a reformatory for bad governments. It is supposedly an association of those who are already "peace-loving," and who are "able and willing to carry out their charter obligations," and the basic obligation is not to use force, except in defense against armed attack.

The Chinese Communist Government has a record of successive armed aggressions, including war against the United Nations itself, a war not yet politically settled but discontinued by an armistice. The regime asserts not only its right, but its purpose, to use force if need be to bring Taiwan under its rule.

Under the Charter the Republic of China is entitled to a permanent seat and "veto power" in the Security Council. Should a regime which in seven years has promoted five foreign or civil wars—Korea, Indochina, Tibet, the Philippines, and Malaya; which itself has fought the United Nations and which today stands condemned by the United Nations as an aggressor; which defies the United Nations decision to reunify Korea; and which openly proclaims its continuing purpose to use force—should that regime be given a permanent seat, with veto power, in the body which under the Charter has "primary responsibility for the maintaining of international peace and security"?

Communist Russia, with its veto power, already seriously limits the ability of the United Nations to serve its intended purposes. Were Communist China also to become a permanent, veto-wielding member of the Security Council, that would, I fear, implant in the United Nations the seeds of its own destruction.

Now let me turn to the matter of trade and cultural relations, which could exist, to a limited degree, even without recognition.

Normal peacetime trade with China, from which American and Chinese people would benefit, could be in the common interest. But it seems that that trade is not to be had in any appreciable volume.

Trade with Communist China is not normal trade. It does not provide one country with what its people want, but cannot well produce for themselves, in exchange for what other people want and cannot well produce for themselves.

Trade with Communist China is wholly controlled by an official apparatus and its limited amounts of foreign exchange are used to develop as rapidly as possible a formidable military establishment and a heavy industry to support it. The primary desire of that regime is for machine tools, electronic equipment, and, in general, what will help it to produce tanks, trucks, planes, ammunition, and military items.

Whatever others may do, surely the United States, which has a heavy security commitment in the China area, ought not to build up the military power of its potential enemy.

We also doubt the value of cultural exchanges, which the Chinese Communists are eager to develop. They want this relationship with the United States primarily because, once that example were given, it would be difficult for China's close neighbors not to follow it. These free nations, already exposed to intense Communist subversive activities, could not have the cultural exchanges that the Communists want without adding greatly to their peril.

Now these are considerations which argue for a continuance of our present policies. And what are the arguments on the other side?

There are some who say that we should accord diplomatic recognition to the Communist regime because it has now been in power so long that it has won the right to that.

That is not sound international law. Diplomatic recognition is always a privilege, never a right.

DISPOSAL OF THE *de facto* ARGUMENT

Now, of course, the United States knows that the Chinese Communist regime exists. We know that very well because they fought us in Korea. And also, we admit of dealings with those Chinese

Communists in particular cases where that may serve our interests. We have dealt with it in relation to the Korea and the Indochina armistices. For nearly two years we have been, and still are, dealing with it in an effort to get free our citizens from prisons and to obtain reciprocal renunciation of force.

But diplomatic recognition gives the recognized regime valuable rights and privileges, and, in the world of today, recognition by the United States gives the recipient much added prestige and influence at home and abroad.

Now, of course, diplomatic recognition is not to be withheld capriciously. In this matter, as others, the United States seeks to act in accordance with principles which contribute to a world society of order under law.

A test often applied is the ability of a regime actually to govern. But that is by no means a controlling factor. Nations often maintain diplomatic relations with governments-in-exile. And they frequently deny recognition to those in actual power.

Other customary tests are whether, as Thomas Jefferson put it, the recognized government reflects "the will of the nation, substantially declared"; whether the government conforms to the code of civilized nations, whether it lives peacefully and whether it honors its international engagements.

Always, however, recognition is admitted to be an instrument of national policy, to serve enlightened self-interest.

One thing which is clear beyond a doubt: There is nothing automatic about recognition. It is never compelled by the mere lapse of time.

Now another argument sometimes beginning to be heard is that diplomatic recognition is inevitable, so why not now?

First of all, let me say emphatically that the United States need never succumb to the argument of "inevitability." We, with our friends, can fashion our own destiny. We do not accept the mastery of Communist forces.

And let me go on to say that these Communist despotisms are not so immutable as they sometimes appear. Time and circumstances work also upon them.

There is often an optical illusion which results from the fact that police states, suppressing differences, give an external appearance of hard permanency; whereas the democracies, with their opposition parties and often speaking through different and discordant voices, seem to be unstable, pliable members of the world society.

The reality, of course, is that a governmental system which tolerates diversity has a long life expectancy, whereas a system which seeks to impose conformity is always in danger, and that results from the basic nature of human beings. Of all the arguments advanced for recognition of the Communist regime, the least cogent is the argument of "inevitability."

CHINESE SPLIT WITH RUSSIA?

Now there are some who suggest that if we assist the Chinese Communists to wax strong, they will eventually split with Soviet Russia and that that is our best hope for the future.

No doubt there are basic power rivalries between Russia and China, but also, the Russian and Chinese Communists are bound together with close ideological ties.

Perhaps, if the ambitions of the Chinese Communists are inflated by successes, they might eventually clash with Soviet Russia.

Perhaps, too, if the Axis powers had won the Second World War, they would have fallen out among themselves.

But no one suggested that we should tolerate and even assist an Axis victory because in the end they would quarrel over the booty —of which we would be part.

We seek to appraise our China policies with an open mind and without emotion, except for a certain indignation at their prolonged abuse of American citizens in China. We have no feeling whatsoever that change is to be avoided merely in the interest of consistency or because change might be interpreted as admitting past errors.

We always take into account the possibility of influencing the Communist regime to better ways if we had diplomatic relations with it, or if, without that, we had commerical and cultural contacts with it. But the experience of those who now recognize and deal with the Chinese Communist regime convinces us that, under present conditions, neither recognition, nor trade, nor cultural relations, nor all three together would favorably influence affairs in China. The probable result would be just the opposite of what we hope for.

Internationally, the Chinese Communist regime does not conform to the practices of civilized nations; does not live up to its international obligations; has not been peaceful in the past, and gives no evidence of being peaceful in the future. Its foreign policies are hostile to us and our Asian allies. Under these circumstances, it would be folly for us to establish relations with the Chinese Communists which would enhance their ability to hurt us and our friends.

You may ask, "What of the future?" Are our policies merely negative? Do we see any prospect of resuming the many friendly ties which, for many generations, the American people have had with the Chinese people, and which we want to have again?

Do we see any chance that the potentially great Chinese nation, with its rich and ancient culture and wisdom, will again be able to play a constructive part in the councils of the nations?

We confidently answer these questions in the affirmative.

We know that the materialistic rule of international communism will never permanently serve the aspirations with which human beings are endowed by their Creator.

Communism is repugnant to the Chinese people. They are, above all, individualists.

And we read the recent brave words uttered within Red China

by the University lecturer: "To overthrow you cannot be called unpatriotic because you Communists no longer serve the people."

We can confidently assume that international Communists' rule of strict conformity is, in China as elsewhere, a passing and not a perpetual phase. We owe it to ourselves, our allies, and the Chinese people to do all that we can to contribute to that passing.

If we believed that this passing would be promoted by trade and cultural relations, we would have such relations.

If we believed that this passing would be promoted by our having diplomatic relations with the present regime, we would have such relations.

If we believed that this passing would be promoted by some participation of the present regime in the activities of the United Nations, we would not oppose that.

We should be, and constantly are, testing our policies, to be as certain as we can be that, in the light of conditions as they are from time to time, our policies serve the great purposes to which our nation was dedicated since its foundation—the cause of peace, justice and human liberty.

Our policies are readily adjustable to meet the requirements of changing conditions. But there are occasions when not we, but others, should provide the change. Nothing could be more dangerous than for the United States to operate on the theory that if hostile and evil forces do not quickly and readily change, then it is we who must change to meet them.

The United States exerts an immense influence in the world today, not only because it is materially powerful, but because we stand for peace, for national independence, and for personal liberty. Many free nations seek to coordinate their foreign policies with ours. And such coordination is indeed indispensable if the free world is to have the cohesion needed to make it safe.

But United States policies will never serve as a rallying point for free peoples if the impression is created that our policies are subject to change to meet Communist wishes for no reason other than that communism itself does not want to change. If communism is stubborn for the wrong, let us be steadfast for the right.

The capacity to change is an indispensable capacity. Equally indispensable is the capacity to hold fast that which is good. Given those qualities, we can hopefully look forward to the day when those in Asia who are yet free can confidently remain free, and when the people of China and the people of America can resume their long history of cooperative friendship.

CHAPTER 8

A Program for Survival in the Nuclear Age

Any program for survival in the nuclear age involves sacrifice, hard work, huge costs, difficult judgments and imaginative research. We are faced, as the launching of the Soviet satellites has made clear, with a tough competitor, whose rate of progress in military development in the past five years has outpaced our own.

We still have some enormous strategic and military advantages, but we are behind the Soviet Union in certain fields, and we are unbalanced in some aspects of military strength.

Here are some of the areas of weakness that deserve immediate attention, highest possible priorities and maximum funds.

LONG-RANGE BALLISTIC MISSILES

The Soviets' lead in some phases of the development of long-range giant rockets, though probably slight, is real, and only major effort will overcome it. Limitations have been removed and more funds provided, and there has been a consequent speed-up in the

This discussion by Hanson Baldwin first appeared in the February 5, 1958 issue of *The New York Times* as one of a series of articles entitled "A Series of Articles Appraising the United States Military Position in Relation to the Soviet Union in the Nuclear Missile Age" and published in *The New York Times* from February 2 to February 7, 1958. Copyright 1958 by *The New York Times*. Reprinted by permission of Hanson Baldwin and *The New York Times*.

Thor and Jupiter intermediate range [1,500 miles] ballistic missiles programs and in the Atlas ICBM [5,500 miles] program.

But the more advanced Titan ICBM has not been speeded, and many authorities consider that our sights are still much too low in the long-range missile field. Our objectives contemplate, as of today, very few ICBM missiles in the 1960 fiscal year; more should be ordered now.

POLARIS GETS HIGH PRIORITY

The Navy's ship-based Polaris IRBM, under development for submerged submarine launching, has—and should have—very high priorities. This is not only because it is launched from a mobile base difficult to detect and destroy, but also because the Polaris is undoubtedly the prototype of the ballistic missile of the future. It is a solid-propellant rocket, and hence is free from the technical difficulties and the long "count-down" or check-off necessary before the firing of a liquid-fueled rocket.

The Army is developing solid-propellant rockets up to 1,000-mile range, and the Air Force is initiating work on a solid-propellant intermediate-range ballistic missile.

SHORT REACTION TIME NEEDED

But in addition to the Atlas and the Titan, which are liquid-fueled rockets, a third intercontinental ballistic missile project should be initiated, with a solid-propellant motor. For a solid-propellant rocket will not only be far more mobile and require less ground support equipment than a liquid-propelled one, but it should materially reduce the time required to react—with offensive measures of our own—to enemy attack or threat of attack.

And the shortest possible reaction time is of tremendous importance in the age of possible surprise attack when the distance between continents has been narrowed to a thirty-minute time span.

Development of ICBM and IRBM capability from bases overseas, bases in this country and bases at sea (ships and submarines) will greatly strengthen our nuclear retaliatory power and hence our deterrent power against any massive enemy aggression.

ANTI-MISSILE MISSILE SYSTEM

An effective defense to blunt any enemy's attack and to preserve our power to retaliate and our viability as a nation is an essential part of any nuclear deterrent.

The North American Air Defense Command is just commencing to achieve the capability of a good defense—though never a 100 per cent one—against piloted aircraft, but the nation has no defense and no warning system against long-range ballistic missiles.

Missile-warning radar with a range of 3,000 nautical miles has been proved technically feasible. Funds to start the construction of three such warning stations in Greenland, Alaska and north of Canada have been asked in a supplemental budget. Such a radar might give at most fifteen minutes' warning of a missile attack, but nine B-52's can take off, when in an alert status, from one airstrip in fifteen minutes, and between them they can carry millions of tons of explosive power in the form of thermonuclear weapons.

START OF BUILDING URGENT

It is a matter of urgency that construction of these warning stations be started during this Arctic summer. Tracking radar to supplement them should be built when it has been developed, and an entire anti-missile missile system, with its intricate system of search, acquisition, and control radars, should have the highest priority.

At present—even when and if such a system is developed (1962–63 is the earliest target date)—an initial 25 per cent "kill rate" against ICBM's is the optimum hoped for. Air defense in general needs more funds and more imagination.

MISSILE-FIRING SUBMARINES

The mobile base capable of launching ballistic missiles with nuclear warheads provides, because of its mobility, the greatest immunity to enemy surprise attack. Thus, a nuclear-powered submarine that is able to stay submerged indefinitely and hence adds invisibility to mobility poses, when equipped with missiles with nuclear warheads, an almost insoluble problem to any aggressor.

No surprise attack can hope to eliminate an entire fleet of missile-firing submarines dispersed at sea. The sea base has another advantage; it would attract the lightning of any enemy's blow away from our shores.

Today, the Navy has two conventionally powered submarines of short submerged endurance equipped to fire, when surfaced, the Regulus winged air-breathing missile. Two other Diesel-electric submarines to fire the Regulus II winged missile are under construction. A nuclear-powered submarine, to be equipped with the faster and longer-range Regulus III, is being built.

FUNDS FOR SUBMARINES

Funds have been provided in a supplemental appropriation bill approved by Congress for three nuclear-powered submarines equipped to fire the Navy's solid-propellant intermediate-range ballistic missile—the Polaris. Nine of these submarines can be built at a cost of about $1 billion including missiles.

Two missile-firing submarines in service and six new ones building or authorized are an unimaginative—and far too modest—beginning for what may prove to be a strategic weapon of revolutionary importance. Again, the nation needs to raise its sights.

ANTI-SUBMARINE WARFARE

The same threat posed to the Soviet by the Polaris-type submarine can, in time, be deployed against us.

Moreover, the Soviet submarine fleet of 475 vessels is the largest in the world. It could threaten our sea lines of communication with our allies, even though the Soviet has as yet (as far as we know) no nuclear-powered submarine and no operating missile-firing submarines.

The nuclear depth charge and other technological breakthroughs in the complex science of anti-submarine warfare have probably given us a qualitative edge in the A.S.W. field, compared to present Russian submarines.

But the Soviets may soon have nuclear-powered submarines that will greatly complicate the problems of our defense. In any case the Navy does not have today enough surface escort vessels or anti-submarine planes. A speed-up in procurement of equipment for A.S.W. and high priority for research and development in this field is essential.

EQUIPMENT FOR LAND WARFARE

The United States Army's fifteen divisions are, under present plans, to be reduced to fourteen next year. Many of them are committed overseas. These divisions plus the Marines' three divisions are the nation's emergency force for "brush-fire wars"—peripheral and limited conflicts.

If the nation retains its present capability of massive nuclear retaliation these small limited conflicts are the kind most likely to occur—in the Middle East, Africa or Asia. Our capability for fighting these non-nuclear wars has steadily declined, and in the last year, for the first time in history, the Soviet Union has, in general, surpassed the United States in the quality as well as the quantity of its Army equipment.

NINE U.S. DIVISIONS ABROAD

Eight United States Army divisions and one Marine division are committed to specific areas overseas. Three divisions are, in effect, training divisions; only five of the fourteen divisions will be available quickly for a global emergency.

This is a minimal force; our calculated risk would be considerably less if the Army were increased by one or two divisions, fully equipped, with the most modern arms and highly mobile.

The United States is weak—relative to Russia—in tanks (particularly light tanks), mortars, some field artillery, and some types of tactical missiles. Above all, the strategic, or long-range, mobility of the Army and Marines is still much too limited in both quantity and speed.

The Navy's amphibious vessels and transports are still largely World War II types. The Army, dependent upon the Air Force for airlift, could count in emergency upon only enough planes to transport about half a division simultaneously across the ocean.

NEW LANDING CRAFT REQUIRED

New high-speed amphibious vessels and new types of ships, such as a large nuclear-powered submarine transport, as well as new high speed naval auxiliaries, are needed to increase the nation's naval and amphibious mobility.

The Army needs more transport aircraft permanently assigned to it; some authorities have suggested that troop-carrier aircraft should be transferred from the Air Force to Army control and operation.

Speed and mobility are essential if the nation is to create a military "fire brigade" capable of preventing small wars from becoming big ones. Without this strategic mobility the Army and the Marines lose much of their usefulness. A speeded procurement program for ground equipment is also necessary.

PILOTED AIRCRAFT

The United States has today a tremendously powerful fleet of piloted aircraft—4,000 to 5,000 planes each capable of carrying a thermonuclear weapon of megaton [equivalent to million tons of TNT] destructive power.

Yet anti-aircraft missiles with nuclear warheads and piloted interceptors with air-to-air missiles are sharply reducing the offensive utility of our present high-altitude piloted bombers.

The Strategic Air Command and the nation have a tremendous investment in the Boeing B-47 medium bomber and the Boeing B-52 heavy bomber, and the Navy has a sizable investment in the

Douglas A3D attack plane. All of these aircraft are subsonic high-altitude bombers, whose span of military usefulness in their present form is now limited.

Instead of ordering more of these planes—the nation already has a tremendous "over-kill" capability with its piloted bombers provided they can get to their tragets—our efforts should be to strengthen them with air-to-surface missiles, decoys, electronic protection and other devices that would extend materially their useful military life.

A B-52, equipped with a 300-mile to 400-mile supersonic guided missile with a nuclear warhead could stand out of range of enemy anti-aircraft missile batteries and yet deliver its weapon to the target.

An air-to-surface missile of this type—the North American GAM-77, already ordered—should have the highest priority, for only by modernization of our bomber fleet will our present lead in piloted aircraft continue to be useful.

At the same time, our modest production program for the Air Force Snark 5,500-mile missile [an air-breathing pilotless aircraft], and for the Navy's supersonic winged missile, Regulus II, should be expanded.

The bomber-launched air-to-surface missile and the Snark and Regulus, if available in some quantities within the next eighteen months, can "cushion" the Soviet lead in long-range ballistic missiles.

The nuclear-powered plane, because of its great cruising endurance, could be the ultimate version of an aerial missile-launching base. Several of these planes, constantly cruising in the skies above the world and equipped with long-range missiles, could present a deterrent to aggression which would be almost impossible to eliminate.

At the same time the nation should develop rapidly new low-flying attack planes capable of penetrating enemy defenses beneath the beams of radar, and very high-altitude light bombers capable of penetration above the range of present anti-aircraft missiles.

There is no need in the future to build tremendous heavy bombers when small fighter bombers can carry megaton bombs. The lighter and smaller supersonic bomber, the Convair B-58, is a trend in the right direction; more should be ordered. But the piloted bomber of tomorrow—if it is to continue to be useful in the age of the missile, and present indications are that it will be—must be smaller than the B-58.

Fewer planes but better ones is the need for tomorrow.

But aircraft development must not be keyed solely to the requirements of a nuclear war. The piloted plane for reconnaissance, close-support, pin-point attack and interdiction is still essential for limited war.

The trend in design has been toward higher-flying faster aircraft that have little utility for accurate surface support. More research and development of specialized aircraft for non-nuclear missions is essential.

The vulnerability of our bomber bases to sabotage or surprise attack is in part the product of the tremendous numbers of piloted aircraft the nation possesses. Congestion on our bases has been caused by sheer growth in numbers—in the Strategic Air Command, for instance, from about 850 combat aircraft in 1950 to far more than 2,000 today.

But this vulnerability in the age of the missile must be reduced rapidly by the construction of new subsidiary air strips, by more dispersed parking areas, by the construction of "alert" facilities to enable quicker take-offs. S.A.C. also requires more Boeing KC-135 jet tankers for air refueling and advance bases for these tankers in northern Canada.

PERSONNEL

Man is still the heart of battle, and despite all the recent accent upon new weapons and new machines, man is probably the weakest element in the American formula for security.

Most of the men in our armed forces are not capable of utilizing at optimum capability the weapons they have. The turnover is tremendous, re-enlistment rates nowhere near high enough, and far too many promising officers are resigning.

The morale of some key units is high but across the board it is indifferent. All of the services are experiencing difficulty in retaining their highly trained technical men. The Strategic Air Command, for instance, keeps only about 17 per cent of its jet engine mechanics beyond their first enlistment.

About 1,500 men out of a crew of 2,500 aboard the aircraft carrier *Saratoga* left the ship in the last six months of 1957 and were replaced by new men, most of them green to the Navy. The old professional high-spirited "band of brothers" of the former services does not exist today except in a few exceptional units.

INCREASED PAY URGED

Implementation of the Cordiner report, which would provide increased pay based on merit rather than longevity, improved incentives for specialists, better housing and other benefits, would, the services believe, help to create the truly professional forces needed for the nuclear-missile age.

But the Department of Defense and the services themselves should improve and simplify their own personnel policies. The Defense Department, in the name of common personnel policies, has almost eliminated the elite unit concept and has tended to reduce all to the same common denominator.

Career guidance has become a fetish rather than a tool; it too often puts square pegs in round holes. Cost accounting has become more important than combat effectiveness.

Longer enlistments, more stability, the elimination of the short-term officer, the pre-selection of officers primarily on the basis of motivation and character; selective reduction in numbers but improvement in quality—and above all, a rigorous standard for leadership—are essential if United States soldiers, sailors and airmen are to become tough, disciplined, intelligent, professional forces capable of matching and over-matching the armed men of the Soviet Union.

LONG-TERM PROJECTS

There are a number of major long-term projects with no clear or immediate military application that should have high priority. Many of these projects—man's first steps into space—deal with some form of upper atmosphere, or space, research. Some of them could have in the future tremendous political, psychological and scientific significance and might produce important military by-products.

All of them must depend upon the military missile programs for support and hence must be closely associated with the military no matter under what management.

The Pied Piper and other satellite reconnaissance programs, a project investigating the feasibility of weather control, explorations of outer space, and manned and un-manned rocket flights to the moon are among the programs that must receive firm support.

A first flight to the moon by a rocket made and launched in the United States would appear to be the only way in which, in the eyes of the world, America's tarnished technological prestige might be restored.

CHAPTER 9

Should the U. S. Ever Strike the First Blow?

[At some time between, roughly, April, 1958, and December, 1959, it is probable that the Communist enemy will possess an intercontinental ballistic missile capability which will render the Free World highly vulnerable. Since the Communist world has already started World War III and since a surprise attack on the United States by Soviet missiles would probably result in fifty million or more casualties and incalculable destruction, individual Americans must reconsider seriously the "let the enemy strike first" philosophy.]

The United States learned once the danger of letting an enemy strike the first blow. That happened in 1941, when Japan attacked Pearl Harbor by surprise.

That attack by Japan was made with what we now contemptuously call "conventional" weapons. Yet it dealt the U.S. a blow from which it took this country more than three years to recover.

Today, with nuclear weapons, the danger of letting an enemy strike the first blow has greatly increased. Transoceanic missiles will further increase this danger.

Yet the U.S. Government appears still willing to "let the other

The noted military analyst, Captain W. D. Puleston, U.S.N., presented his views on this subject in an article entitled "Should the U.S. Ever Strike the First Blow" and published in the December 13, 1957 issue of *U.S. News and World Report*. Reprinted from *U.S. News and World Report*, an independent weekly news magazine published at Washington. Copyright 1957 United States News Publishing Corporation.

fellow strike first." The Eisenhower Administration is continuing to rely on the policy of "massive retaliation"—the theory that the threat of American retaliation will deter Soviet leaders from attack.

Secretary of State John Foster Dulles has declared that the United Nations Charter "binds us not to use armed force against any country unless first an armed attack occurs."

Once an enemy attacks, the Eisenhower Administration's plan is that the U.S. Strategic Air Force will strike back, with devastating nuclear power.

When we retaliate, our employment of "area bombing" will be no more merciful than the Reds' attack. The American plan specifically calls for destruction of sources of raw materials and key agricultural areas, as well as of strictly military targets. Our policy only demands that Americans be killed first, before we strike.

Now, however, the increasing flexibility and power of thermonuclear weapons compels the U.S. to review this policy of conceding the first blow to Moscow.

When first constructed, A-bombs could be delivered only by large planes, and only in large sizes that resulted inevitably in wide destruction. But now we have developed smaller bombs whose power can be limited to that necessary to destroy strictly military targets. These new bombs can be pinpointed on military targets. They can be delivered by planes, by submarines, by guns and by missiles. They can be used for offense or for defense. Like all weapons, they are offensive when they threaten you, defensive when they threaten your enemy.

We know that our Strategic Air Command can launch an all-out attack without mobilization, that our submarines can deploy in positions to attack targets deep in Red territory.

We must assume that, likewise, Soviet planes and submarines can attack our cities, mechant marine and men-of-war with little or no warning.

After such an attack by Russia, would our armed forces be able to retaliate?

Certainly, our armed forces could deliver a more effective attack if their attack were made before they had sustained heavy losses. Certainly, thousands of Americans will be reprieved from death if our Government refuses to concede Moscow the first blow. Certainly, we can help our allies more before our Navy, our merchant ships and our coastal cities are exposed to Red submarines and our military shore establishments and our industrial areas are desolated by bombs.

Today we are pledged to aid any nation in the Middle East which is attacked by international Communism. We are blocking Red China's entry into the United Nations and the advance of Red Russia in the Middle East.

Secretary Dulles admits that previous experience indicates that a fundamental conflict like that now existing between international Communism and the Free World ultimately erupts into war. He seems confident that his skillful diplomacy can avert war. President Eisenhower apparently agrees with him, and they accept this calculated but unpredictable risk for their country.

It must not be forgotten, however, that Moscow—as well as Tokyo did in 1941—appreciates the advantages of striking the first blow. Moscow has been told that we will await her attack—that we will not strike first.

It is perilous to assume that in the future the Red general staff will be deterred from attack by fear of retaliation. In 1941, Stalin deliberately risked provoking Hitler rather than abandon Russian ambitions in the Balkans. The Kremlin, we may assume, would not hesitate to strike if it considered success probable—regardless of what Soviet leaders may say for public consumption. President Eisenhower just recently said, "Respect for Russia's word is at a new low."

If the Kremlin retains its present hold on its satellites, obtains a few more friendly nations in the Middle East, increases and improves its atomic bombs and the means of their delivery, will the Kremlin resist the temptation, on some favorable occasion, to strike the United States in order to remove the most stubborn opponent of Russia's further expansion?

On the other hand, if satellites grow more restive, if Communist Party control in Russia is menaced, will not party leaders be equally likely to strike the United States, whose radio broadcasts openly urge captive nations to regain their freedom? And will not the knowledge that Soviet armed forces can make their plans for striking the first devastating blow without fear of a prior attack be an additional inducement for the Kremlin to strike?

At one time, there was evidence that the American high command was carefully reviewing its defense policy of conceding Moscow the first blow. More than a year ago, the President said: "In any combat where these things [tactical A weapons] with limited destructive power can be used on strictly military targets, I can see no reason why they should not be used just as you would a bullet."

Recently the President announced that "we have learned to make weapons which would reduce fall-out to a minimum and whose destructive force can be concentrated on military objectives."

Subsequently, Charles E. Wilson, then Secretary of Defense, told a House subcommittee: "We are depending on atomic weapons. Our strategy is geared to their use."

Adm. Arthur W. Radford, former Chairman of the Joint Chiefs of Staff, has warned Americans that "no country would allow itself to be defeated without using its best [most effective] weapon."

These approaches to a more realistic appraisal of our situation vis-à-vis the Soviet Union have been halted by the super-loyalty of Secretary Dulles to the United Nations. This country still remains in the position of awaiting the first blow.

Our country should never adopt a policy of seeking to gain advantage by a sudden, unprovoked assault.

There is, however, a prudent and honorable alternative to conceding an enemy the first blow. The United States is not forced to choose between awaiting a holocaust or delivering one.

Our planes now can deliver tailor-made nuclear bombs very close to purely military targets. Hostile air bases, navy yards, army garrisons and closely related auxiliaries such as railways, munition factories and power plants can be destroyed without resorting to indiscriminate area bombing that devastates a whole province or destroys a city, needlessly killing hundreds of thousands of helpless civilians.

Our Sixth Fleet can assist our European allies in a matter of minutes and—without devastating huge areas—could break up formations of ground troops such as those which suppressed the Hungarian revolt.

What this country should do is to adopt a policy once proposed and then abandoned by Mr. Dulles—a policy which permits the U.S. to choose the time, the place and the weapons of attack.

Our Government today should tell the world what areas the United States will fight to defend. It should be made unmistakably clear to the Soviets where they cannot go and what they cannot do without inviting attack by the U.S.

Then, if the Russians or their satellites should attack any nations of the Free World which the U.S. has pledged to defend, the U.S. could reply with nuclear weapons tailor-made for the type of war which would be necessary to defend this nation.

But that is not all.

Our Government also should make it equally clear to the Soviets that we will not stand idly by and wait to be attacked—that we will not permit any nation to prepare and mount a surprise attack upon this country or any of its allies.

If Russia—or any other nation—should give positive evidence that it is preparing such an attack, the United States should immediately:

1. Alert its armed forces and deploy them for instant attack upon the threatening nation.

2. Serve immediate notice upon the threatening nation that, unless it dismounts the attack preparations within a specified brief

period of time, the United States will attack in self-defense, without waiting to be hit first.

Then, if the Russians or their satellites should defy this warning, the U.S. would be in a position to get at least an even break. If the enemy should attack, we could attack simultaneously. If the enemy should persist in its preparations to attack, we could—with honor—attack first, and thus gain the initial advantage instead of conceding it.

With the tailor-made nuclear weapons now available, this defensive attack would not need to result in wholesale slaughter and widespread devastation. The attack could be pinpointed on military targets to destroy the enemy's capability of waging war without ravaging his entire country. The holocaust of indiscriminate nuclear warfare could be avoided.

Any other plan of dealing with Red Russia will jeopardize the future of the United States. Communist leaders certainly will use atomic bombs before surrendering control of their own country. Nor will they hesitate to launch an atomic attack upon the United States the moment that they are confident that they could win the war.

The best evidence we possess today that we are still superior to the Reds in the production and delivery of thermonuclear weapons is Russia's failure to launch such an attack.

Isn't it absurd to assume that a regime which murdered and enslaved millions of its own people to establish Communism would hesitate to destroy the one nation left that is strong enough to defeat them?

Americans and their Government must cease shuddering about atomic war and soberly consider the probable effects of such a war. The world now is only on the outer rim of the nuclear era.

Optimists pinning their hopes on limitation of armaments or disarmament should recall the repeated failures of such remedies between the two world wars and since. If some miracle would eliminate all existing weapons tomorrow, more potent ones would quickly emerge from test tubes of the modern research laboratories, unless the rivalries between international Communism and the free world are diminished.

Improvements in weapons hinge upon scientific and industrial progress. They are extremely costly. Only fear of being defeated in a nuclear war has reconciled American citizens to the burden of providing modern weapons.

Governments which advocate disarmament one day denounce each other the next. Whether international Communism and the free world can reconcile their differences remains to be seen. But of one fact Americans can be sure: Thermonuclear weapons are here to stay.

During this dawn of the nuclear era it is more necessary than ever for our Government first to consider its obligations to its own citizens, next to its allies. Meeting these responsibilities will tax its resources. Its first responsibility is to survive as a great power, so that it can protect its own citizens from a surprise thermonuclear attack on the continental United States.

Only a vigilant Administration, resolved to defend its citizens, their homes, farms, mines and factories, can shield them from a treacherous enemy attack during this nuclear era. And then it can be done only by the timely anticipation of a projected enemy attack with an earlier and deadlier attack of our own.

Such a policy as outlined here would not be in violation of international law.

No principles or precepts of international law—past or present—require an independent nation to await an attack by another.

International law specifically recognizes the right of any state to go to war to protect its interests, and the state is the sole judge of its jeopardy. In 1907, the Second Hague Conference almost unanimously rejected a resolution of the Netherlands delegation "that hostilities should not commence until a lapse of 24 hours from the time of a definite declaration of war." Instead, Article I of the Conference reads: "Hostilities must not commence without a previous and unequivocal warning . . . either by a declaration of war . . . or of an ultimatum with a conditional declaration of war."

According to Dr. G. B. Wilson, for many years professor of international law at Harvard and the U.S. Naval War College: "In modern times the practice of a formal declaration of war before recognizing the existing war and capturing enemy property has fallen into disuse. Actual hostilities determine the date of commencement of war . . . although no proclamation was used . . . no declaration made . . . and [hostilities] began without action of the legislative branch [Congress]."

By far the greater number of wars in recent years have been carried on and concluded without a declaration. Professor William Edward Hall, an English authority on international law, writes: "The use of a declaration does not, of course, exclude surprise . . . only . . . that notice shall be served an infinitesimal space of time before a blow is struck."

The Japanese attack on Pearl Harbor would have been legal if Ambassador Nomura had been able to present Secretary of State Hull a message tantamount to an ultimatum at 1 p.m., Washington time, as directed by his Foreign Minister in Tokyo. Decoding the long message delayed its delivery until 2:30 p.m. Japanese pilots hit on schedule about an hour previously. Technically, they were guilty of violating international law. They had not waited "an infinitesimal time" after the ultimatum was delivered because they did not know its delivery had been delayed.

When the "cold war" with Russia developed, President Harry S. Truman, Secretary of State Dean Acheson and Gen. Omar Bradley, Chairman of the Joint Chiefs of Staff, naturally were reluctant to launch the first "atomic" attack on the Soviet Union. Moreover, if our planes had attacked Russia, her ground troops could have advanced into Western Europe.

Our Government at that time wisely depended upon our prior possession of the atomic bomb to deter a Red attack on our European allies.

Since then, however, Russia has improved and increased her arsenal of fission and fusion bombs. She also has improved her means of delivering them to American targets. The Kremlin claims to have developed an intercontinental ballistic missile that will reach the United States from Russia with a nuclear warhead. We know that the Russians have launched successfully two earth satellites.

A "Pearl Harbor" of today would not be aimed at an island possession. It would be aimed at the continental United States. It would not just sink a few ships and knock out an air base. It could wipe out entire cities, lay waste entire States.

The time in history is past when this nation can afford to let the enemy deliver the first blow.

PART II

The Internal Communist Threat and How to Combat It

CHAPTER 10

Communism U.S.A.

COMMUNIST THEORY IN REGARD TO THE UNITED STATES

The conquest of the United States is the ultimate objective of Soviet foreign policy. Therefore, international Communism is constantly striving to weaken the United States internally and to isolate it in world affairs. Soviet propaganda portrays the United States as the bulwark of "decadent capitalism" and "imperialism," whose very existence makes war inevitable. So long as the United States remains non-Communist, Soviet leaders cannot rest, for their announced goal is the creation of a Soviet dictatorship in this country. America must, then, be destroyed through the application of the most advanced techniques of cold and hot warfare.

William Z. Foster, leader of the American Communists, once declared under sworn testimony: "When a Communist heads the government of the United States—and that day will come just as surely as the sun rises—the government will not be a capitalist government but a Soviet government, and behind this government will stand the Red Army to enforce the dictatorship of the proletariat." American Communists consider themselves advance echelons of the Soviet army, preparing the way for "liberation." It is the task of the American Communists to weaken America through industrial strife, racial and religious conflicts, and infiltration into the key areas of influence: government, the mass media, industry, and education. This latter infiltration is to be accomplished (and has been accomplished in the past) largely through the intermediary of "front" organizations, that is, organizations which are controlled by the Communists but which appear to be merely "liberal" or "progressive." These fronts usually have an impressive list of sponsors recruited from the traditionally gullible "intellectuals" who are in a position to influence policies in government, the mass media, industry, and education, where outright Communist propaganda might be rejected. After the 1948 presidential election, J. Edgar Hoover, head of the Federal Bureau of Investigation, placed the number of non-Communist fellow travelers who worked for Communist fronts at 400,000. This meant that for every Communist there were available to the party ten Americans willing to work for the benefit of the Soviet Union, without, however, accepting the risks and responsibilities of actual party membership.

The American Communists are not just another political party. They admit that their first allegiance is to the Soviet Union and international Communism. By their ideology and their actions, they have placed themselves outside the limits of the "loyal opposition." Contrary to the behavior of other Americans, the Communists follow the lead of the Soviet Union and international Communism blindly and without deviation. When the Soviet Union tells them to obey William Foster, they obey William Foster; when the Soviet Union tells them to follow Earl Browder, they follow Earl Browder. In 1939, and for twenty months thereafter, American Communists supported the Hitler-Stalin pact and, led by millionaire Frederick Vanderbilt Field, picketed the White House with placards reading: "The Yanks Aren't Coming." On June 23, 1941, American Communists suddenly—overnight—changed their views to jibe with the new position of the Soviet Union. Until the end of 1944, there was great agitation for all-out war against Hitler by means of unlimited aid to Soviet Russia and the opening of a second front (during all of which time the Soviet Union retained its alliance with Japan in the Far East). In 1945, the American Communists, ordered to do so by Moscow, repudiated Browder and adopted Foster as their new leader. When the war was over, they changed their tune from temporary friendship for America to antagonism toward America and claimed that the United States was guilty of "imperialism" in Europe and Asia. From 1945 to mid-1948, the American Communists strongly supported Tito. Thereafter, in line with the new Soviet attitude, they denounced Tito as a "deviationist."[1] After the brutal Soviet repression of freedom in Hungary, American Communists duly agreed that the Soviet troops had to intervene to preserve "workers' Socialism" from foreign-inspired reactionaries.

The head of the Communist party, U.S.A., makes it clear that the Communist "classics," or works, of Marx, Engels, Lenin, and Stalin contain the fundamental principles of Communism and that these principles are accepted by all Communist parties. The works of the "masters" teach and advocate the overthrow and destruction of government by force and violence; indeed, both Lenin and Stalin specifically repudiated "peaceful means." The Communist party, U.S.A., teaches these principles by means of party schools in which the "classics" are the basic texts and in which lectures and study outlines based on them are presented.

William Z. Foster wrote in 1949: "These books are Communist classics. They contain the fundamental principles and program of Communism. They are universal in scope and they are accepted by all Communist parties. . . . They are the scientific guides of humanity to a freer, fuller life. . . . We American Communists apply them strategically and tactically in the need of specific American conditions."

One of the most important of the "classics" is Stalin's *Problems of Leninism.* The 1947 edition of this book defined strategy and tactics for international Communism as follows: "Strategy is the determination of the direction of the main blow of the proletariat at a given stage of the revolution, the elaboration of a corresponding plan for the disposition of the revolutionary forces, the fight to carry out this plan throughout the given stage of the revolution. Tactics are the determination of the line of conduct of the proletariat in the comparatively short period of the flow or ebb of the movement, of the rise or decline of the revolution, the fight to carry out this line by means of replacing old forms of struggle and organization by new ones, old slogans by new ones. . . . While the object of strategy is to win the war . . . tactics concern themselves with . . . winning a particular engagement or a particular battle. . . . Tactics are a part of strategy, subordinate to it and serving it."

Party leader Foster made it clear that "Communist parties always enunciate their policies with complete frankness, as the *Communist Manifesto* so dramatically points out. If any books speak out more forthrightly and frankly upon the question of force and violence than Lenin's *State and Revolution,* or Stalin's *Foundations of Leninism* (which we daily circulate), I cannot imagine what they could be."

In his book *Foundations of Leninism,* Stalin states: "The dictatorship of the proletariat cannot arise as the result of the peaceful development of bourgeois society and bourgeois democracy; it can only arise as the result of the smashing of the bourgeois state machine, the bourgeois army, the bourgeois bureaucratic machine, the bourgeois police." In the same book, Stalin sums up the purposes of the world revolution: "Objective: to consolidate the dictatorship of the proletariat in one country, using it as a base for the overthrow of imperialism in all countries. The revolution is spreading beyond the confines of one country; the period of world revolution is at hand."

Some American-Soviet apologists have tried to claim that Marx at one time held there would not have to be a revolution in England and America. Lenin answers as follows: "The argument that Marx in the 'seventies granted the possibility of a peaceful transition to socialism in England and America is the argument of a sophist, or to put it more bluntly, of a swindler who juggles quotations and references. First, Marx regarded this possibility as an exception even then. Second, in those days monopoly capitalism, i.e., imperialism, did not yet exist. Thirdly, in England and America there was no military then—as there is now—serving as the chief apparatus of the bourgeois state machine." Stalin, writing along the same lines, concluded that "the law of violent proletarian revolution, the law of the smashing of the bourgeois state machine . . . is an inevitable law of the revolutionary movement in the imperialist countries of the world. . . . Therefore Lenin is right in saying: 'The proletarian revolution is impossible without the forcible destruction of the bourgeois state machine and the substitution for it of a new one.'"

GOVERNMENTAL COUNTERACTION

Gradually recognizing that the Communist movement in America was outside the pale of the loyal opposition, the United States government initiated certain steps aimed at its control. In 1940, the Alien Registration Act (Smith Act) was passed by Congress. It provided that "whoever knowingly or willfully advocates, abets, advises, or teaches the duty, necessity or desirability, or propriety of overthrowing or destroying the Government of the United States, or the government of any state, territory, district or possession thereof, or the government of any political subdivision therein by force and violence, or by the assassination of any officer of any such government, or whoever, with intent to cause the overthrow or destruction of any such government, prints, publishes, edits, issues, circulates, sells, distributes or publicly displays any written or printed matter advocating, advising or teaching the duty, necessity, desirability or propriety of overthrowing or destroying any government in the United States by force and violence, or attempts to do so, or whoever organizes or helps or attempts to organize any society, group or assembly of persons who teach, advocate or encourage the overthrow or destruction of any such government by force and violence, or becomes or is a member of, or affiliates with, any such society, group or assembly of persons, knowing the purposes thereof—shall be fined not more than $10,000 or imprisoned, or both."

Under the terms of this law, the top eleven American Communist leaders were tried and convicted in 1949, as were a number of state Communist leaders. In 1951, the Supreme Court, in a 6-2 decision, upheld the constitutionality of the Smith Act. But six years later a somewhat different Court, voting 6-1, upheld the contention of fourteen convicted Communist leaders in California that the law was improperly applied against them. The majority held that it was not a crime to "organize" the Communist party and that a distinction should be made between advocating violent overthrow in the abstract and advocating it in the concrete. Dissenting Justice Clark labeled the distinction "an exercise in semantics."

The McCarran Internal Security Act (not to be confused with the McCarran-Walter Immigration Act) was the next step taken by the government against the Communist party and Communist fronts. This law, passed in 1950, forces the party to list all its officers and members every year; to give a comprehensive annual accounting of how it gets its money and how it spends it; to name all its contributors; and to label all mail and literature it sends out. The law also forces Communist-front organizations, after a proper hearing, to register with the Attorney General of the United States. The first twelve such fronts were asked in April, 1953, so to register, as a prelude to forcing the remaining 200-odd fronts to do likewise. These fronts were: the Labor Youth League, the International Worker's Order, the Civil Rights Congress, the American Committee for the Protection of the Foreign Born, the National Council on American-Soviet Friendship, the Joint Anti-Fascist Refugee Committee, the Jefferson School of Social Science, the United May Day Committee, the Veterans of the Abraham Lincoln Brigade, the Council on African Affairs, the Committee for a Democratic Far Eastern Policy, and the American Slav Congress. These organizations and similar ones to be named later were given ample time to argue before the Subversive Activities Control Board that they were not front organizations. But neither Communists nor Communist fronts have registered with the Attorney General, pending a Supreme Court decision on the constitutionality of the law.

The Internal Security Act also provides that in time of war (and the United States was engaged in war for several years after the enactment of the statute), American Communists should be placed in detention camps. This part of the law was not enforced during the Korean War.

In addition to the Smith and McCarran acts, the United States Government tries to protect itself through a loyalty program (later called the Security Program) designed to keep Communists and persons of doubtful loyalty out of the federal civil service.[2] Under this program the Civil Service Loyalty Review Board found that there was a question of doubtful loyalty in the cases of John Stewart Service, John Carter Vincent, Oliver Edmund Clubb, and many other prominent career officers.[3] The first two played key roles in American Far Eastern policy during the fateful years when China was overrun by Communism. Service gave top military and diplomatic secrets to the editor of a Communist magazine (*Amerasia*) yet held key posts in the State Department for six years thereafter. It was not until Senators McCarran and McCarthy began to publicize the case that action was taken. Indeed, in many instances government agencies refused to heed FBI warnings about actual or potential subversives until after Congressional committees publicized the cases. For example, the FBI warned President Truman repeatedly from November, 1945, to January, 1946, that Undersecretary of the Treasury Harry Dexter White was involved in espionage, but Mr. Truman failed to fire him.

The scope of the Security Program was considerably reduced by a Supreme Court decision in 1956 which exempted so-called "non-sensitive" federal employees' jobs from the operation of the program. This means that Communists and other security risks could obtain and hold some one million federal jobs. Congress can, of course, correct this situation by making clear its desire to include *all* federal employees in the Security Program.

In August, 1954, Congress passed the Communist Control Act, authored by Senators Butler and Humphrey. It sought to prevent

Communist unions from becoming bargaining agents with the National Labor Relations Board and to deprive the Communist party of legal status. This law, in addition to the increasingly effective perjury weapon used against "Fifth Amendment Communists," seemed to indicate more resolute governmental action against Communism. Unfortunately, however, some governmental leaders and molders of public opinion continued to spend more time attacking Congressional investigating committees (which had done much of the work in uncovering Communists and loyalty and security risks) than in attacking the Communists themselves.

Another way in which American society can protect itself against subversion is through the Immunity Act of 1954. Under this law, certain witnesses who might otherwise invoke the Fifth Amendment's anti-self-incrimination clause can be granted immunity from prosecution, and then they must testify. On March 26, 1956, the Supreme Court ruled that Soviet espionage agent William Ludwig Ullman must testify before a Congressional committee, having been granted immunity under the law.

However, during 1957, the Supreme Court struck down most of our internal security program in the name of "civil rights." This action will be discussed in the next chapter.

CHAPTER 11

The Impact of the 1957 Supreme Court Decisions on Communism

[A committee of the American Bar Association looks at recent Supreme Court rulings and raises these questions: Is the Court leaning too far backward in defending theoretical rights of Communists? Are the Court's decisions tying the hands of the U.S. government against Communism? To overcome the effects of the Court's rulings, new legislation is suggested. This study comes from the American Bar Association's Committee on Communist Tactics, Strategy and Objectives. It is presented here by Committee Chairman Herbert R. O'Conor, former Senator from Maryland.]

Modern history is filled with the wrecks of republics which were destroyed from within by conspiracies masquerading as political parties. The nine justices of the Supreme Tribunal of Germany refused to see that the Nazis were a conspiracy against the very existence of the German Republic. The Kerensky Government of Russia thought it could tolerate and co-exist with the Communist conspirators. The Communists responded to this toleration by disbanding the Constituent Assembly at bayonet point and destroying the newborn republic of Russia. The republics of Czechoslovakia,

The material in this chapter first appeared in a report adopted by the American Bar Association Special Committee to Study Communist Tactics, Strategy and Objectives. The report was submitted by Chairman Herbert R. O'Conor and the Committee at the annual meeting of the American Bar Association held at London in July, 1957. Reprinted by permission of Mr. O'Conor.

Poland and China tried valiantly to co-exist with the Communist Party in their midst, but were unable to do so.

We are spending more to equip and defend ourselves and our allies from Communist aggression than we ever spent to stop Japanese aggression. The Japanese found it difficult to purloin our military secrets, but the Communists have stolen many of our military secrets, including vital details of the atomic and hydrogen bombs which were known to the traitors Dr. Klaus Fuchs and Dr. Bruno Pontecorvo.

The cynical cruelty with which the Kremlin crushed the Hungarian patriots and executed their leaders is proof by deeds that "the spirit of Geneva" was always a tactic and a sham. Likewise, the admission of Mao Tse-tung in his recently published Peiping speech of February, 1956, that the Chinese Communists completed the "liquidation" of 800,000 persons between October, 1949, and January, 1954, and the report published June 15, 1957, by the Senate Internal Security Subcommittee that, in fact, more than 15 million persons have been executed in Red China since 1951 prove the fatuity of those who argue that Red China should be admitted into the family of nations and recognized by our Government.

The Communists have conquered large areas of the world according to a carefully enunciated plan. In 1903, Lenin established Communism with 17 supporters. In 1917, the Communists conquered Russia with 40,000. In 1957, the Communists are in iron control of 900 million people. Their advance since the end of World War II has been especially tragic.

The Korean war proved that aggression does pay because it was followed by Communist aggression in Tibet, Indo-China and Hungary. After Soviet tanks rolled into Hungary, the Communists succeeded by clever propaganda in electing their first government by forms of democratic processes—in the state of Kerala, in India. To the Communists "peaceful co-existence" means Communist conquest without war.

The greatest asset the Communists have at the present time is not the hydrogen bomb, certainly not soviet satellites, but world ignorance of their tactics, strategy and objectives. The biggest need today is for the free peoples to develop an awareness of the menace of Communism and the ability to isolate the Communist line so that it can be detected no matter who utters it. One speech from the mouth of an important American innocent can be worth a truckload of "Daily Workers" in advancing the international Communist conspiracy. The current Communist line includes the following:

1. Repeal or weaken the anti-Communist legislation on the books, especially the Smith Act, the Internal Security Act, and the Subversive Activities Control Act.

2. Discredit and hamper the Senate Internal Security Subcommittee, the House Un-American Activities Committee, and State officials investigating Communism.

3. Weaken the effectiveness of the FBI and reveal its sources of information.

4. Destroy the federal security system.

5. Recognize Red China and admit her to the United Nations.

6. Oppose the possibility of the United States' breaking off diplomatic relations with Soviet Russia.

7. Enlarge East-West trade, especially in items in short supply behind the Iron Curtain.

8. Revive the idea that the Communist Party is just another political party.

9. Use the recent shake-up in the Kremlin as a guise to revive the Communist peace offensive, just as a previous shake-up in the Kremlin brought about the "spirit of Geneva."

In the last 15 months the United States Supreme Court has decided 15 cases which directly affect the right of the United States of America to protect itself from Communist subversion:

1. Communist Party v. Subversive Activities Control Board
   The Court refused to uphold or pass on the constitutionality of the Subversive Activities Control Act of 1950, and delayed the effectiveness of the Act.

2. Pennsylvania v. Steve Nelson
   The Court held that it was unlawful for Pennsylvania to prosecute a Pennsylvania Communist Party leader under the Pennsylvania Sedition Act, and indicated that the antisedition laws of 42 States and of Alaska and Hawaii cannot be enforced.
3. Fourteen California Communists v. United States
   The Court reversed two federal courts and ruled that teaching and advocating forcible overthrow of our Government, even "with evil intent," was not punishable under the Smith Act as long as it was "divorced from any effort to instigate action to that end," and ordered five Communist Party leaders freed and new trials for another nine.
4. Cole v. Young
   The Court reversed two federal courts and held that, although the Summary Suspension Act of 1950 gave the Federal Government the right to dismiss employees "in the interest of the National Security of the United States," it was not in the interest of the national security to dismiss an employee who contributed funds and services to a not-disputed subversive organization, unless that employee was in a "sensitive position."
5. Service v. Dulles
   The Court reversed two federal courts which had refused to set aside the discharge of [John Stewart] Service by the State Department. The FBI had a recording of a conversation between Service and an editor of the pro-Communist magazine "Amerasia," in the latter's hotel room in which Service spoke of military plans which were "very secret." Earlier the FBI had found large numbers of secret and confidential State Department documents in the "Amerasia" office. The lower courts had followed the McCarran amendment which gave the Secretary of State "absolute discretion" to discharge any employee "in the interests of the United States."
6. Slochower v. Board of Education of New York
   The Court reversed the decisions of three New York courts and

held it was unconstitutional to automatically discharge a teacher, in accordance with New York law, because he took the Fifth Amendment when asked about Communist activities. On petition for rehearing, the Court admitted that its opinion was in error in stating that Slochower was not aware that his claim of the Fifth Amendment would *ipso facto* result in his discharge; however, the Court denied rehearing.

7. Sweezy v. New Hampshire
   The Court reversed the New Hampshire Supreme Court and held that the Attorney General of New Hampshire was without authority to question Professor Sweezy, a lecturer at the State University, concerning a lecture and other suspected subversive activities. Questions which the Court said that Sweezy properly refused to answer included: "Did you advocate Marxism at that time?" and "Do you believe in Communism?"
8. United States v. Witkovich
   The Court decided that, under the Immigration and Nationality Act of 1952, which provides that any alien against whom there is a final order of deportation shall "give information under oath as to his nationality, circumstances, habits, associations and activities and such other information, whether unrelated to the foregoing, as the Attorney General may deem fit and proper," the Attorney General did not have the right to ask Witkovich: "Since the order of deportation was entered in your case on June 25, 1953, have you attended any meetings of the Communist Party of the U.S.A.?"
9. Schware v. Board of Bar Examiners of New Mexico
   The Court reversed the decisions of the New Mexico Board of Bar Examiners and of the New Mexico Supreme Court which had said: "We believe one who has knowingly given his loyalties to the Communist Party for six to seven years during a period of responsible adulthood is a person of questionable character." The Supreme Court substituted its judgment for

that of New Mexico and ruled that "membership in the Communist Party during the 1930s cannot be said to raise substantial doubts about his present good moral character."

10. Konigsberg v. State Bar of California
The Court reversed the decisions of the California Committee of Bar Examiners and of the California Supreme Court and held that it was unconstitutional to deny a license to practice law to an applicant who refused to answer this question put by the Bar Committee: "Mr. Konigsberg, are you a Communist?" and a series of similar questions.
11. Jencks v. United States
The Court reversed two federal courts and held that Jencks, who was convicted of filing a false non-Communist affidavit, must be given the contents of all confidential FBI reports which were made by any Government witness in the case even though Jencks "restricted his motions to a request for production of the reports to the trial judge for the judge's inspection and determination whether and to what extent the reports should be made available."
12. Watkins v. United States
The Court reversed the Federal District Court and six judges of the Court of Appeals of the District of Columbia, and held that the House Un-American Activities Committee should not require a witness who admitted, "I freely co-operated with the Communist Party" to name his Communist associates, even though the witness did not invoke the Fifth Amendment. The Court said: "We remain unenlightened as to the subject to which the questions asked petitioner were pertinent."
13. Raley, Stern and Brown v. Ohio
The Court reversed the Ohio Supreme Court and lower courts and set aside the conviction of three men who had refused to answer questions about Communist activities put to them by the Ohio Un-American Activities Commission.
14. Flaxner v. United States

The Court reversed two federal courts and set aside the conviction of Flaxner of contempt for refusing to produce records of alleged Communist activities subpoenaed by the Senate Internal Security Subcommittee.

15. Sacher v. United States

    The Court reversed two federal courts and set aside the conviction of Sacher of contempt for refusing to tell the Senate Permanent Investigations Subcommittee whether he was or ever had been a Communist.

The Communist "Daily Worker" described the effect of these decisions as follows: "The Court delivered a triple-barreled attack on (1) the Department of Justice and its Smith Act trials; (2) the freewheeling congressional inquisitions; and (3) the hateful loyalty-security program of the Executive. Monday, June 17, is already a historic landmark. . . . The curtain is closing on one of our worst periods."

The Watkins case decided that it is not "pertinent" for a congressional committee, established for the investigation of un-American activities, to ask a witness to give information concerning persons known to him to have been members of the Communist Party.

The courts have repeatedly said: "The power to legislate carries with it by necessary implication ample authority to obtain information needed in the rightful exercise of that power, and to employ compulsory process for that purpose."

Although many people consider the congressional investigations into Communism by the House Un-American Activities Committee [which was a particular target of the Watkins opinion] and the Senate Internal Security Subcommittee [which was ruled against in the subsequent decision of Flaxner v. U.S.] as primarily the information type of inquiry, they have resulted in a considerable quantity of important legislation. This includes the Smith Act, the Subversive Activities Control Act of 1950, the Internal Security Act of 1950, the Summary Suspension Act of 1950, certain sections of the McCarran-Walter Immigration Act, the Immunity Act of 1954, the Communist Control Act of 1954 and considerable State legislation such as the United States Supreme Court-approved New York Feinberg and Maryland Ober laws. . . .

The repeal or the weakening of these anti-Communist laws and committees is in the forefront of the program of the Communist Party of the United States.

Until the Watkins case, the Court had never interfered with the work of the House Un-American Activities Committee, and had on four occasions specifically refused to set aside contempt convictions imposed on witnesses who balked at testifying before this Committee.

Until the Watkins case, the Court had upheld the information function of legislative committees, and had always refused to interfere with the work of congressional committees investigating Communism. In a unanimous decision which was considered for more than two years before its pronouncement, the Supreme Court said:

"A legislative body cannot legislate wisely or effectively in the absence of information respecting the conditions which the legislation is intended to effect or change: and where the legislative body does not itself possess the requisite information—which not infrequently is true—recourse must be had to others who do possess it."

In defending the congressional power to investigate the Teapot Dome scandals, Mr. Justice Felix Frankfurter (then a professor) wrote:

"The question is not whether people's feelings here and there may be hurt, or names 'dragged through the mud' as it is called. The real issue is whether . . . the grave risks of fettering free congressional inquiry are to be incurred by artificial and techncial limitations upon inquiry . . . the abuses of the printing press are not sought to be corrected by legal restrictions or censorship in advance because the remedy is worse than the disease. For the same reason, congressional inquiry ought not be fettered by advance rigidities because, in the light of experience, there can be no reasonable doubt that such curtailment would make effective investigations almost impossible . . . the power of investigation should be left untrammeled."

In defending the congressional power to investigate the abuses of business, Mr. Justice Hugo L. Black (then a Senator) wrote:

"Witnesses have declined to answer questions from time to time. The chief reason advanced has been that the testimony related to purely private affairs. In each instance with which I am familiar the House and Senate have steadfastly adhered to their right to compel reply, and the witness has either answered or been imprisoned. . . .

"Public investigating committees . . . have always been opposed by groups that seek or have special privileges. That is because special privilege thrives in secrecy and darkness and is destroyed by the rays of pitiless publicity."

In refusing to enjoin Senator Black's lobby-inquiry committee from what was widely charged to be improper use of the congressional power of exposure, the Court said: "It is legislative discretion which is exercised, and that discretion, whether rightfully or wrongfully exercised, is not subject to interference by the judiciary."

If it is proper for congressional committees to investigate businessmen, it is surely proper to investigate Communists. If congressional inquiry into dishonesty "ought not to be fettered by advance rigidities," neither should congressional inquiries into disloyalty.

The Watkins opinion points to the Royal Commissions of Inquiry as something to be imitated by congressional committees because of the commissions' "success in fulfilling their fact-finding missions without resort to coercive tactics."

The report of the Canadian Royal Commission on Espionage, which was created on Feb. 5, 1946, to investigate the charges of

Igor Gouzenko, and which is the Royal Commission most nearly comparable in purpose to the House Un-American Activities Committee, reveals the following differences between the methods used by a Royal Commission investigating subversion and the methods used by a Congressional committee investigating subversion:

1. A Royal Commission can arrest and jail witnesses. A congressional committee has no such power.

2. A Royal Commission can hold witnesses without bail and incommunicado for many days and until after they are questioned. A congressional committee has no such power.

3. A Royal Commission can compel witnesses to testify and impose sanctions for refusing to testify. It does not recognize a "fifth amendment" or privilege against self-incrimination, as do our congressional committees.

4. A Royal Commission can have its police agents search witnesses' homes and seize their papers. A congressional committee has no such power.

5. A Royal Commission may forbid a witness to have his lawyer present at the hearing. Congressional committees permit a witness to have his lawyer present and even to consult with him before answering each specific question.

6. A Royal Commission can require all concerned in the inquiry, including witnesses, to take an oath of secrecy. The questioning by the Commission can be secret and, since only selected excerpts from the testimony are then made public, it is impossible to know whether a fair selection was made. Most congressional committee hearings are public and open to the press.

7. A Royal Commission is not subject to or under the control of the courts, Parliament or the Cabinet, and a Commission "is the sole judge of its own procedure." Congressional committees are completely subject to Congress, and they need the assistance of the courts in dealing with contemptuous witnesses.

We do not approve, or urge, all of the foregoing practices, but cite them to show what other freedom-loving nations do to protect their security.

Our Committee deems the bill introduced to overcome the effect of the Steve Nelson decision to be in the public interests. Serious considerations must be given to legislation which will:

1. Safeguard the confidential nature of the FBI files;

2. Give to congressional committees the same freedom to investigate Communists and pro-Communists that these committees have always had to investigate businessmen and labor leaders;

3. Sanction the right of the Federal Government to discharge security risks even though they occupy so-called nonsensitive positions;

4. Vest in the Department of Justice the right to question aliens awaiting deportation about any subversive associations and contacts;

5. Correct the notion that the Smith Act was not intended to prohibit advocacy and teaching of forcible overthrow as an abstract principle;

6. Permit schools, universities, bar associations and other organizations to set standards of membership high enough to exclude those who refuse to testify frankly and fully about their past activities in furtherance of Communist plans to conquer the free world by subversion.

In recent weeks the New York "Daily Worker" has been replete with articles and editorials proclaiming that the usefulness of FBI informants in future prosecutions has been destroyed; that the Smith Act is now ineffective and for all practical purposes invalidated; that the effectiveness of congressional inquiries into subversive activities has been curtailed and that the Government loyalty-security program is under serious attack. In reporting on its current fund drive the "Daily Worker" has stated it has experienced an enlivening of contributions which it attributed to renewed hope by its supporters for its future.

The reaction of the Communist Party to the recent Supreme Court decisions clearly depicts the resilience of the organization and the speed with which its leadership recognizes an advantage and presses to capitalize to the fullest extent on circumstances conducive to the growth of the organization.

Some Americans may wonder whether an organization the size of the Communist Party, U.S.A., with a consistent decline in membership in recent years represents a danger to the security of this country. It must be remembered that numbers alone do not mean everything. The party has never boasted of a large membership but rather has continually endeavored to confine its membership to hard-core members who have adhered to Communist discipline down through the years and who can be relied upon to carry out the party's orders without question.

Our Committee believes that special mention should be made of the June 3, 1957, decision of the United States Supreme Court in *Jencks* v. *United States* and legislation subsequently introduced in Congress to define the scope of the rule announced by the Court in that case.

In the Jencks case the Court held that one accused by the United States of a criminal offense is entitled to inspect, for purposes of impeachment, prior statements and reports which the prosecution witnesses had previously made to the Government and which touch upon the subject of their testimony at the trial. Further, the defense need not first lay a foundation of inconsistent testimony in order to obtain production of these documents.

We are in firm agreement with the Court's view that the accused's right to make an adequate defense must not be jeopardized by an arbitrary withholding of pertinent documents by the prosecution.

We are equally strong in our belief, however, that the rules by which these documents are produced should be defined with sufficient restriction that one accused of subversion against this nation and its people will not be allowed to rummage at will through

Government documents containing confidential information important to the national security and of no relevance whatever to the defense of the accused. There is danger of such a result.

The Attorney General himself testified before the Congress only recently, declaring that a grave emergency resulted from the Supreme Court decision in the Jencks case. He asserted that some trial courts have interpreted the Jencks decision to require that the Government submit to the defense not only those reports and statements specified by the Supreme Court, but also the investigative report of the case, much of which is neither relevant nor material to the defense of the accused.

We believe the effect of such interpretations is to weaken immeasurably the proper and necessary defenses of society, without granting to the accused any additional information which he rightfully needs to make his defense. We also point out that the investigative reports sometimes contain the names of third persons who originally were linked to the case in a manner subsequently found to be innocent. To release the names of these innocent people from the bond of Government secrecy would not promote the interests of justice. On the contrary, it would be injustice of the rankest sort.

Accordingly we believe that a firm stand should be taken in support of legislation, already introduced in the Congress, which would recognize the rights of the accused as defined by the Supreme Court in the Jencks decision, but at the same time prohibit those rights from being used by criminals and subversives as a lever to pry out of the Government files information to which they are not entitled and the release of which can serve no purpose but to jeopardize the rights of innocent persons and the public at large.

Your Committee calls attention to the report to the Congress which was recently made by the Commission on Government Security, of which Loyd Wright, past president of the American Bar Association, is chairman. This report points out the critical situation with respect to national security. We urge the careful study and consideration of this report by the lawyers of our country and, further, that the efforts to strengthen our internal-security defenses have wholehearted support and co-operation.

Chairman Wright, his fellow members of the Commission on Government security, the advisory group and staff of the Commission are entitled to the commendation and gratitude of the citizenry for their monumental undertaking, which has been so efficiently and painstakingly performed. It is heartening to note the unselfish efforts exerted by Chairman Wright and his colleagues to achieve the desired goal of Government security, at the same time safeguarding the legitimate interests of everyone involved in the considerations of Government security.

This committee again commends President George Meany of the AFL-CIO for his prompt detection of the current Communist line and his warnings to his fellow Americans of the folly of trying to do business with a government which has violated every agreement that it ever signed.

We also commend Mr. Albert Hayes, of the International Association of Machinists, for promptly dismissing three organizers who took the Fifth Amendment when asked by the Senate Internal Security Subcommittee about their Communist activities. It is hoped that leaders in other fields of American life will react with equal courage to current Communist tactics.

We desire to record emphatically our approval of the organization and functioning of the two congressional committees, which have given special attention to the problem of subversive activities, namely: the Senate Internal Security Committee and the House Un-American Activities Committee. It is our considered opinion, for close observation of the work of these two groups, that they have rendered immeasurable service to the American people and that their operations have been of inestimable value in the defense of our country against those who would undermine our basic institutions.

It is also our privilege to comment upon the painstaking and intelligent efforts of the Federal Bureau of Investigation. Under the able leadership of Director J. Edgar Hoover, this devoted group has become a tower of strength in the all-out effort to detect and to apprehend subversion, among their other important undertakings. We praise their work and urge the American people to give continuous aid and provisions to uphold and support the operation of this protective agency.

Lawyers, by training and tradition, know and appreciate the vital importance of an independent judiciary. Wherever we find it, we respect it. Where the independence is exercised with courage and soundness, we revere it—for then we have justice under law. Our training has also given us, and we must impart the benefit of it to the American people, a tolerance and an understanding of difference of viewpoint.

The Judicial branch is one of the three cornerstones of our constitutional government—and the ultimate determinant of our individual rights—but, as we said in our brief to the Supreme Court in the Communist Party case, "There can be no individual rights or freedoms without national security."

For the reason that our Committee has been charged with the duty of studying the problems caused by international Communism and we have observed the Communist tactics and realized the danger to American life and to the free world, we must urge an unremitting effort to maintain a judicial system which will ever function as impartial, resolute and vigilant. There must ever be one standard of justice under law for both high and low, for those who are accused of serious offenses as well as for lesser crimes.

There must never be different and varying schedules for determination of rights or duties or violations applicable to cases involving Communist problems as compared to other issues.

It must be remembered that it is one of the cardinal policies of the Communist movement not to be concerned with actions, proceedings, charges or indictments so much as their ultimate determination and consequences. For that reason, the strategy of delay is employed by them in every case and at every stage.

It should not happen that sound and established concepts of law and standards are disregarded and different standards employed simply because the problem involved Communist activity. To conjure hypothetical fears not involved in a case submitted for determination is neither sound judicial administration nor good government. Again, to quote from our brief in the Communist Party case, may we repeat, "Where no constitutional or statutory provision is violated, the Courts are no more immune from the duty to safeguard the nation than is the Congress or the President."

The criterion of justice must in this country be high—but it must be human—and cannot be perfect. We believe and shall always strive for the same high standard of justice for any Communist or Communist organization as for any loyal American citizen or any legal entity, but likewise, we will deplore special and extraordinary treatment for Communists or Communist organizations.

The momentous and dangerous times in which we live present serious problems to every branch of Government and entail sacred responsibilities. It is imperative that our bench and bar must be sound as well as courageous, realistic as well as idealistic.

The desire to preserve liberty in all its forms and the absolute necessity of protecting our countries and our families from international Communism pose a problem that is admittedly very difficult. On the one hand, England and the United States have for centuries cherished the ideal that uniformity of opinion among the citizens is neither desirable nor obtainable; on the other hand, we are not so blind as to think that Communism is merely another shade of political opinion. The dilemma that confronts our two countries is monumental.

The duty of the bar to play an important part in finding a solution to the dilemma is self-evident. We must strive to find the proper degree of balance between liberty and authority.

It is traditional and right that our courts are zealous in protecting individual rights. It is equally necessary that the executive and legislative branches take effective action to gird our country in defense against Communist infiltration and aggression.

If the courts lean too far backward in the maintenance of theoretical individual rights, it may be that we have tied the hands of our country and have rendered it incapable of carrying out the first law of mankind—the right of self-preservation.

CHAPTER 12

Communist Penetration into the United States

SOVIET ESPIONAGE IN AMERICA

Spies for the U.S.S.R. and those in a position to spy are numerous and often well protected inside the United States. In 1953, Soviet diplomatic and official personnel in the United States numbered 407. This count included employees of the Soviet Embassy in Washington; delegates to the United Nations; officials of *Amtorg*, the trade agency, with headquarters in New York City; correspondents connected with the *Tass* news agency, *Pravda*, and the U.S.S.R. radio; and the dependents of these employees. In addition, Communist satellite states have several hundred officials and dependents in the United States. All of the Soviet functionaries in the United States have official status of one sort or another. Diplomats and their staffs enjoy special immunity. Officials of *Amtorg*, *Tass*, and *Pravda* carry special visas that give them an extra measure of protection and privilege. The Soviet spy Gubitchev, although not certified as a diplomat, claimed that as an official he had a measure of immunity; this claim helped to set him free. Neither William Oatis nor Robert Vogeler, however, could claim special protection from the American government, which was seemingly unable to aid them when they were held behind the Iron Curtain.

Russia's diplomats, *Amtorg's* businessmen, and Russian reporters are free, for the most part, to travel where, when, and as they wish.[1] They send telegrams, make telephone calls, use the mails, take pictures, subscribe to technical journals crammed with vital information, and drive as many cars as they wish. Nobody stops them for unexpected searches. A correspondent of *Pravda* filed a story from Detroit in 1952 detailing effects of military-production contracts in that key U.S. industrial center. American correspondents in Russia would not be allowed to get within miles of an industrial center like Detroit.

In 1952, Georgi N. Zarubin became the new resident of the mansion at 1125 Sixteenth Street, N.W., in Washington. Zarubin was the new Soviet Ambassador to the United States. Wherever Russia's Zarubin has moved in, active spy operations have developed. When he was Ambassador to Canada, the Communist spy ring in that country reached its highest state of efficiency. Then Ambassador Zarubin moved to London. Klaus Fuchs, now known as the most dangerous spy in history, did some of his work under the Zarubin regime. It was then, too, that Bruno Pontecorvo, a leading atomic scientist in Britain, defected to the side of the Communists, carrying top secrets with him. During Zarubin's stay in London, two British diplomats, Donald McLean and Guy Burgess, disappeared behind the Iron Curtain, carrying diplomatic secrets of the highest importance.[2]

When Zarubin moved to Washington, he found a situation almost made to order. Russian officials had the freedom of the city. Agents of the *Tass* news agency had access to the White House, to Congress, to nearly all federal agencies. They attended Presidential press conferences, as well as those of the Secretary of State and other high officials. When Zarubin took over his new post, he saw at first hand that spies for Russia were operating in the United States with considerable success. Some American Communists spying for the Soviets have been exposed and prosecuted (Harry Gold, the Rosenbergs, Judith Coplon, Alger Hiss), yet the spy activities that break into the open are only a small visible part of the whole. Beneath the surface, the spying still goes on.

One of the most skillful practitioners of the Soviet undercover technique in the United States was Alger Hiss. On August 3, 1948, Whittaker Chambers, senior editor of *Time* magazine, appearing before the House Un-American Activities Committee, named Alger Hiss and nine other government officials as Communists working for a Soviet ring. Among those named were Harry Dexter White, former Assistant Secretary of the Treasury; Nathan Witt, former general counsel of the National Labor Relations Board; John Abt, former Assistant Attorney General; and Lee Pressman, former general counsel of the Works Progress Administration, later chief counsel for the CIO. Chambers testified that he had first told this story of Soviet espionage to A. A. Berle, then an official of the State Department, and that Berle had told it to President Roosevelt, who laughed it off.

Chambers' testimony supplemented that of Elizabeth Bentley, who had named twenty-nine government employees as members of a Soviet spy ring, including William Remington, official in the Commerce Department; Lauchlin Currie, a White House assistant; Nathan Silvermaster of the Board of Economic Warfare; and Victor Perlo of the War Production Board.

Hiss was called for his side of the story, and he denied knowing Chambers. President Truman denounced the whole investigation as a "red herring." He said that the Congressional committee was infringing on the Bill of Rights and claimed that "no American secrets leaked out during the war." Meanwhile, Hiss admitted that he might have known Chambers under the name of "Crosley" but denied being a Communist or a spy. When Hiss and Chambers confronted each other in public, Hiss called Chambers a liar. The latter, however, had previously given the Committee conclusive proof that he had known Hiss some years before.

After some delay following this public exposure of Hiss, Hiss sued Chambers for libel. Chambers produced a stack of typewritten and handwritten copies of secret documents given him by Hiss in 1938. This evidence was quickly impounded by the Justice Department, and frantic efforts were made to keep it from the public eye. Chambers was threatened with prosecution for illegal possession of government documents. On December 1, 1948, the Justice Department informed the press that it was "about ready" to drop the entire investigation. Thereupon Chambers showed Representative Richard Nixon and investigator Robert Stripling microfilmed copies of additional State Department documents hidden in a pumpkin. The "pumpkin papers" became famous, revealing that a steady stream of information had flowed to the Soviet spy ring in 1938. Experts identified four documents as being in the handwriting of Hiss and the remainder as the product of his typewriter. After the first Hiss jury deadlocked eight to four in favor of conviction on two counts of perjury (Hiss could not be indicted for espionage because the three-year statute of limitations had run out), a second jury found him guilty on January 21, 1950. Six hours later, Secretary of State Dean Acheson declared: "I do not intend to turn my back on Alger Hiss."

I asked former President Harry S. Truman, on a television program in Milwaukee on September 3, 1956, why he had not acted when he was warned by FBI Director J. Edgar Hoover in 1945 that Harry Dexter White (Assistant to the Secretary of the Treasury) and other security risks were engaged in espionage against the United States. Mr. Truman denied that Hoover had so warned him and claimed that White was not "guilty of anything."[3] Yet this is what Hoover said in his letter to the White House dated November 9, 1945: "The investigation, however, at this point has indicated that the persons named hereinafter were actually the source from which information passing through the Soviet espionage system was being obtained.... Dr. Gregory Silvermaster (Department of Agriculture), Harry Dexter White, George Silverman (War Department), Lauchlin Currie (former Administrative Assistant to the late President Roosevelt), Victor Perlo (formerly with the War Production Board), Donald Wheeler (formerly with the Office of Strategic Services), Major Duncan Lee, Julius Joseph, Helen Tenney, and Maurice Halperin (all with the O.S.S.), Charles Kramer (formerly on Senator Kilgore's staff), Captain William Ludwig Ullmann (Army Air Corps), and Lt. Col. John H. Reynolds (U.S. Army)."

During the same program, I asked Mr. Truman if he thought Alger Hiss was a Communist spy. The former President replied: "No, I do not."

Millions of Americans who may be killed by Soviet nuclear weapons in World War III can thank Klaus Fuchs, Harry Gold, Morton Sobell, and Julius and Ethel Rosenberg—convicted atomic spies. These traitors turned over information and materials on the atomic weapon which advanced the development of the Soviet A-bomb. In 1944, Fuchs went to Los Alamos, New Mexico, where he worked under Hans Bethe, originator of the theory on which the hydrogen bomb is based. When the first test explosion of an atomic bomb took place, Fuchs was on hand.

Harry Gold was the anonymous courier to whom Fuchs entrusted the priceless information he gathered in the most closely guarded of all American military projects. Gold was responsible to Soviet agents Semenov and Yakovlev in New York. Gold also got information for the Soviets from David Greenglass, Morton Sobell, and the Rosenbergs. Julius Rosenberg recruited Greenglass for the spy ring in 1945 and directed his activities in Los Alamos for at least four months. On March 28, 1951, a New York jury returned a verdict of guilty. The Rosenbergs were sentenced to death; Gold and Sobell got thirty years and Greenglass fifteen (Greenglass cooperated with the prosecution and turned state's evidence). Fuchs was tried and convicted in Britain.

In February, 1957, a federal grand jury charged that Jack Soble, his wife Myra, and Jacob Albam conspired with Soviet intelligence agents to transmit to Russia information about the national defense of the United States. Later in 1957, George and Jane Zlatovski, American citizens living in France, were also indicted by a federal grand jury on five counts of spying for the Soviet Union. At the end of the year, Col. Rudolf I. Abel, who had resided in New York, was convicted as a Soviet spy.

The Department of State was forced to grant Mrs. Zlatovski a passport in 1955, when Judge Burnita S. Matthews ruled that it could be withheld only if the State Department divulged full knowledge of the espionage activities of which she was a part. This the Department refused to do. Thus the United States government was unable to prevent a known Soviet spy from leaving the country.

THE STORY OF THE INSTITUTE OF PACIFIC RELATIONS

The loss of China to Communism and the subsequent casualty lists in Korea are to a large degree attributable to the disastrous influence which the Institute of Pacific Relations had on American Far Eastern policy. An international organization supported by wealthy patrons, including pro-Communist Frederick Vanderbilt Field, the IPR came to be dominated by Communists and their allies. It wielded tremendous influence, not only in government circles, but in the universities and the mass media, and was instrumental in shaping the Far Eastern policy of these organizations. No wonder so many people became prejudiced against anti-Communists such as Chiang Kai-shek and Syngman Rhee, although there had been no prejudice so long as they were fighting the Japanese. No wonder so many unwitting Americans came to believe that the Chinese Communists were only agrarian reformers.

Frederick V. Field, Owen Lattimore, Philip Jessup, and Edward Carter ran the IPR. The Senate Internal Security Subcommittee, after an eighteen-month investigation, concluded that the IPR was "considered by the American Communist party and by Soviet officials as an instrument of Communist policy, propaganda, and military intelligence"; it described Lattimore as a "conscious, articulate instrument of the Communist conspiracy"; it held that "John Carter Vincent was the principal fulcrum of IPR pressures in the State

Department"; it stated that the IPR "possessed close organic relationships with the State Department through interchange of personnel, attendance of State Department officials at IPR conferences, constant exchange of information, and social contacts."

On June 18, 1941, with the Hitler-Stalin pact still in force, Lattimore and Edward Carter lunched with Soviet Ambassador Oumansky in Washington, shortly after Presidential Assistant Lauchlin Currie had succeeded in getting Lattimore appointed as presidential advisor to Chiang Kai-shek. Neither Lattimore nor Carter has satisfactorily explained what sort of business they transacted with the ambassador of a country associated with the Axis in war against America's allies, Britain and China.

During 1941, two IPR groups sought to dissuade Japanese militarists from attacking Russia (and by implication, to encourage Japan to expand southward). One of these was the Lattimore-Currie-Harry Dexter White group in the United States; the other was the Soviet spy ring of Richard Sorge in the Far East, which included such IPR leaders as Hotsumi Ozaki, Kinkazu Saionji, Agnes Smedley, and Gunther Stein. Whereas these people later favored appeasement of Communist Far East aggression, in 1941 they vehemently insisted on military action against the Japanese aggressor.

IPR leaders held several conferences attended by leading State Department officials and published books and pamphlets to influence public opinion along pro-Communist lines. The most important pro-Communist writers were Maxwell S. Stewart, Lawrence K. Rosinger, and T. A. Bisson. Rosinger refused to tell the Senate subcommittee whether or not he was a Communist. Bisson used the pen name "Frederick Spencer," which happened to be Frederick V. Field's name in the Communist party. He and Field were editors not only of IPR publications, but also of the Communist magazines *Amerasia* and *China Today*.[4]

In 1945, John Stewart Service, top State Department political officer in China during the war, absconded with government secrets and gave them to the editor of *Amerasia.* Not until Senator McCarthy became interested in his case in 1950 did the State Department take action against him. In 1951, the Civil Service Loyalty Review Board found him to be of doubtful loyalty to the United States. During the war, both Service and John P. Davies worked with State Department Far Eastern Chief John Carter Vincent, in cooperation with the IPR, to encourage the Chinese Communists. They described the "democratic nature" of the Communists and concluded that "a coalition Chinese Government in which the Communists find a satisfactory place is the solution of this impassee most desirable to us."[5]

In January, 1944, Soviet agent Vladimir Rogoff met Lattimore and John Carter Vincent in New York. Increased pressures by Lattimore and Vincent resulted in an American policy which treated the Chinese government and the Communist rebels as equals. General Marshall was sent to China to tell Chiang to bring Communists into the Chinese government or do without American aid. When Chiang quite naturally refused, Marshall cut off all aid to Chiang; this, in addition to the concessions the U.S.S.R. obtained at Yalta and Soviet aid to the Chinese Reds, set the stage not only for Communist conquest of China, but also for the attack on Korea.

Having done much to help the Communists to victory in China, the IPR proceeded to send its top men (including Lattimore and Rosinger) to dominate a State Department conference on China in October, 1949. This conference contained an IPR majority which agreed with Rosinger and Lattimore that Communist China should be recognized. Three months earlier, Lattimore had written: "The thing to do in Korea is to let south Korea fall, but not let it look as though we pushed it."

By 1953, Service and Vincent were out of government employment, thanks to the Senatorial investigation and the Security Program, and most of the others had been exposed. Rosinger refused to deny allegations that he was a Communist, Field was definitely proven a Communist,[6] Lattimore was indicted on seven counts of perjury,[7] and John P. Davies was shifted from his key post in Bonn, Germany, to an obscure job in South America and was later discharged for incompetence. The situation had improved, but much damage had been done. As late as 1952, the Rockefeller Foundation granted thousands of dollars to the IPR; a year earlier it had given Rosinger approximately $8,500 in grants—all this while American blood flowed in Korea.[8]

It must not be assumed, however, that the above-mentioned men no longer influence public opinion. John Carter Vincent lectured under the auspices of the Foreign Policy Association after his enforced departure from the government, and John S. Service was given his old State Department job back again when, in 1957, the Supreme Court held that Secretary of State Acheson had violated a technicality in firing Service under the Security Program.

COMMUNISM AND THE INTELLECTUALS

Congressional exposures and subsequent court actions revealed massive Communist penetration into government, industry, the mass media, and, most recently, education. What was most shocking was that large numbers of "intellectuals" who had made crystal clear their militant opposition to Nazism and Fascism refused to take the same stand against Communism. Indeed, many of them had fraternized with the Communists during the New Deal era and, of course, during the period of the U.S.-Soviet alliance. They seemed to think that whereas Ku Klux Klanners, racial supremacy advocates, and Bundists deserved no place in American society, Communists were different and deserved considerate treatment in the name of "civil rights."

Ten of the top academic collaborators with Communist fronts and enterprises since 1933 have been: Corliss Lamont (Columbia), Harry F. Ward (Union Theological), Bernard J. Stern (Columbia), Henry P. Fairchild (New York), Robert Morss Lovett (Chicago), Colston E. Warne (Amherst), Dorothy Brewster

(Columbia), Dirk J. Struik (M.I.T.), Edwin P. Burgum (New York), and Kirtley F. Mather (Harvard). Ward, Fairchild, and Lovett are now deceased.[9]

One of the most influential Communist-front organizations has been the National Council of the Arts, Sciences, and Professions. On March 25, 1949, the NCASP convened a "Cultural and Scientific Conference for World Peace" in New York, whose purposes were to serve the greater glory of the Soviet Union. Seven college presidents served as sponsors. World-famous scientists, including Albert Einstein, Linus Pauling, and Norbert Wiener were also sponsors. Harvard contributed astronomer Harlow Shapley, geologist Kirtley Mather, and philosopher Ralph Barton Perry. Cornell was represented by nuclear physicist Philip Morrison, who worked on the Manhattan A-bomb project. Columbia Professors Corliss Lamont, Gene Weltfish, and Mark Van Doren were there; so was Frederick L. Schuman of Williams College, whose textbooks on international politics are widely used in American colleges and universities.[10]

Other "intellectuals" who have collaborated with Soviet and Communist-dominated organizations up to and including the era of the Berlin blockade (by which time they presumably should have known better) include: T. A. Bisson (formerly of California), Derk Bodde (Pennsylvania), Rudolf Carnap (Chicago), Dorothy Douglas (Smith), Kermit Eby (Chicago), Thomas I. Emerson (Yale), Fowler V. Harper (Yale), Mervin Jules (Smith), Oliver Larkin (Smith), Halford E. Luccock (Yale), Louise Pettibone Smith (Wellesley), John B. Thompson (Chicago), and Leroy Waterman (Michigan). Of the top academic collaborators, including the above, who have been affiliated with at least ten units of the Communist-front apparatus up to and including the Berlin blockade, seventy-two of the leading one hundred are listed in *Who's Who*.[11]

Perhaps most important from the point of view of American security was the academic collaboration with the enemy of a number of scientists. The names of Professor Alan Nunn May, Klaus Fuchs, Harry Gold, and Julius and Ethel Rosenberg are well known to the American public. Much less familiar are those of Joseph Weinberg, Ken Max Manfred, Irving D. Fox, David J. Bohm, Giovanni R. Lomanitz, and Clarence Hiskey. Incontrovertible evidence linked these "professors" with the Communist party. Weinberg, Manfred, Fox, Bohm, and Lomanitz were members of a Communist cell in the radiation laboratory of the University of California. All of them took refuge, when questioned about party membership, in the Fifth Amendment to the Constitution. Yet with the exception of Hiskey, who was linked with the Soviet atom spy Arthur A. Adams, all of these Communist collaborators received good jobs in reputable universities *after* their membership in the Communist cell at the University of California had been exposed.

As J. B. Matthews points out, "the undeniable fact . . . is that little or nothing has ever been done to remove any Communist from any faculty anywhere in the United States until the pressure of legislative investigation has been applied." He cites the cases of Professors Ralph Gundlach, Joseph Butterworth, and Herbert Phillips at the University of Washington, Professors Bernard Riess and Henrietta Friedman of Hunter College, and Professors Harry Slochower and Melba Phillips of Brooklyn College as examples. He also cites the case of Edwin B. Burgum, who was not discharged by New York University until he refused to tell the Senate Internal Subcommittee whether or not he was a Communist.[12]

In July, 1954, no less a person than Dr. J. Robert Oppenheimer was declared by the Atomic Energy Commission to be a security risk on the basis of Communist affiliations. Oppenheimer, who had called the atomic targets in Japan in 1945 "too small," suddenly claimed to have moral qualms about building nuclear weapons which might have to be used against Communism. He opposed the H-bomb program and delayed the development of the bomb. Dr. Oppenheimer is today head of the Institute of Advanced Study at Princeton, N.J.[13] In 1957, certain "liberal" columnists, panicked by

Soviet missile claims, launched a hue and cry that Oppenheimer had been the victim of "McCarthyism" and urged his return to government employment. The next year, they claimed credit for the resignation of Atomic Energy Commission Chairman Lewis Strauss, whom they had attacked because he and Dr. Edward Teller refused to stop our nuclear tests in the Pacific.

COMMUNISM AND LABOR

An index of Communist strength in the labor movement, with its potential of serious harm to American defense in emergency, can be gleaned from the list of the unions which were under Communist domination in 1949 and have largely remained under that domination. These CIO unions were:

The American Communications Association, headed by Joseph Selly, veteran Communist.

The Food, Tobacco, Agricultural, and Allied Workers of America, headed by Donald Henderson, who headed the old Red-ruled union in this field.

The International Fur and Leather Workers Union, headed by Ben Gold, open Communist.

The International Longshoremen's and Warehousemen's union, headed by Harry Bridges, convicted of perjury for swearing he was not a Communist.

The International Union of Mine, Mill, and Smelter Workers, headed by Morris Travis.

The United Public Workers of America, headed for years by Eleanor Nelson.

The National Union of Marine Cooks and Stewards, headed by Hugh Bryson.

The United Furniture Workers of America.

The United Office and Professional Workers of America. (Communist Domination of Certain Unions, Report of Senate Sub-Committee on Labor and Labor-Management Relations, Document 89, 82nd Congress, 1st Session.)

All of the above unions were expelled from the CIO in 1950.[14] Among those not expelled were the following:

Transport Workers Union of America, which under the leadership of Michael Quill broke with the Communist party.

The National Maritime Union, which under the leadership of Joseph Curran likewise repudiated previous Communist control.

The United Electrical, Radio, and Machine Workers Union, actually led by James Matles, official representative of the Politburo in that union, which dropped affiliation with the CIO before charges could be filed.

In addition, there was Local 65 of the Wholesale and Retail Workers Union, headed by Arthur Osman, who later headed the Distributive, Processing, and Office Workers of America (DPOWA).

Both President Walter Reuther of the CIO and President James B. Carey of the International Union of Electrical Workers, CIO, have been engaged in a grim fight with the Communists. But, unfortunately, both Reuther and Carey give ammunition to the Communist cry for "labor unity" and to the contention that any curb of the Communists injures labor. At the convention of the American Association of School Administrators on February 17, 1953, Mrs. Agnes E. Meyer, wife of the publisher of the *Washington Post*, made an extreme attack on the investigation of Communist professors and teachers. The Communist press, together with its allies and friends, made Mrs. Meyer's speech the occasion for widespread propaganda to cover up and defend the conspiracy. Walter Reuther followed Mrs. Meyer on the speaker's platform and advocated the same anti-anti-Communist line. Said Reuther: "The growing attack by the apostles of fear, hatred, and hysteria against academic freedom and civil liberties generally must be met by an effective counteroffensive." His words seem to imply that all attempts to uproot the infiltrators from our educational system must be halted.

The newsletter *Counterattack* stated in its issue of March 20,

1953: "It makes sense when the CP plugs this line and gives publicity to Reuther when he does . . . just as it has given publicity to his attacks on the Internal Security Act of 1950 and the Smith Act, under which the Politburo and other CP leaders have been tried and convicted of conspiracy. But it doesn't make sense when Reuther plugs it. When he does he is actually, though unintentionally, identifying the interests of the CIO, the UAW, and all labor with those of the CP."

At the 1950 convention of the CIO, Reuther sponsored a resolution criticizing the Smith Act, which did so much to cripple the Soviet fifth column until its effectiveness was lessened by Supreme Court decisions. This criticism was repeated by the 1953 convention of the UAW under his leadership. The Communists, while playing up in their press this anti-anti-Communist attitude, at the same time assail Reuther for breaking "labor unity" by opposing them within the UAW. It is small wonder that, with such a convenient cover as Reuther's own statements, they were able to rout his forces in the big Ford Local 600, the spearhead of their drive into the UAW. They won this victory despite the exposure of specific officers of Local 600 as members of the Communist conspiracy by the House Committee of Un-American Activities.

In view of the way in which the Communists, Communist fronters, and those influenced by them work from the top of organizations to attain their ends, it is significant that the counsel for the UAW is Harold Cranefield, leading member of the National Lawyers Guild, which the House Committee on Un-American Activities declared to be the "legal arm" of the Communist party.

With President James B. Carey of the IUEW, the story has been the same. In February, 1953, for instance, Carey appeared on the American Forum of the Air to assail Congressional investigations and to indicate that a greater threat to the United States than Communism was the attempt of "reactionaries" to destroy it. He claimed that this led to lack of faith by the American people, in one another and in their institutions. Carey has made other statements to the same effect. This has given another convenient cover to the Communists. Partly because of this, the Communist party-directed United Electrical, Radio, and Machine Workers Union won a National Labor Relations Board election at the North American Cyanimide Company plant of the International Harvester Company, early in 1953. The Red-ruled union also made marked headway among electrical workers in Pittsburgh and Erie, Pennsylvania, and in parts of New Jersey.[15]

The attitude expressed by Reuther, Carey and other labor leaders along this line is in strange contradiction to the statement repeatedly made by the CIO committees that "the Communist Party does not believe in trade unions. It believes in using trade unions. And it believes in using them for the purposes of the Soviet Union." If that is so, then the Communists are the enemies of the free labor unions, as they have proved to be by their splitting tactics in non-Soviet countries and by their complete crushing of genuine unionism wherever the Soviet dictatorship is established.[16]

Clearly anti-Communist is George Meany, head of the AFL-CIO. In an address to the National Labor and Religious Foundation in 1956, he shocked liberals with these words:

"Too many in the Free World are still prisoners of the illusion that Communism is, historically speaking, a progressive system—extreme liberalism temporarily making bad mistakes. Actually, Communism represents darkest reaction. . . . Too many in the Free World seem to have lost their capacity for moral indignation against the most brutal inhumanities when they are perpetrated by Communists. They never find the time to utter a word of condemnation against the Communist imperialist destruction of the national independence and democratic rights of hundreds of millions of people in Europe and Asia. Many people in our country who call themselves liberals are stone silent about the Soviet concentration camps. . . . Communism is the very opposite of liberalism. Communism is the deadliest enemy of liberalism. Liberals should be the most consistent and energetic fighters against Communism. Liberals must be on guard against developing a certain type of McCarthyism of their own. They must shun like the plague the role of being anti-anti-Communists. Only by refusing to be thus entrapped can liberals shed every vestige of subconscious and conscious regard for Communism as a movement with which they have something in common."[17]

Few Americans have expressed so succinctly why some liberals have a blind spot in their thinking when it comes to Communism.

THE PROBLEM OF THE UNITED NATIONS

Evidence came to light at the end of 1952 that Communist countries have been using the UN as a ready-made means of funneling a massive amount of information about the United States back to Russia. During 1952, some one hundred Americans in the UN were fired or allowed to resign on security and loyalty grounds. This included top-level administrators who refused to say whether or not they were Communists: Alfred Van Tassel, Joel Gordon, Frank Bancroft, Stanley Graze, Eugene Wallach, and Frank Coe. The last, former head of the International Monetary Fund, refused even to tell a Senate subcommittee whether or not he was at that moment spying against the United States.

On December 3, 1952, a New York federal grand jury issued the following warning on the matter of Communist influence in the UN:

"This jury must, as a duty to the American people, advise the court that startling evidence has disclosed infiltration into the United Nations of an overwhelmingly large group of disloyal United States citizens, many of whom are closely associated with the international Communist movement. This group numbers scores of individuals, most of whom have long records of federal employment, and at the same time have been connected with persons and organizations subversive to this country. Their positions at the time we subpoenaed them were ones of trust and responsibility in the United Nations Secretariat and in its specialized agencies. . . . Our sole concern and effort has been directed toward possible violations of law by United States citizens whose activities are indisputably within our jurisdiction.

"Our attention was first sharply directed to this concentration of disloyal Americans in the UN while we were investigating a possible espionage violation by a U.S. citizen. . . . This witness . . . refused to state whether or not he was still engaged in espionage activities against this country; whether or not he was still a Communist party member; whether or not he would support this nation in case of war with the Soviet Union. The evidence before us establishes that: (a) Over a score of these United States citizens employed at the UN . . . refused to answer questions concerning past and present Communist party membership and activity, including in some instances past and present espionage activity against the United States; (b) a number of other witnesses admitted past and hitherto unrevealed Communist party membership and activity. At least one admitted involvement in the Communist party underground. Still others admitted continuing sympathy with the Communist movement. . . .

"Almost without exception these same subversive employees were formerly employed in various departments of our own Federal Government. They were transferred from one federal department to another, finally ending up in key positions in the UN. The evidence shows this is not coincidental but part of a definite, planned pattern. It appears to result from the contrivance of certain highly placed officials who have surrounded themselves in each Government agency and then in the UN with personnel who share their disloyal convictions. One such official, a division director, has executed this procedure with alarming success. He has placed in important United Nations posts at least four officials who have invoked the self-incrimination privilege before us, and one person whom the Senate Judiciary Committee has declared to be a "conscious, articulate instrument of the Soviet conspiracy." Despite public revelation of his conduct, this division director remains to this day in his post of dangerously high responsibility in the UN. . . .

"The United Nations today is engaged in a bloody war in Korea. Its implications are world survival of the democratic nations against the Communist threat. United States citizens whose loyalties are to the world Communist movement cannot be faithful to the UN Korean undertaking."

As a direct result of the findings of this grand jury, and upon receiving an opinion from a commission of three international jurists advising him that disloyal nationals could be discharged by their governments from the UN, Trygve Lie, then UN Secretary General, proceeded to co-operate with American officials to weed out a number of officials classified as doubtful security risks. Unfortunately, however, the International Court decided in July, 1954, to grant life pensions to the UN employees who had been thus discharged.[18]

During 1956, the Soviet legation of the UN kidnapped several Russians who had defected from the Soviet Union and had sought asylum in the United States. As a result, two Soviet UN officials were declared *persona non grata* and were asked to leave the United States. On September 24, 1953, a defected Polish diplomat, Dr. Marek S. Korowicz, told the House Un-American Activities Committee: "The United Nations is considered one of the most important platforms for Soviet propaganda in the world." Experience has shown that the Communist regimes in the UN utilize their status primarily for purposes of propaganda, espionage, threats, and kidnappings of former citizens of central and eastern Europe.

CONCLUSION

On October 3, 1952, Dwight D. Eisenhower warned a Milwaukee audience:

"All of us—citizens, jurists, officials—must remember that the Bill of Rights contains no grant of privilege for a group of people to join together to destroy the Bill of Rights. A group—like the

Communist conspiracy—dedicated to the ultimate destruction of all civil liberties, cannot be allowed to claim civil liberties as its privileged sanctuary from which to carry on subversion of the Government.

"At the same time we have the right to call a spade a spade. That means in every proved case, the right to call a Red a Red. The time is past when we can hide our heads in the sands of stubborn ignorance or spend our days in the leisurely indulgence of abstract argument. . . .

"Having done this, let us make one more fact plain: To work for the United States Government is a privilege, not a right. And it is the prerogative of the Government to set the strictest test upon the loyalty and the patriotism of those entrusted with our nation's safety.

"Every official of Government must bear clear responsibility for the loyalty and fitness of his own immediate subordinates. And every official of the Federal Government—on every level—must ever be ready to answer any question from appropriate sources touching upon his loyalty and devotion to the United States of America."

But five years after this campaign talk, the Eisenhower administration's security program was weakened, and Supreme Court decisions rendered impotent much of the countersubversion program. Eisenhower appointees, including Chief Justice Warren and Associate Justice Brennan, voted almost every time with Justice Douglas and Black, whose judicial opinions reveal an incredible naïveté about the Communist conspiracy.

CHAPTER 13

Why Do People Become Communists?

THE VARIOUS APPEALS

Communism, like other fanatical ideologies which preceded it, does have a power of attraction for some individuals. In the first place, Communism offers answers to questions. Why, the human mind has asked through the millennia of history, is the world in such a sad state?

The great religions of the world offer answers—but for some their answers are too intangible, too difficult. Christianity offers an answer that insists upon the personal responsibility of every individual soul for the free and constant choice between good and evil, between life everlasting and death everlasting. This ancient answer of religion is reiterated by democratic ethics, which insist upon the element of individual responsibility in the political field. Science, far from disagreeing with religion, asserts that only the individual's recognition of what is true and what is false and the application of this knowledge can enable man to understand and control his environment.

The Communist faith often invokes the fervor of a new religion. The party member feels that he is a member of an elite group, the germ of the new world of tomorrow. The nonparty infidels, he thinks, are living in outer darkness in a world that is decadent and doomed. For the apostles and prophets of religion, he substitutes Marx, Lenin, and Stalin.

People do not become Communists primarily because they are

poor or hungry. A large percentage of the party consists of mission-minded intellectuals who have constituted themselves the exponents of the interests of labor, although labor wants no part of them. William Bledsoe, former editor of the *Screen Guild Magazine,* describes Communism in Hollywood thus: "I saw social consciousness quicken and come to a boil in actors, writers, and directors. . . . I followed the insurrection mass meeting by mass meeting, cocktail party by cocktail party, until many a Big Name was more or less secretly enrolled in the Communist Party or tagging along solemnly in one of the 'front' committees. . . . Hollywood is a city of unhappy successful people. And that, it seemed to me, was the basis for Communism with two butlers and a swimming pool. . . . Actors, writers, and directors . . . joined party 'fractions' which met in Beverly Hills, Bel Air and Brentwood underground cells to hear the party line." Another observer of this phenomenon has written: "We listen to speeches and sign pledges, and feel that warming glow which comes from being packed in close with a lot of people who agree with you—a mild hypnotism, and exhilarating pleasurable hysteria."

The Communist party, like the National Socialist or Fascist movements, also has an appeal for psychologically maladjusted individuals. Neurotic persons are baffled by the complexities of modern society, and the Marxist-Leninist formula offers a ready-made answer to all questions. To the neglected social rebel, the Communist party, for its own insidious purpose, offers security and friendship. It will befriend the writer, artist, teacher, or actor who is angry at the "system" and offer him remunerative outlets. After accepting Communism under these conditions, the neurotic or social rebel begins to feel himself superior to his parents and the adult world around him. As a member of a secretive organization, he now has all the answers; he has a certain confidence and sense of assurance. The Communist movement offers attractive bait to those who crave companionship and excitement. It offers relief from boredom.

Once an individual enters the Communist movement, he lives in a world which is hermetically sealed off from the outside by an increasingly impenetrable iron curtain of continuous indoctrination to which he gradually becomes accustomed, to the exclusion of all other outside sources of information and thought. He relies upon party literature, schools, and spokesmen for his views and information. More and more of his social activity is carried on within the party. Within this closed circle, the Communist hears the same Communist clichés over and over again. He can be sure of approbation and sympathy, since he is always moving among his ideological kinfolk. He is never isolated. Added to this is the excitement of picket lines, strikes, mass meetings, parades, demonstrations, tiffs with the police, and arrests. There are Communist meetings every day, often several each day. There is never a dull moment.

There is no doubt that the Communist network holds an attraction for adventurous spirits who thrive on the conspiratorial atmosphere within the party, the secret meetings, the resort to aliases, the paraphernalia of illegality and opposition to constituted authority. Those who tend to rebel against tradition and convention—Bohemians and nonconformists of all kinds—are naturally attracted to the Communist movement. By its repudiation of so-called capitalist ethics and moral standards, the party provides a welcome philosophical sanction for the lunatic fringe.

The party is a vehicle for anyone with an axe to grind, for anyone who has become embittered. Second-rate artists, lawyers without clients, doctors without patients, writers without outlets, underpaid teachers with inferiority complexes—all these are soothed by the thought that it is all the fault of the capitalist system. They find, in the party, an instrument to vent their spleen against the imagined source of injury, as well as a receptive audience.

Lest it be assumed that individuals join the Communist party solely because of certain psychological aberrations, for idealistic reasons, or because of the party's intellectual appeal, it should be realized that the organization is in a position to offer attractive material benefits. There are businessmen dependent for contracts upon the good graces of the Soviet Union. Communist lawyers, accountants, and insurance men draw generous incomes from their services to Communist unions, front organizations, other Communists, and pro-Communists. Certain writers, musicians, actors, and artists find it extremely profitable to cater to left-wing intellectual circles. The Communist patronage machine, with its wide ramifications, is extremely solicitous of its faithful followers. Communist-front organizations, schools, and unions offer jobs to their friends and supporters.

Many Communists and pro-Communists have more than occasional doubts about slave labor camps, aggression in Korea, Soviet anti-Semitism, conditions in Hungary, etc., but they lack the spiritual and moral courage to make a break. Having become completely dependent upon his Communist surroundings and associates for his spiritual and physical sustenance, having isolated himself from non-Communist friends and influences, the doubting Communist looks upon the very thought of a break as a personal tragedy. He dreads being cast out of the holy of holies, the temple of Soviet worship. He fears the vilification and slander which will be directed against him as a "renegade" by the Communist smear apparatus. If he is employed through a Communist union, school, or front organization, it may mean the loss of his job. The party threatens with exposure those who have become disaffected. It is much easier for the weak character to swallow his pride and his principles and just go along.

Communism, as Elizabeth Janeway points out,[1] presents an absolute answer designed to lead interested persons to a heaven on earth—a solution most appealing to the materialistic mind. The condition of the world, according to Communism, is the result of economic forces which can be charted by Marxist-Leninist-Stalinist dialectic and channeled through decisions and orders made in

Moscow. Through the act of becoming a Communist, the individual can, in effect, stop thinking and accept the pronouncements of the Soviet leadership in Moscow as the truth. Communism offers a retreat to those who cannot face facts or bear the responsibility of individual action. The Communists try to make the convert feel that he is part of a team which is riding on to inevitable victory. By joining, he simultaneously "takes it out" on his boss, his church, his country, his enemies, his secret fears and uncertainties.

Everybody has something of the idealistic in him. Some former Communists have tried to explain their behavior by the challenge of the question: In prosperous America have I the right to be comfortable in the face of tragedy abroad? Communism, discovering these and other souls distressed by problems of evil and unhappiness, exploits their concern by offering answers for each type of malcontent and sincerely disturbed "liberal." There are well-to-do actors and celebrities with uneasy consciences and naïve political dispositions who can be led into contributing some of their earnings to organizations with a number of abstract nouns in their titles and a number of fellow travelers on their letterheads. There are churchmen deeply distressed over American supremacy in atomic bomb development. They can be persuaded to sign the Stockholm Peace Pledge and contribute to its circulation. After all, who is opposed to peace?

There is no doubt that Communism, like other totalitarian systems, appeals to the individual whose life has been a shambles and who seeks a neat and plausible solution to a situation he feels he can no longer control. Whittaker Chambers was a young man whose personal life had been a nightmare. The household in which he grew up included a mad grandmother who wandered the house at night, a brother who committed suicide, a father who lived in stony isolation from the rest of the family. In trying to impose order upon this chaos, a man of great intellect found in the Communist system a theory which seemed to tie up his bundle of problems with the neat strings of dialectic method. As a student at Columbia, he fell prey to the same Communist influences at work on lonely, "intellectual," and materialistic students all over America. Unless such a student has influences at home or at church to counteract the campus Communist, the odds are that he will fall for Communism either as a militant participant or as a fellow traveler who blames all his difficulties and inadequacies on the "rotten capitalistic system." Chambers, as he acquired religious conviction, broke with the party and helped his country fight the Communist conspiracy.

Klaus Fuchs may have been shaped for Communism along similar lines. His mother killed herself in 1932; his father was imprisoned by the Nazis; his sister threw herself under a train in 1939. Having joined the anti-Nazi camp as a youth, Fuchs was led to believe that Communism was the only consistent, relentless foe of Nazism. He once said: "The idea which gripped me most was the belief that in the past man has been unable to understand his own history and the forces which lead to the further development of human society; that now for the first time [with Marxism], man understands the historical forces and he is able to control them, and that therefore for the first time he will really be free. I carried this idea over into the personal sphere and believed that I could make myself into what I should be."

Stephen Spender also became enmeshed in the Communist apparatus via the Fascist issue. During the period of the "United Front" (1935–1939), when many materialistic and misguided "intellectuals" were drawn into Communism, Spender testified that "by being anti-Fascist I created a rightness for myself beside which personal guilt seemed unimportant."

Persons who have for one reason or another failed in their careers, or who feel insecure in their communities, may tend to blame "the system," and attribute all their hatreds and frustrations to "capitalism." These people seek a way out of personal responsibility and accountability by joining the mass collectivity of Communism. Here they are told that "in the Morgan-Rockefeller-Du

Pont empire the working man has only one right—to serve as human raw material fit only to be exploited." Refusing to stop and consider the fact that officially sanctioned exploitation exists primarily in Communist countries, such persons espouse escapism in the form of Communism because of an occasional inequity in the United States.

THE HATE ASPECT

The hate aspect of Communism's appeal is aptly described by Bishop Fulton J. Sheen in his incisive *Communism and the Conscience of the West:*

"By far the greater appeal of communism is to the disillusioned and the frustrated. Many follow communism not because they are convinced that it is *right,* but because they have a hidden hate against something or somebody. Those who feel individually impotent to vent their hate upon a person or a class or an institution feel that if they joined communism they could find a corporate expression for their pent-up animosities and their dammed-up hate. . . . The appeal of communism to this group is not in its theory, but in its hates. That is why communism always has to have a devil. The first argument every Communist uses is to incite contempt of his devil or his neighbor's devil, whether it be Fascism, which is never defined, or capitalism or democracy or religion or morality. A man who is the husband of one wife and who is refused permission by the Church to marry a second or a fifth time is always a potential member of the Communist Party, because through it he can 'get even' with religion which irritated his conscience. The more he subconsciously feels the wrong he has done, the more violent will be his opposition to religion. That is why the greatest persecutors of religion are those who have been baptized. 'The corruption of the best is the worst.' Hitler, Mussolini, Stalin, and Marx were all baptized and fell away. . . . In the same connection, those who started out with a great lust for wealth and never achieved it, or who became frustrated capitalists, will join the Communist Party to get even with the capitalists whose wealth they envy, and which they now want to possess by expropriation. Those who have more money than they know what to do with, or who have made it too easily, will seek to compensate for their ill-gained wealth by espousing anti-social causes to justify their uneasy consciences. At bottom their love of communism is due to an extreme form of pocket-consciousness. Those who have felt the sting of uncharitable fellow men who made fun of their race or color and refused to give them the hand of fellowship are also likely material for communism, not because communism can give them recognition, which it does not in practice, but only because they get a chance to get even with those who were unkind. Those, too, who have never been able to think clearly, and who have by much reading and little thinking taken more than they can digest, flock to communism where they will have to do no thinking whatever, but where their very obedience to a dictator will give them the illusion of power. Because they became disillusioned with their freedom, which produced chaos in their souls, they look for a communist dictatorship outside themselves to organize their chaos. Because they lost the power of self-regulation from within, they seek a communist-imposed regulation from without; because they lost the goal of existence and the purpose of life, they invite a communist tyranny to impose a goal and dictate a purpose; because they have been isolated from their fellow men, they seek a restoration into a community not on the basis of spirit and love, but of matter and force.

"The supreme advantage of all these hates is that they enable the frustrated and the disillusioned to combine the strongest social affirmations with the most contemptuous disregard for personal betterment. They could not become Christians—which in their hearts they want—because Christianity would demand personal righteousness and justice by hating the wrongs of others without any obligation to better their own individual lives. . . . The charges these frustrated souls bring against society are very often justified, but in their zeal to cure the baby of whooping cough they accept the solution of cutting off its head."

DISCIPLINE AND FEAR

But Communism is a disciplined force. And whereas a majority of its adherents may have begun as alienated individuals seeking a magic cure for the troubles of living, a different form of development soon sets in. Once within the reach of the party, even those who joined for purely emotional reasons are dominated by a directing force which is not crackpot, not neurotic. For as Elizabeth Janeway puts it: "At the center of Communist intent is the simple drive for power: power within the Government, the United Nations, labor unions, liberal organizations, the arts, the sciences, education, and the churches."[2]

The gravest danger hovering over America is not Soviet propaganda, effective as it is. It is the power of the Soviet state, and this suggests to the faithful a major power of attraction in the thought that they are going to be on the winning side. This conviction must surely be supported when they see Communism expanding inexorably from the Soviet heartland, when they see American military forces restrained from achieving military victory in Korea, when they hear the President of the United States declare that he will not go to the aid of the East German workers or Hungarian patriots in their struggle to gain their freedom from Communism. An examination of Soviet military and diplomatic successes, especially since 1941, strengthens a growing conviction that the United States prefers "peace" to victory, whereas the Soviet empire not only wants to win, but actually is winning.

The conviction that Communism must inevitably conquer the world means that the ranks of the neurotic Communists are augmented by the power hungry, who, like Laval, Bose, Mosely, and Quisling, place their money on the winning horse.[3] They may be seduced into the movement through hatred, ignorance, "campus

Communism," belief in "scientific" Marxism, or love for power—but love of power is the element that ultimately dominates. Hitler, Stalin, Khrushchev, and Mao Tse-tung, all these men cared more for power than for ideology. If it became necessary to trim their ideological sails in order to meet an immediate situation, they inevitably did so, in order to retain or increase their power. Naturally they consistently utilized ideological arguments to appear before the faithful as the bona fide exponents of their particular totalitarian persuasion.

Communism also wins adherents through blackmail and "brainwashing." Harry Schwartz, writing in the *New York Times*, described the process as follows: "Blackmail is a potent weapon in some cases. Communist agents who have discovered some ruinous facts in an individual's personal history can threaten him with exposure unless he goes over to their side. Homosexuals are particularly open to such blackmail. . . . The essence of Communist 'brain washing' appears to be a process of disintegrating the victim's powers of resistance and his original mental health. It involves impressing upon him the complete hopelessness of his position, a hopelessness emphasized in some cases by physical punishment and in others by endless interrogation and psychological torture." The object is, first, to reduce him to such a state that all his past beliefs and experiences are virtually effaced and he finds hope or the possibility of survival only in finding favor with his captors, who are his sole link with humanity. Then begins the process of "re-education and the creation of a new personality on the Communist model."

FELLOW TRAVELERS

Some distinction should be made between Communist-party militants and fellow travelers. More often than not the party militant is a fanatic, obsessed with the conviction of ultimate Communist victory and believing that only Soviet "science" can cure the world's ills, by achieving a world U.S.S.R. The militant has swallowed the Communist bait, hook, line, and sinker. His ability to think and reason objectively is obscured by an irrational fanaticism. The fellow traveler, on the other hand, has not "progressed" or "developed" (as the Communists phrase it) to the point of being a militant. He is at least temporarily taken in by the "peace" campaign or anti-Fascism;[4] he thinks he is fighting racial intolerance or strengthening civil liberties. Again, however, there are shades and degrees. A fellow traveler who has joined but two or three "front" organizations may be different from one who has affiliated with thirty or more. Sometimes, of course, it is difficult, if not impossible, to determine whether a fellow traveler (for example, one who has remained affiliated with five or more fronts since the Berlin airlift in 1948) is only that or whether he is a secret party member. Evidence produced by such FBI plants within the Communist party as Philbrick, Calomiris, and Cvetic makes it quite plain that often persons are under party discipline although not, apparently, actually members of the party. Budenz, Bentley, Chambers, and Bella Dodd have shown Congressional committees how even outwardly conservative non-Communists have worked for the party and the Soviet government.

One of the most important feeder lines into Communism or fellow traveling is the education field. A young boy or girl, with no other ideological conditioning by home or church, may easily be seduced into Communist or pro-Communist campus activities. College clubs, professors, and publications can, over a four year period, profoundly influence young people. Such a young man or woman, upon graduating, may easily be convinced that America is rotten and that humanitarian social and economic policies, as well as policies dedicated to world peace, are being advanced by Soviet Russia and the "people's democracies." Such persons are most likely actively to enter the political arena in the important areas of opinion molding—government, education, the mass media, or labor relations. Many college texts in the social sciences stress the seamy side of American life while tending to be uncritical of

Soviet Russia and Communism. Furthermore, anti-anti-Communist professors and influences have succeeded in swaying many Americans into believing that any criticism of their activities is "hysteria," "McCarthyism," or an attack on "academic freedom."[5]

THE DISILLUSIONED

Why do Communists become disillusioned? One reason is a growing understanding of what Soviet reality is. When it gradually dawns on the idealistic "intellectual" that the glowing promises of social equality and "economic democracy" and peace have not been carried out in and by the Soviet Union—when he realizes the ugly truth of the slave labor camps and aggression—there ensues a revulsion which ultimately causes him to leave the party. The brutal Soviet repression of the Hungarian patriotic uprising in 1956 disillusioned many Communist sympathizers, although few actual members broke with the party.

Another factor is the ideological one. Most, if not all, Americans have an idealistic streak in them which leads them to espouse some cause. If an individual does not believe in Christianity, he may tend to be attracted by the economic determinist approach of Marxism. After joining the pseudo religion of Communism, which promises him a heaven here on earth, he is satisfied ideologically for a time. But if and when the break with Communism comes, it is very apt to come because Communism no longer adequately serves his deep spiritual and ideological needs. Such a person frequently leaves Communism to embrace a religious faith—witness the cases of Whittaker Chambers, Louis Budenz, Bella Dodd, Elizabeth Bentley, and Douglas Hyde. There are, of course, convinced Socialists and other materialists who, after toying with or espousing Communism, leave it to try to relive or rediscover an ideological satisfaction in Socialism or some type of humanitarianism divorced from religion.

People behind the Iron and Bamboo curtains know Communism better than most Westerners. Every week, thousands of them flee into Berlin, Vienna, Hong Kong, and other border stations on the fringes of the Soviet empire. In Korea, two-thirds of the Korean and Chinese Communist war prisoners chose not to return to Communism. These people know tyranny at first hand and are in a position to educate the starry-eyed college graduate in America who thinks the Soviet Union brings peace and plenty. This is particularly true in the case of major defecters from the Soviet Union itself, such as Barmine, Kravchenko, Gouzenko, Petrov, Krivitsky, Khokhlov, Rastvorov, and Bogolepov. These men, like many other ex-Communists, defected (as many have no opportunity to do) not only in revulsion against terror and tyranny, but also in protest against the dictation of a party leader who must be followed through all the twists and turn of Soviet policy. Some rebelled after years in which party membership and obedience to the Soviets took precedence over family, home, patriotism—and truth. Human beings, forced to abandon or suppress the basic loyalties of human hearts and minds in order to remain in good standing with the party must inevitably be shaken in their devotion to the party. The beginnings of doubt and uncertainty may ultimately lead them to break with the party. For even monolithic Communism cannot change the essential nature of man: a creature of God with a conscience and a sense of individual responsibility.

CHAPTER 14

Identifying Communists and Communist Fronts

Naïvely unaware of the conspiratorial nature of the Communist party, some Americans demand the production of a party membership card or other documentary evidence before they will believe that an individual is a Communist. Some even accept as truth denials of party membership on the part of those charged. Actually, such records as are kept are secret, and Communists are instructed to conceal their affiliations when it seems expedient.

Section 5 of the Communist Control Act of 1954 (Butler-Humphrey Act) contains fourteen excellent guides to determine membership in the Communist party. The most important of these are:

1. Has the accused been listed as a member in any . . . document of the organization?
2. Has the accused made financial contribution to the organization?
3. Has the accused made himself subject to the discipline of the organization?
4. Has the accused executed the orders, plans, or directives of the organization?
5. Has the accused been accepted to his knowledge as a member of the organization?
6. Has the accused communicated . . . directives or plans of the organization?
7. Has the accused indicated by word, action, conduct, writing . . . the objectives or purposes of the organization?

8. Has the accused participated in the activities, planning, actions . . . of the organization?

There are various gradations of membership in the Communist apparatus: (1) open party members; (2) secret party members; (3) nonparty members; (4) nonparty volunteers. The two latter categories include those not technically in the party but under party discipline, together with those who voluntarily and knowingly support the party, its activities, and its campaigns. In addition to the above, there are the "fellow travelers." This category has two gradations: (1) conscious fellow travelers; and (2) unwitting (one is tempted to say "unconscious") fellow travelers. The first are motivated by a definite sympathy for the Soviet Union or the Communist party; sometimes they consider Chiang Kai-shek, Syngman Rhee, Senator William Knowland, or Congressman Francis E. Walter to be a greater threat than Communism (if they consider Communism a threat at all). The second occasionally support Communist-inspired enterprises in the belief that such enterprises are accomplishing some meritorious social purpose; they are presumably unaware of the Communist inspiration of the organization or activity. Degrees of fellow traveling can be judged by the following non-rigid criteria:

1. The number of associations with Communist-controlled organizations.
2. The importance of post or posts occupied in these organizations.
3. The extent of activity and how recent.
4. Adherence to these organizations despite public exposure of their Communist character.
5. The fellow traveler's standing in the Communist press.
6. Public statements and writings regarding the U.S.S.R., the Communist party, and Communists.
7. Personal associations with Communists or those consistently sympathetic to Communism.

How strong is the Communist movement numerically? An FBI

breakdown of Communist party membership in 1951 showed New York State to be in the lead with 15,458 members, trailed by California with 4,295, Illinois with 1,596, and Pennsylvania with 1,441. The only other two states with more than 1,000 members were Ohio and New Jersey. It is interesting to compare these figures with the 1948 popular vote by states for the Progressive party of Henry Wallace (created and controlled by the Communist party). The Progressive party polled 501,167 votes in New York, 190,381 in California, 55,161 in Pennsylvania, 42,683 in New Jersey, and 37,596 in Ohio. It was not on the ballot in Illinois. The Progressive vote in Massachusetts and Michigan was more than 38,000 for each state (ahead of Ohio), although there are twice as many Communists in Ohio as in either Massachusetts or Michigan. Fellow travelers took up the slack in these states. Over 25,000 votes were cast for Henry Wallace in each of the following states: Minnesota, Washington, and Wisconsin. Almost invariably, Communist-Progressive strength is centered in the large cities and industrial areas.

Communist party membership has declined since 1951, but Communist influence cannot be estimated properly merely by comparing its votes or membership with those of bona fide political parties. Those who declare that the Communist party is no menace because its membership and voting strength constitute but a relatively small percentage of American voters are deluding themselves and others. There are many instances (Russia included) in which Communists took over with a tiny minority.

Each party member or sympathizer must be evaluated in terms of his political, social, and economic weight and influence and the fact that he is being supported by a major foreign power. In a highly sensitive and articulated society like ours, it is not difficult to cause havoc by a strategic dislocation. Communists make a practice of seeking out such points of vantage. Thus a party member or sympathizer may be an official of a labor union, with thousands of members, which can tie up an entire industry. He may be an unpublicized government official who prepares memoranda on policy affecting the entire nation. He may be an atomic scientist with access to highly secret information vital to our security. He may be a writer, a preacher, or a radio or television broadcaster with a vast audience. He may be a script writer whose message reaches millions. He may be an actor whose popularity is exploited by the party to sponsor its front organizations and public appeals. He may be the idol of a racial or foreign language group. In each case the individual's influence radiates to ever widening circles with an effect similar to that of a stone thrown into a pool.

Government agencies are sometimes confronted with cases in which individuals claim that they have resigned from the Communist party. Under no circumstances should such a statement be accepted at its face value. Party members have been known to use this device when they are convinced that their previous Communist affiliations are known and provable. In other cases, as for instance in connection with the signing of non-Communist affidavits, the party will instruct members who are trade-union officials to resign formally while remaining under party discipline. In order to judge the legitimacy and sincerity of an alleged "resignation" from the party, the following questions should be asked:

1. What was the real motive for resignation?

2. Was he (the one who resigned), or the Communist party, or a Communist-controlled organization in a position to benefit thereby?

3. What was the attitude of the Communist press toward the action?

4. Do his views, writings, readings, associations, and general attitude indicate that he is still loyal to the party line or that he has, in fact, repudiated it?

5. Can he corroborate this claimed repudiation of the party with written evidence or the statements of known anti-Communists?

6. Has he willingly co-operated with the FBI and Congressional committees in helping to expose former fellow conspirators?

The FBI and Congressional committees investigating Communist influences must rely heavily on "plants" within the party (such as Herbert Philbrick, Angela Calomiris, and Matt Cvetic) and former Communists in order to combat successfully the Soviet conspiracy in our midst. Only these people can provide the United States government with the necessary "inside" information which can lead to governmental action against treason and sedition, actual or potential. It is small wonder that the Communist and pro-Communist press directs campaigns of invective against former Communists with the intention of casting doubt on their credibility.

In judicial and deportation proceedings thus far, including the cases of Alger Hiss, Harry Bridges, Harold Christoffel, the national and state Communist leaders, and many others, the testimony of ex-Communists has demonstrated a high level of credibility under the most rigorous cross-examination and investigation. It is not easy for ex-Communists to help their government in this task. They are not only subjected to a smear campaign by the Communist and pro-Communist press and labeled "stool pigeons" and "informers," but they are also often the victims of physical violence as well. The Communist Gestapo murdered Walter Krivitsky as he was about to defect; the same thing happened to George W. Alberts, Juliet Stuart Poyntz, and Laura Law. In 1948, a young U.C.L.A. student named Everitt Hudson was murdered by Communist fellow students as he was about to quit the party.

Communists speaking openly in the name of the Communist party and frankly as disciplined agents of the Soviet Union would make very little progress in subverting the United States or in winning converts. Their strength lies in a calculated policy of deception. One of the most important instruments of Communist deception is the front organization. Without the aid of its front organization, the Communist party would be an isolated, insignificant sect. With the aid of its network of fronts, the Communist party can and does exercise influence out of all proportion to its actual membership.

A Communist-front organization may be broadly described as an organization formed at the initiative of the Communist party or the

Cominform (formerly Communist International) and operating under Communist control to achieve some short-term Communist objective. Normally, the actual aim of the front is not openly stated, but is concealed behind a high-sounding and attractive reform objective. Occasionally a Communist front is the result of the capture by the Communist party of an originally non-Communist organization.

As part of Soviet psychological warfare against the United States, Communist fronts seek to paralyze America's will to resist Communist aggression by idealizing Russia's aims and methods, discrediting the United States, and spreading defeatism and demoralization. Among these fronts have been the American Peace Crusade, the Committee for Peaceful Alternatives to the Atlantic Pact, the Congress of American Women, American Youth for Democracy, and the Committee for a Democratic Far Eastern Policy. Some fronts specialize in pro-Soviet propaganda; these include the National Council of American-Soviet Friendship, the American-Russian Institute, the magazine *New World Review* (formerly *Soviet Russia Today.*) Fronts designed to appeal to special groups in American society have been the Labor Youth League (formerly American Youth for Democracy), the Congress of American Women, the National Negro Labor Council, the International Worker's Order, the American Committee for Protection of the Foreign Born, and various language publications of the Communist apparatus. The Communists operate occupational fronts such as the National Lawyer's Guild, the National Council of the Arts, Sciences, and Professions, the Photo League, and Farm Research.

To defend Communists in trouble with the law, fronts have been devised making special appeals in behalf of civil liberties. Among these are the Civil Rights Congress, the Emergency Civil Liberties Committee, the National Committee to Repeal the McCarran Act, the Committee to Secure Justice in the Rosenberg Case, the Joint Anti-Fascist Refugee Committee. When the Communist party itself is under fire, these fronts offer a bulwark of protection.[1]

On the political level, Communist operatives work through such parties as the American Labor party and the Progressive party; here they run their candidates under labels other than that of Communism. In the field of religion, Communists have achieved some influence through such groups as the Methodist Federation for Social Action, the American Jewish Labor Council, and a magazine called *The Protestant*, as well as through various pacifist and "peace" groups. In the realm of news dissemination, Communists control the Allied Labor News Service, the Federated Press, and the Labor Research Association.

Many Americans do not realize that there are in the United States several Communist training schools offering courses in various phases of subversion. The two most important are the Jefferson School of Social Science in New York, and the California Labor School in San Francisco.[2] Instructors, for the most part, are Communists, and the Communist press urges its readers to enroll. Most Communist leaders in this country are graduates from these schools, and some teach there now themselves.

Communist fronts frequently change their names or disband after they have outlived their usefulness. In the early 1930's the line was openly anti–United States, and it was propagated by the American League Against War and Fascism. Then during the period of the united front, the American League for Peace and Democracy advocated collective security against Fascism. During the era of the Hitler-Stalin pact, the American Peace Mobilization opposed aid to Britain and France against Germany and stressed peace as any price; when Germany attacked Russia, the Communists suddenly became stridently anti-Nazi and urged opening up of the second front. The National Committee to Win the Peace pressured America to make maximum concessions to the Soviets at international conferences for the sake of postwar coexistence. The "peace with Russia at any price" theme was then carried on by the American Peace Crusade and the Committee for Peaceful Alternatives.

Many Communist fronts are but national adjuncts of international Communist fronts. Among these are: World Federation of Democratic Youth, International Union of Students, World Federation of Democratic Women, World Peace Congress, World Federation of Scientific Workers, International Organization of Democratic Journalists, and International Association of Democratic Lawyers. All of the above work in close harmony with the Communist-dominated World Federation of Trade Unions.

Since Communist fronts have a way of changing names from time to time and from place to place, no specific list can serve as a permanent safeguard to insure their detection. The following criteria will be useful in spotting a Communist front.

1. Since Communist fronts must start with a working nucleus of party members or reliable sympathizers and since the party depends for its continual control of these organizations upon this nucleus, the presence of certain names frequently found as sponsors and officials is often a good clue. The Senate Internal Security Subcommittee report *The Communist Party of the United States of America* (December 21, 1955) lists the most active and typical sponsors of Communist fronts in the past as follows: Josephine Truslow Adams, Edward K. Barsky, Mrs. Charlotta Bass, Elmer Benson, Hugh Bryson, Edward Berry Burgum, Morris Carnovsky, John W. Darr, Jerome Davis, W. E. B. DuBois, Robert W. Dunn, Thomas I. Emerson, Philip Evergood, Henry Pratt Fairchild, Howard Fast, Hugo Gellert, Ben Gold, William Gropper, Dashiell Hammett, Marion Hathway, R. J. Havighurst, Lillian Hellman, Charles J. Hendley, Alphcus W. Hunton, Grace Hutchins, James Imbrie, V. J. Jerome, Robert W. Kenny, Rockwell Kent, John A. Kingsbury, Freda Kirchwey, Alfred Kreymborg, Corliss Lamont, Millard Lampell, John Howard Lawson, Robert Morss Lovett, Robert S. Lynd, Albert Maltz, Thomas Mann, Kirtley F. Mather, Clifford T. McAvoy, John T. McManus, Jack R. McMichael, Carey McWilliams, Clyde R. Miller, Philip Morrison, Hugh N. Mulzac, Dorothy Parker, William L. Patterson, Linus Pauling, Anna M. W. Pennypacker, Arthur Upham Pope, Walter Rautenstrauch, Anton

Refregier, Bertha G. Reynolds, Paul Robeson, Rose Russell, Frederick L. Schuman, Harlow Shapely, Guy Emery Shipler, Herman Shumlin, William B. Spofford, Johanes Steel, Vilhajalamur Stefansson, Bernhard J. Stern, Donald Ogden Stewart, Maxwell S. Stewart, I. F. Stone, Fred W. Stover, Leon Straus, Dirk J. Struik, Maurice Sugar, John R. Thompson, Alexander Trachtenberg, Maurice Travis, Willard Uphaus, Mary Van Kleeck, Harry F. Ward, Colston E. Warne, Gene Weltfish, Doxey A. Wilkerson.

2. Does the organization receive publicity and promotion in Communist publications?

3. Does the organization hold meeting in halls used by Communist organizations, or does it have its offices in premises ordinarily used by Communist organizations?

4. Is literature of the Communist party or other front organizations to be found at headquarters and at meetings?

5. Are speakers and entertainers employed who are frequently associated with other Communist fronts or with the Communist party or its press?

6. Are facilities used in common with the Communist party or its front organizations (printers—see printers' union label—mimeograph services, addressing, stationers, picnic grounds, accountants, real-estate agents, doctors, lawyers, artists, promotion agents, public-relations counselors, radio commentators, etc.)?

7. Great care should be taken in determining the character of those who actually run the organization, ignoring such figureheads as the honorary chairman. What is the loyalty record of the executive secretary, president, and functioning members of the executive committee, members of the staff, the organization secretary, educational director, editor, etc.?

8. Does the organization, and especially its official organ, follow the Communist party line on issues and campaigns publicized in the *Daily Worker*? Does it invariably support and defend the Soviet Union? Does it adhere to its avowed purpose or inject issues of the above character?

9. Does the organization co-operate with other fronts and with the Communist party in election campaigns, May Day parades, peace campaigns, petitions, tag days, and other projects promoted in the *Daily Worker*?

10. Does the organization co-operate with Communist-controlled unions?

11. Does the organization furnish direct or indirect revenue to the Communist party, its publications, its fronts or establishments, through orders for printing, stationery, advertisements, donations, and services of various kinds?

12. Is the organization repudiated as Communist-controlled by such outstanding organizations as the American Federation of Labor, the American Legion, or its own former constituents? What is its history? How long has it existed?

13. Does it furnish financial statements issued by unknown and unreliable public accountants?

14. Is the organization actually controlled by its membership or by an outside Communist clique or group?

15. Does it interchange mailing lists with the Communist party, its front organizations, or its publications?

The September 30, 1956 issue of the Communist *Daily Worker* announced that most front organizations were to be abolished because they were too openly connected with Communism. Communist leaders urged the cadres of these defunct front groups to penetrate such non-Communist groupings as the League of Women Voters, Parent-Teacher Associations, and religious and fraternal organizations in order to penetrate more deeply into American life. This stratagem was part of the new campaign to return to the Trojan horse tactics of the 1930's, when Communists posing as "liberals" and "progressives" reached the highest echelons of American government.

The American Forum for Socialist Education was created in April, 1957, with Communists Albert Blumberg and Doxey Wilkerson as two of the leading officers. Other leaders include the Reverend A. J. Muste (pacifist minister), Professors Mulford Q. Sibley (University of Minnesota), Kermit Eby (Chicago), Paul Baron (Stanford), Derk Bodde (Pennsylvania), William A. Williams (Oregon), H. H. Wilson (Princeton), Stringfellow Barr (formerly president of St. Johns College), Farrell Dobbs (Trotskyite), and Dorothy Day (editor, *Catholic Worker*). This coalition of Marxists, pacifists, neutralists, and anti-anti-Communists, totally unconcerned about the recent bloodbath in Hungary, began to espouse many causes dear to Communism. Harry Schwartz of the *New York Times* called it "the broadest spectrum of [leftist] political thought since the Progressive Party of 1948."[3] Denounced by Herman Singer, National Secretary of the Socialist Party, the Communist influence within this united front was soon exposed.[4]

The Communist movement has recently stressed the following propaganda in its publications and organizational activities:

1. Since Geneva, Russia wants peace, but the United States persists in continuing the cold war.

2. American nuclear tests are contaminating large areas of the world and should be stopped.

3. Red China should be recognized and brought into the UN.

4. The offshore islands of Quemoy and Matsu should be given to Communist China.

5. Germany should be neutralized and NATO disbanded.

6. Africa and Asia should side with Russia in the fight against "colonialism."

7. The FBI should be forced to reveal its informants within the Communist apparatus.

8. Anti-Communist legislation should be scrapped, in keeping with the "spirit of Geneva."

9. Congressional committees investigating Communism should be investigated.

10. The Loyalty and Security programs should be scrapped because "innocent reputations" are hurt and "civil liberties" endangered.

As part of the international Communist apparatus, the Communist party, U.S.A., is furthering the interests of the U.S.S.R. in trying to bring about the establishment of a Soviet Republic in the United States. It works ceaselessly to penetrate all key areas of American life in order to bring victory in World War III to the Communist world.

If Communist expansion continues at the same rate in the future as during the years from 1943 to 1955, the Soviets will have conquered the world by 1980. Whether or not they succeed depends on what the United States does and, particularly, what American citizens do. The Defense Department's Advisory Committee on Prisoners of War (in Korea) concluded: "The responsibility for the maintenance and preservation of the United States and all it stands for is one which must be shared by every citizen. Every American is in the front line in the war for the minds of men. The battlefield of modern warfare is all inclusive. Today there are no distant front lines, remote no man's lands, far-off areas. The home front is but an extension of the fighting front."

CHAPTER 15

How to Spot a Communist

INTRODUCTION

Events of recent years have made it obvious that there is no foolproof way of detecting a Communist. The Communist individual is no longer a "type" exemplified by the bearded and coarse revolutionary with time bomb in briefcase. U.S. Communists come from all walks in life, profess all faiths, and exercise all trades and professions. In addition, the Communist Party, USA, has made concerted efforts to go underground for the purpose of infiltration.

If there is no foolproof system in spotting a Communist, there are, fortunately, indications that may give him away. These indications are often subtle but always present, for the Communist, by reason of his "faith" must act and talk along certain lines.

The following chapters contain some of these indications which may help in recognizing as such the individual who belongs to the Communist Party as well as the sympathizer and fellow-traveler of all shades.

THE "COMMUNIST LANGUAGE"

In LENIN'S writings, there are repeated references to the "Aesopian Language" which he assertedly used to evade arrest and punishment as a revolutionary under the tsarist regime. The term

The material in this chapter was first issued by First Army Headquarters in a pamphlet entitled "How to Spot a Communist." It was reprinted by *U.S.A.* in a special supplement on June 22, 1955. Copyright 1955 by *U.S.A.*, An American Magazine of Fact and Opinion. Reprinted by permission of *U.S.A.*

is derived from AESOP, famed fabulist of ancient Greece, who attempted to hide the contemporary significance of his fables by satirizing animals rather than human beings. In LENIN's case, the term described the method of "writing in hints" in order to fool the censors. Ever since 1917, Communists in all countries have taken up and practiced the art of "Aesopian Language" and, wherever possible, have refined it.

Through this process of refinement, Communists in the United States have developed what might be called a "Communist Language." It is not defined in dictionaries or taught in schools but can be of considerable help in identifying a Communist. The two distinguishing marks of this language are sentence structure and vocabulary.

The Communist's eternal preoccupation with Marxist theory appears to prod him to constant imitation of Marxist style at its most involved. The imitation is not limited to purely political discussions or writings and finds its way into the Communist's private life. Here are some sample sentences taken at random from Communist publications:

"The American go-getters counted on getting these resources into their clutches and exploiting them in the grand colonial manner, by taking advantage of the weakness of the tsarist government and the venality of the tsarist officials."

"If we stand at the brink of destruction, we also stand at the brink of something else, at the brink of a new dawn, in which the human race, in all of its complex and fascinating difference, will come to the conclusion that it must live in a peaceful brotherhood that will include this multitude of difference."

"It is rejection of finality, rejection of the idea of *knowing* the truth, rather than seeking it; it is the elasticity and experimentalism that come with this which, . . . , is at the heart of the finest American tradition, is the essence of true radicalism."

While a certain heaviness of style and preference for long sentences is common to most Communist writings, a distinct vocabulary provides the second and more easily recognized feature of the "Communist Language."

Even a superficial reading of an article written by a Communist or a conversation with one will probably reveal the use of some of the following expressions: integrative thinking, vanguard, comrade, hootenanny, chauvinism, book-burning, syncretistic faith, bourgeois-nationalism, jingoism, colonialism, hooliganism, ruling class, progressive, demagogy, dialectical, witch-hunt, reactionary, exploitation, oppressive, materialist.

This list, selected at random, could be extended almost indefinitely. While all of the above expressions are part of the English language, their use by Communists is infinitely more frequent than by the general public.

In speaking of a "Communist Language" it must be clearly understood that the use of certain terms and structures can never constitute proof of a charge as serious as subversion. Nevertheless, since the distinguishing marks of that language are in fact parts of the American Communist's life, they might well be considered as a danger signal.

THE "COMMUNIST RELIGION"

The proverbial devotion to the "cause" found in most hard-core Communists and many sympathizers is more than merely an intellectual response to an idea. The case of the ROSENBERG atom spies and the appearance of numerous Communists before Federal and State Committees show that most of these men will sacrifice their careers and families and some their lives if required by Party discipline.

While it is generally believed that Communists are atheists as a result of their political indoctrination, it appears likely that many find in Marxist philosophy a substitute for religion in which they had previously lost faith. William R. Kintner writes in his book *The Front is Everywhere!*

"Communism has become a faith to warlike men set adrift from certainty in an unbelieving world. The faith appeal of Communism has important implications. It should lead us to reject the notion that all Communists are crackpots, although many of them may be."

Once the Communist has accepted his new faith, he rejects all others as a rule, and his attitude toward organized religion becomes one of hostility. Nevertheless, when speaking or writing for the public, he will usually pretend to be indifferent rather than hostile. William Z. Foster, National Chairman of the CP, USA, recently wrote in a Communist publication:

"I find that the dialectical materialist viewpoint fully satisfies me in meeting the everyday problems of life, as well as in confronting the perspective of eventual natural dissolution by death. In my outlook on life, there is no place for religion."

The tell-tale signs of this "Communist Religion" are not easy to detect. There is, above all, a rigidity in views insofar as they pertain to the Communist doctrine. This is not to say that the Communist lacks persuasiveness or variety of expression. It does mean, however, that he will stubbornly cling to the "line" even when proven wrong in debate. The Communist has implicit faith in Marxist philosophy and in the truth of the "line" as transmitted from Moscow. Because of this faith, he cannot and will not give ground when challenged on basic Marxist issues or political pronouncements made by his leaders. The possibility of compromising on these issues is utterly beyond his comprehension.

Frequently, the Communist's slavish adherence to Moscow edicts becomes absurd. A classic illustration is the "Daily Worker" edition of 23 August 1939. On this day, when the USSR concluded an non-aggression pact with Nazi-Germany, the Communist newspaper's columns were filled with denunciations of "Hitlerism barbarism." On the very next day, after receiving the news of the pact, the "Daily Worker" spoke glowingly of Hitler's "peaceful intentions" and sharply condemned those "imperialistic jackals," Great Britain and France. There is no indication in this and many other cases that the frequent changes in the "line" evoke any doubt or even wonder in the minds of U.S. Communists.

His "religion," then, can give away the Communist. His naive and unquestioning acceptance of the "line," his refusal to accept criticism are excellent indications. Last but not least, the Communist feels a strong compulsion to speak his "faith" and can frequently be spotted by his never-ceasing attempts at conversion of others.

THE "COMMUNIST'S LOGIC"

The Communist's logic is a natural product of his "religion" which has been discussed in the preceding chapter. His peculiar logic is based on a rigid mind which serves merely as a storehouse for pre-conceived and pre-digested ideas.

This logic is diametrically opposed to our own. Thus, the Communist refers to the iron curtain police states as "democracies," and any defensive move on the part of the Western powers is condemned as "aggression." The Communist thus builds for himself a topsy-turvy world with a completely distorted set of values. For this reason, it is practically impossible to win an argument with a hard-core Communist. For one thing, he is trained to accept unquestioningly the ready-made views disseminated through the national party organization. In addition, the Communist mind cannot and will not engage in a detached examination of ideas. Talking to a Communist about his own ideas, then, is like listening to a phonograph record. His answers will invariably follow a definite pattern because he can never admit, even hypothetically, that the basis for his ideas may not be sound. This attitude is typical not only for the individual but also on a national scale. Western protests against incidents provoked by Communist nations invariably meet with the same stereotype answer asserting that the complainants are completely wrong while they, the Communists, are just as completely right. This answer is final and no arguments are permitted so far as the Communists are concerned.

The Communist, then, is not really "logical." The finality of his arguments and the completeness of his condemnation marks him clearly, whether as a speaker, a writer or a conversation partner.

THE COMMUNIST'S APPROACH TO OTHERS

The fact that the Communist has a very rigid set of values has a profound influence on his approach to others, whether as an individual or as a member of a group. For this reason, it is possible to some extent to predict and generalize Communist techniques.

In general, two aspects of Communist tactics are plainly distinguishable. Excessive condemnation is one. The Communist, when criticizing, goes all out in condemning a situation, an idea, or an individual. He will not admit to a single good aspect of anything which has been selected as a target by virtue of the "line." This procedure is in sharp contrast to non-Communist critics who frequently realize that admission of "good" points only increases the weight of their arguments against others. The hard-core Communist, then, denounces ALL of the U.S. foreign policy, ALL of a piece of legislation or ALL members of an organization which he dislikes.

Another general Communist principle is the customary procedure of seizing on any, even the most insignificant, occurrence or issue to create uncertainty and unrest. Thus, the arrest of a Negro (for perfectly legitimate reasons) has given rise to an organization against "police brutality," and a case of a suspended college professor (for lawful reasons) has provoked well organized propaganda campaigns, charging "suppression of academic freedom."

In addition to these very general principles common to Communist tactics, a number of specific issues have been part of the Communist arsenal for a long period of time. These issues are raised not only by Communist appeals to the public but also by the individual Party member or sympathizer who is a product of his Communist environment. They include: "McCarthyism," violation of civil rights, racial or religious discrimination, immigration laws, anti-subversive legislation, any legislation concerning labor unions, the military budget, "peace."

While showing standard opposition to certain standard issues, the U.S. Communist has traditionally identified himself with certain activities in the hope of furthering his ultimate purposes. Such hobbies as "folk dancing" and "folk music" have been traditionally allied with the Communist movement in the United States. Groups of Communists and sympathizers have been formed for the express purpose of following these hobbies. The reason for their choice is not altogether an attempt to hide political activities. The Communist's fondness for everything that comes from "the people" is not an entirely theoretical preference and has found expression in his everyday life. Most Communists are likely to show preference for group activities rather than such bourgeois forms of recreation as ballroom dancing.

In discussing the Communist's tactics, a mention of outright Communist propaganda is indicated. The Communist knows well that a direct approach would most likely meet with hostility among a population alert to the Communist danger. Consequently, the direct approach has largely been abandoned in favor of bringing up issues which have no direct bearing on Communist philosophy. The Communist correctly assumes that this procedure makes it extremely difficult to differentiate between Communist and non-Communist inspired arguments.

THE COMMUNIST'S AFFILIATIONS

Communism as a social philosophy becomes meaningful only when practiced in groups. The individual Communist, "security-conscious" as he may be, will at one time or another engage in group activities. The nature of the groups with which he affiliates can then serve as a good indication of his own convictions.

The Communist Party itself has largely gone underground. Meetings therefore have definite characteristics. Only a very few members, sometimes not more than three or four, assemble at one time. Meeting places are street corners, automobiles, private homes and even public places such as restaurants, department stores and railroad terminals. In all cases, secrecy to avoid detection by law enforcement agencies is the primary concern of all who attend the meetings.

Both CP members and sympathizers who are not Party members frequently belong to one or more organizations referred to as "Communist Fronts." Some of these have been declared subversive by the U.S. Attorney General under Executive Order 10450 or cited by Congressional Committees. Many others carry on their work of disseminating the CP line without that stigma. Generally speaking, it is well to be wary of those organizations which stand for wholesale condemnation of the U.S. Government, a legitimate political party, or groups of individuals. Communist fronts have consistently shown preference for such issues as "Civil Rights," anti-subversive legislation and restrictions on immigration. In addition, these groups frequently seize on any controversial subject from fluoridation of drinking water to "police brutality" in order to promote their nefarious schemes.

Membership in one or more of such organizations is another danger signal. It is to be noted that many of these groups spring up spontaneously and go out of business after a comparatively short time only to make room for others.

CONCLUSION

A study such as this can lead to only one certain conclusion: There is no sure-fire way of spotting a Communist. Certain criteria, some of which were discussed above, provide clues in determining an individual's political leanings. They never provide proof.

It is obvious, then, that the job of "spotting a Communist" is a highly responsible one. The principal difficulty involved is the distinction between the person who merely dissents in the good old American tradition and the one who condemns for the purpose of abolishing that tradition.

In attempting to find the answer to the question: "Is this man a Communist?" a checklist such as this can prove helpful, although in itself it cannot provide the answer:

Does the individual use unusual language? ("Communist Language")

Does he stubbornly cling to Marxist ideals without being willing to question them?

Does he condemn our American institutions and praise those of Communist countries?

Does he pick on any, even the most insignificant occurrences in this country for his criticism?

Is he secretive about certain of his contacts?

Does he belong to groups exploiting controversial subjects?

Above all, the approach to the problem of discovering Communists must be detached and completely free from prejudice. Using some of the clues mentioned in this study in connection with a factual approach provides the best system at present of spotting a Communist.

CHAPTER 16

How You Can Fight Communism

Armed with the salient facts of Communist aggression and subversion, anyone can step into the arena of public debate and discussion and influence the course of developments in his community, state, and even throughout the nation.[1] All that is required is intelligent and accurate use of the known facts and a little courage and boldness. As an individual, you have no right to complain about Soviet aggression and fifth-column activity unless you are willing to do something, *personally*, about it. The small Communist minority in the United States works hard every day and influences millions of Americans, largely through its "front" organizations and collaborators strategically placed in the press, radio, television, theatre, motion pictures, education, industry, and government. For example, a pro-Communist reporter in Korea during early 1953 sent back several slanted dispatches designed to turn public opinion against the anti-Communist Korean Republic of Dr. Rhee in favor of meeting the Communist demands at Panmunjom. An indefatigable pro-Communist student worked for weeks to gather petitions in behalf of the Rosenberg atom spies. A pro-Communist professor wrote several dozen letters every day for a month to his colleagues urging nonco-operation with Congressional committees investigating Communism in education. A "housewife" organized a chain letter campaign to a TV program director attacking an anti-Communist newscaster and succeeded in having his program canceled. These active Communist and pro-Communist influences represent at best but 2 per cent of the population, but their actual influence makes up almost 40 per cent of the headlines and opinion-molding. If an active group of Americans no larger than 2 per cent of the population did the same thing in behalf of America, the Communist influences would at least be neutralized. If this pro-American and anti-Communist element grew to 5 per cent, the battle at home would be all but won.

The difficulty is that some anti-Communists have good intentions but lack adequate knowledge and know-how. It cannot be sufficiently stressed that before you can act against the enemy, you have to know the enemy and how he operates. A doctor cannot operate on his patient without adequate training and an intensive study of the patient's case history. He also consults with other doctors who have handled similar cases. A university professor does not go into the classroom to deliver a lecture without many years of training and a thorough knowledge of his subject. A businessman does not make a decision involving thousands or millions of dollars without many weeks of study, conferences, and investigation.

The Soviet Union and its Communist and pro-Communist agents abroad have been working at their task for forty years. They have developed elaborate techniques and stratagems which cannot successfully be countered overnight. The business of fighting Communism is not as simple as some would have it. It is a deadly, earnest game in which defeat is permanent. It should not, however, discourage those millions of Americans who want to fight Communism. Some can do more than others, but everyone can help if he is willing to learn the basic facts, and to act upon these facts coolly and effectively.

There is no substitute for the personal approach in fighting Communism. The anti-Communist forces in America are no better than the individuals who make up these forces. It does little good for an organization to pass a resolution condemning Communism unless the individual members sustain that resolution actively in their daily work. Communist groups and their "fronts" work unceasingly in behalf of a Soviet victory in America. Unless and until pro-American groups work with the same zeal and effort, a Communist victory is assured.

The personal, individual approach calls for utilizing more of one's free time to win people to intelligent anti-Communist action and spending less time on frivolous and wasted efforts which the Communists disdain. You seldom find a Communist wasting time; he is busy influencing people at his place of work, writing letters to his newspaper and to radio and TV stations, and influencing lawmakers in Washington and his state capital. The Communists make their 2 per cent of the population count. Whereas there were no American demonstrations against the murders of Nikola Petkov, Willi Goettling,[2] or the ten thousand American war prisoners in Korea, American Communists mobilized thousands of non-Communists into strident protests against the execution of atom spies Julius and Ethel Rosenberg—who served a cause which killed or maimed 150,000 Americans in Korea.

What can the individual do? Here are some examples. He can strengthen or develop anti-Communist thinking by discussing with others the Communist atrocities in Hungary, Korea, and Viet-Nam, Soviet slave labor camps, and the effects of treason as perpetrated by Hiss, Fuchs, the Rosenbergs, and others. Kravchenko's book on Soviet tyranny, Elinor Lipper's book on slave labor, Chambers' story of treason, and the UN report on Hungary can serve as points of departure. Incidents such as the torturing of Robert Vogeler and the shooting down of American and Allied planes by Communist planes are constantly recurring, and the good anti-Communist does not let them pass by without translating indignation into personal or group action. Senator Knowland's demand that the United States break off diplomatic relations with the U.S.S.R. after Soviet fighter planes shot down an American patrol plane over the Sea of Japan on September 6, 1954, is an example. During the Korean War, as more and more shiploads of American dead passed through the Golden Gate from Korea and more and more families were affected, sentiment favorable to the MacArthur and Van Fleet plans of action grew. If it was right to punish Nazi war criminals, why not punish Communist war criminals? When the Soviet tanks crushed the freedom fighters in Hungary during November, 1956, thousands of Americans sent letters or telegrams to the President and the UN, and anti-Communist rallies were organized. The courage of the Hungarian patriots served as an excellent example of anti-Communist action to freedom-loving people all over the world. In 1958, anti-Communist rebels rose up against the pro-Communist Sukarno regime in Indonesia, and many Asians and Americans urged support for them.

The individual approach can be especially effective in giving publicity to anti-Communist books. Maximum support and circulation should be given books listed in the Appendix. Such anti-Communist publications as *U. S. News and World Report, U. S. A., Human Events, National Review, American Mercury, American Opinion, National Republic,* and *Counterattack* can be supported and subscriptions to them given as birthday or Christmas presents. Similarly, gifts and recommendations of anti-Communist books should be made on every possible occasion (Regnery, Devin-Adair, Caxton, and The Bookmailer are publishers specializing in anti-Communist books). Get into the habit of lending copies of anti-Communist books or magazines to others and recommend that they write their Congressman to obtain copies of current Congressional reports on Communism. Among the most important of these are: *Soviet Total War* (House Un-American Activities Committee) and *The Communist Party, U.S.A.* (Senate Internal Security Subcommittee).

Anti-Communist organizations and publications are in a position to recommend good speakers; a list of such speakers can be culled from the authors cited in the Appendix of this book. Pro-Communist groups and front organizations excel in making known the availability of their speakers; the pro-American and anti-Communist groups seldom seem to bother, although in recent years some of them have done good work on very limited budgets. An excellent example has been provided by the conservative student and adult group organized by Mrs. Manion J. Pritchard in Minneapolis.

The possibilities inherent in the individual approach are limitless. An intelligent and realistic discussion of the Communist problem can light a spark of interest in anyone. Action, however, must be induced from this interest: telegrams to the President advocating defense of Quemoy and Matsu; group letters to the *New York Times* or the local newspaper urging appropriate sanctions against Communist violations of the Panmunjom and Geneva agreements; letters to the UN demanding aid to the Hungarian patriots; telephone campaigns to get the widest possible action; mass meetings to protest "Summit" meetings leading to appeasement or to urge that existing anti-Communist legislation be enforced and the work of Congressional investigating committees continued. Most importantly, prominent citizens should be induced to lend their names to your organization or activity. Solicit the support of representative leaders of the community.

If a local or national radio or television commentator, organization, or sponsor consistently follows the Communist line (appeasement of the Communists in China, a neutralized Germany, attacks on Congressional committees, demands to terminate nuclear testing, or the release of traitor Morton Sobell from jail), citizens' groups should look into the situation and get as much information as they can. This can be accomplished by obtaining the advice of specialists or consulting the appropriate Congressional report or publication of the Attorney General. The House Un-American Activities Committee *Cumulative Index*, 1938–1955, is an excellent source; so is the 1918–1956 *Index* of the Senate Committee on Government Operations (July 23, 1956). Queries to the Americanism Commission of the American Legion (Indianapolis, Indiana) or to one of the organizations, publications or writers listed in the Appendix are also recommended. If a pattern of pro-Communist activity can be established (including frequent support of the commentator or organization in the Communist press), a petition or phone-call campaign can be directed to the program director, or sometimes the sponsor if he is amenable, suggesting that a replacement be found, one capable of giving at least equal publicity to the anti-Communist point of view.

Publications of the various Congressional committees, such as the Senate Internal Security Subcommittee, the Senate Permanent Subcommittee on Investigations, and the House Un-American Activities Committee, can usually be obtained gratis from your congressman or the committee involved. The Attorney General's list of subversive organizations and publications can be bought from the U.S. Government Printing Office, Washington 25, D.C. The *Cumulative Index* (cited above) and the the Senate Internal Security Subcommittee report *The Communist Party, U.S.A.* (released December 21, 1955) also contain valuable information.

It should be your duty to see that your public and private libraries have anti-Communist books and magazines. A worthwhile project is to look in the card index file of the library under "Communism" or "U.S.S.R." or "Russia" and see whether there are more Communist and pro-Communist authors than anti-Communist authors. The Bibliography in this book can be used as a guide. Books published by Cameron and Kahn are Communist line. If pro-Communist books appear to predominate, protest to the librarian and recommend the purchase of anti-Communist books. Leading anti-Communist publishers include Regnery, Devin-Adair, the Bookmailer, and The Caxton Press. If the library subscribes to *New Masses, National Guardian,* or the *I.F. Stone Weekly,* ask the librarian if it is library policy to subscribe to publications which consistantly follow the Communist line. If the library contains anti-anti-Communist periodicals such as *Nation, New Republic, Reporter,* or *Progressive,* be sure that the anti-Communist periodicals are also available (including *U.S. News and World Report, National Review, Human Events, New Leader,* and *Counterattack*). When the local newspaper or a well-known national newspaper favorably reviews pro-Communist books and fails to review anti-Communist books or reviews them unfavorably, a letter to the newspaper could suggest that the anti-Communist writers be given equal space and consideration. Bookstores that consistently stock pro-Communist authors and seldom anti-Communist authors can be approached and, if necessary, boycotted. The amount of good that can be done by advocating the cause of anti-Communist and pro-American books, magazines, and commentators is incalculable.

Seldom does a day go by that a Communist or pro-Communist does not write a letter to the editor in support of some aspect of current Communist propaganda. It is an excellent habit to express your anti-Communist views frequently to your newspaper, your congressman, and others in positions of influence. When you learn that a professor sympathetic to Communist China is going to lecture at a public school auditorium, find out what you can about him and let the school board know what you think about the use of tax-supported property to further Communist ends. If you learn that a pro-Communist is being considered for a key government post, you can organize a telegram or letter campaign to Washington in protest and solicit Congressional support. If you learn that the state or federal Un-American Activities Committee may have to give up its work because of lack of funds or because of the pressure of groups allegedly interested in protecting "civil liberties," you can likewise direct an avalanche of protests to the state capital and the local press. Make your protests courteous and seek the signatures and support of prominent citizens.

If your congressman is confronted with a bill which will weaken Communism or expose its activities, make certain that he knows what your views are, as well as the views of all those who agree with you. When UN members start to pressure the United States into recognition of Communist China, you can write to the President or to your congressman suggesting that if the Communist aggressor is invited into the UN, the United States should withdraw from that organization;[3] also support the work of the Committee of One Million Against the Admission of Communist China to the UN. When the local UNESCO leader tries to foist on the school board the 1953 UNESCO bibliography, it should be pointed out that whereas no anti-Communist authors appear on the list, such well-known Soviet collaborators as L. K. Rosinger, Louis Dolivet, and Howard Fast appear several times. Dolivet is a known Soviet agent, formerly editor of *UN World.* Fast and Rosinger refused to tell Congressional committees whether or not they were Communists. Both were unwilling to condemn the Soviet Union as being responsible for aggression. On the positive side, a group of civic-minded citizens could then proceed to draw up a reading list based on the bibliography in the Appendix.

In general, it is better to work against Communists, persistent pro-Communists, and front organizations than against individuals and organizations which you do not care for but which are not actually Communist or consistently pro-Communist. Do not confuse the fight against Communism with other controversial matters. You only hurt your cause by making yourself vulnerable through incorrect statements or by diffusing your strength against organizations and individuals that may be objectionable on other grounds. Protest against their bad influence if you wish, but do not confuse it or associate it with the actual anti-Communist campaign, except where it is warranted by the facts. Do not, in any event, allow these other issues to prevent you from presenting a united front with people of good will whose views you may not completely share. Many Americans disagree with each other on vital questions of the day, but when it comes to actual Communism, these same Americans should be solidly in agreement. Let us first rid ourselves of Communist subversion and Soviet aggression, and then we can proceed to the solution of other problems.

Shortly after the Korean War started in 1950, J. Edgar Hoover, head of the FBI, asked all American citizens to aid the Bureau in assembling data on actual Communist and Soviet activities in the United States. Few Americans heeded the call for co-operation. But in reality, the FBI has so much on its hands that it frequently misses some important piece of information or evidence which might be of tremendous importance. For example, a person living in Palo Alto, California, noticed that every Saturday night his neighbor received a large bundle of newspapers. His curiosity aroused, he discovered that they were copies of the Communist *People's World*— the west coast version of the *Daily Worker*. This bit of information he then passed on to the FBI, and it proved to be conclusive evidence long sought by the Bureau. By keeping your eyes and ears open, particularly when in a position to observe areas or activities known to be Communist infiltrated or of interest to the Communists, you may be able to render real service to local or federal law-enforcement agencies. Do not, of course, annoy the FBI with gossip and unsubstantiated rumor.

If you can prove a pattern of support of bona fide Communist causes and document it fully, you have a basis for action. In determining such a pattern, a knowledge of international Communist tactical changes is essential. In determining patterns of consistent pro-Communist and pro-Soviet actions, it is helpful to keep in mind the eight tactical periods in the history of the world Communist movement. They are:

1. 1917–1921: Calls for world Communist uprisings on the Russian pattern.
2. 1922–1928: Setting up institutional ties with the Comintern.
3. 1929–1934: Strikes and violence to try to gain power during the depression in expectation of "capitalist" collapse.
4. 1935–1939: United front with "liberals" against fascism, war, and existing social and economic conditions.
5. 1939–1941: Hitler-Stalin pact; no aid to Britain; peace with Hitler.
6. 1942–1945: All-out aid to Soviet Russia; open up "second front" concessions to Russia in the name of "allied unity."

7. 1945–1953: Cold war in Europe and hot war in Asia; attacks on "McCarthyism" and Congressional committees.

8. 1954 to the present: Peace at any price, "coexistence," end of U.S. nuclear tests, and attacks on the security program.

If an individual, through his writings, affiliations, and behavior, fits into all of these tactical periods, a strong presumption of collaboration may be established.

An individual, or an organization, who hailed the Soviet Constitution of 1936, condoned the purge trials (1935–1939); supported the Hitler-Stalin pact (1939–1941); opposed American aid to Nationalist China after 1945; attacked the Republic of Korea's fight for survival after 1950; urged recognition of Red China after November, 1950; opposed German rearmamant after 1950; pleaded for the cessation of nuclear testing by the U.S. (but not the U.S.S.R.); or who attacked Congressional committees as more dangerous than Communism itself may fit into the the pattern.

In each issue of *Counterattack* (42 Broadway, New York 4, New York), there is documentation on two or three current Communist activities, concluding with a specific "What You Can Do to Combat Communism" recommendation. Acting upon this, anti-Communist Americans can take effective action every week of the year.

It is an excellent practice at the end of each week to write down on paper what you have done by way of anti-Communist action and what you plan to do the following week. Ask yourself this question: "Am I working as hard for God and country as the Communists are working for Marx and the U.S.S.R.?"

Further suggestions for individuals and group action can be found in the Appendix. Special attention is called to the U.S. Chamber of Commerce's "Check of Anti-Communist Activities," the section on periodicals, organizations (which can also furnish speakers), and reports of Congressional committees, especially those of the House Un-American Activities Committee, the Senate Internal Security Subcommittee, and the Senate Permanent Subcommittee on Investigations. The reader should write to the chairmen of these committees and ask to be placed on their mailing lists. And every reader should:

1. Promote anti-Communist books and periodicals.
2. Obtain the services of anti-Communist speakers.
3. Obtain the reports of Congressional investigating committees.
4. Support anti-Communist legislation.
5. Support such organizations as the Committee of One Million (17 Park Avenue, New York 16, New York) and join such organizations.
6. Encourage ex-Communists.
7. Combat Communist penetration into American life with facts and publicity.
8. Read *Masters of Deceit*, by J. Edgar Hoover.

CHAPTER 17

Counterattack Against Communism in Education

Too many college professors in the United States have a double standard of political morality; Fascism, they believe, is evil, but Communism is something we must try to understand and get along with. In the 1930's, there were faculty and student anti-Fascists congresses, conventions, rallies, and demonstrations. The prevailing sentiment was a willingness to risk war to stop Fascism; legislative investigations of the Bund were enthusiastically welcomed in liberal circles. But where are the faculty and student anti-Communist organizations and demonstrations today?

The plain fact is that they do not exist. Those who suggest a tougher policy against Communism are denounced by liberal intellectuals as "warmongers"; those who welcome legislative investigation of Communism are labeled "McCarthyites." J. Robert Oppenheimer bewailed the fact that the atomic targets in Japan were too small but later demanded the end of nuclear tests and opposed the use of such weapons in any future war.[1] Those professors who supported or sympathized with Alger Hiss or Owen Lattimore were and, in the latter case at least, are legion; those who favored Whittaker Chambers and the McCarran Committee are very few in number.

All of this constitutes a disservice to America by its liberals. In the Popular Front of today, as in the Popular Front of the 1930's, many of these molders of youthful minds look upon Communism and Communists as having something in common with democracy. As George Meany has pointed out, they look upon Communism as a basically humanitarian ideology temporarily off the track. They are most sympathetic with what they call the "social experiments" in Red China and in Yugoslavia—but they throw up their hands in horror at the suggestion of sympathy and support for the republics of Korea and China. Indeed, Max Ascoli, for example, seems to believe that membership in the "China Lobby" is the ultimate sin.

Defense of Fifth Amendment invokers by intellectuals is taken as a matter of course; defense of those who help their government expose the Communist conspiracy is anathema. Professor Herbert Fuchs of American University was fired *because* he was anti-Communist at the same time that M.I.T. restored Fifth Amendment Dirk Struik to its staff and Harvard defended and retained its professors who had invoked the Fifth Amendment. The American Association of University Professors seems to be largely interested in professors who invoke the Fifth Amendment or who have a background of Communist collaboration; anti-Communist professors who are muffled by "liberal" administrations do not appear to be the concern of the A.A.U.P.[2]

Communist penetration of American education is serious and takes many forms. First, there have been the actual Communist educational institutions themselves, such as the Jefferson School in New York and the California Labor School in San Francisco. Some of the professors from these Communist schools lecture on the campuses of leading American universities. Joseph Clark, formerly foreign editor of the *Daily Worker,* Herbert Aptheker, Samuel Sillen, and Alan Max are among those who have recently spoken at such institutions as the University of Wisconsin, the University of Minnesota, Swarthmore, and Cornell. After a controversy in which he was barred from speaking at New York's municipal colleges, *Daily Worker* editor John Gates received an invitation to speak at Columbia University. Columbia officials, it was reported, granted the request to have Gates appear "as a matter of course."

Second, there have been actual Communist units consisting of both faculty and students on college campuses. Such units included the Labor Youth League, the Progressive Citizens of America, and the local and regional groups which were exposed by the House Un-American Activities Committee in Michigan and by the Senate Internal Security Subcommittee in New York several years ago. These groups brought Communist or pro-Communist speakers to the campus, agitated for the end of legislative investigations into Communism and for the end of U.S. nuclear testing, and demanded peace with Soviet Russia and Communist China at any price.

Third, there are those professors who refuse to deny under oath affiliations with Communism. Among these have been Bernhard J. Stern of Columbia, Clarence Hiskey of Brooklyn Polytechnic Institute, Bernard Riess of Hunter College, Moses Finley and Saul Heimlich of Rutgers, and Gene Weltfish of Columbia. With respect to such professors, most schools follow Harvard's example of retaining them on the faculty. This is "academic freedom."

Fourth, we have that impressive number of professors who, over a long period of time, remained persistently affiliated with fellow-traveling organizations designated by the Attorney General or legislative committees as Communist controlled. Among such have been Colston Warne of Amherst, Frederick L. Schuman of Williams, Kirtley Mather and Harlow Shapley of Harvard, Corliss Lamont of Columbia, Robert J. Havighurst of Chicago, Thomas I. Emerson of Yale, H. Hubert Wilson of Princeton, Robert S. Lynd of Columbia, Owen Lattimore of Johns Hopkins, and Edwin B. Burgum of New York.[3] Not only do these men present a distorted, leftist point of view outside the classroom, but they also write textbooks and reference books which are read by students and laymen alike. Schuman's texts on international relations and the Soviet Union are still widely used in our colleges and universities today, and books by Lattimore, Lamont, Wilson, and Lynd have had, and in some instances continue to have, a wide following and influence.

Fifth, there is the vast majority of purveyors of the double standard of political morality: the anti-anti-Communist professors. Although they may occasionally affiliate with left-wing organizations, their main stock in trade is to denounce anti-Communism and anti-Communists. Among these might be included Arthur Schlesinger, Jr., Harold Fisher of Stanford, Malcolm Sharp of Chicago, Nathaniel Peffer of Columbia, William A. Williams of Oregon, Dana F. Fleming of Vanderbilt, and John K. Fairbank of Harvard. Their anti-anti-Communist message reaches thousands via their lectures and books and through the services they render to the government, political leaders, publishers, and tax-exempt foundations. Professor Francis Wormuth of Utah recently praised John Wexley's book about the Rosenberg atom spies in a leading political science journal, calling the Rosenberg trial "America's Dreyfus case."[4] Several academicians in leading universities, notably Professor Packer of Stanford Law School, continue to insist that Alger Hiss was framed by the FBI.

Finally, the double-standard moralists achieve their impact through myriad private organizations interested in American politics and world affairs. In the case of the Institute of Pacific Relations, its effective leadership, which consisted of Edward C. Carter, Frederick Vanderbilt Field, Philip Jessup, and Owen Lattimore, profoundly influenced not only governmental decisions relating to the Far East, but also teaching and research in colleges and universities, and the writing, publishing and reviewing of volumes which were widely read and accepted, even by laymen.

Today, the Foreign Policy Association and the Fund for the Republic carry on in the highest traditions of anti-anti-Communism, subsidized by tax-exempt foundations and inspired and guided by persons generally belonging to categories 4 and 5 outlined above. The Foreign Policy Assocation has for years been led by Vera Micheles Dean, who wrote in 1946: "If we are really honest with ourselves we cannot escape the conclusion that since V-J Day our economic withdrawal, our naked materialism as exemplified by our attitude toward the feeding of starving peoples, our political vacillations, and above all, our moral negativism, have done more to keep the world in turmoil than Russia's actions." This classic message of double-standard morality reaches millions of thinking, adult Americans in most major cities of this land, organized into "World Affairs Councils," as well as student groups on most of our college campuses, known as "International Relations Clubs." Mrs. Dean and her cohorts have large sums of money to spend on guiding the thinking of such organizations along "correct" lines. The FPA organizes special seminars, mails thousands of kits containing bibliographical data and area studies to interested organizations, and sends speakers on tours throughout the United States. Among these is John Carter Vincent, formerly head of the State Department's Far Eastern Division, who was found by the Civil Service Loyalty Board to be of doubtful loyalty to the United States. Needless to say, there is no mention of this fact in the brochure supplied by the speaker's bureau of the Foreign Policy Association. FPA speakers include more than a representative number of "neutralist" ambassadors and consuls representing India, Yugoslavia, Burma, and Indonesia.[5]

The Fund for the Republic has given a cash prize to a pacifist group for not firing a Fifth Amendment employee; it has published a book attacking the Security Program without even trying to present the Government view; it has widely distributed a book on the Fifth Amendment which insists that we must not come to any conclusion about the guilt of one who invokes the Fifth Amendment, and it refuses to give equal space to a dissenting analysis provided by a lawyer better versed in Constitutional law. It offers cash prizes to anyone who can show to the satisfaction of the Fund that his civil liberties have been curtailed. In short, the solicitude displayed by the Fund toward pro-Communism and anti-anti-Communism is prodigious.[6]

Confronted with the spectacle of an American educational structure dominated by a doctrinaire, aggressive, intolerant, well-heeled, and influential fraternity of double-standard moralists, those who do not conform must at least strive to achieve a balance between pro-Communism and anti-Communism, between members of the "Liberal Establishment" and nonmembers. Some bold souls even venture to suggest that some effort should be made to give the pro-American and anti-totalitarian view pre-eminence in the educational structure.

There are some anti-Communists on our college faculties, although many others are casualties of the college cold war who have run afoul of the "Establishment" which dominates our campuses. The number and influence of the anti-Communists on the campus should be increased. Even now they are accomplishing much by presenting the case for freedom and by calling for a critical examination of the theory and practice of Communism. Their purpose is not indoctrination but objective education. Indeed, what they object to in the "Establishment" is its tendency to indoctrinate in behalf of collectivism and anti-anti-Communism.

Some of the smaller foundations have established annual seminars which encourage exchange of views among professors who can properly be described as anti-Communist,[7] and some of these encourage publication. A group of scholars at the University of Pennsylvania, led by Professor Strausz-Hupé, are doing an immense amount of good work with their Foreign Policy Research Institute; some of their publications have been reprinted in such influential media as *U.S. News and World Report,* and their radio programs, sympathetic to liberation, are excellent.

These men also reach the thinking public with articles in such widely read publications as the *Saturday Evening Post, Reader's Digest,* and *U.S. News and World Report,* as well as in such periodicals as *Human Events, National Review, American Mercury, National Republic,* and the newspapers associated with the Spadea Syndicate. *Human Events,* with its weekly Washington commentary and staunchly conservative viewpoint, has outstripped the circulation of two left-wing journals, *The Nation* and *New Repub-*

lic. *National Review,* with its excellent editorial staff (Buckley, Bozell, Burnham, Mitchell, LaFollette), is challenging the left-wing intellectuals at their own level with conspicuous success. In 1957, three new journals, *Modern Age, Orbis,* and *Free World Review,* were launched by men knowledgeable in the Communist field.

A few colleges in the United States now present comprehensive courses devoted to critical analysis of the theory and practice of Communism. Among these are Marquette, Duquesne, Georgetown, Fordham, and the University of San Francisco. In the last named, the course, conducted by militantly anti-Communist Jesuit Father Raymond Feely, is compulsory for all seniors. Professors from these schools and some others have also developed anti-Communist leadership training programs for adults in their communities, with the intention of training community leaders. They are acquainted with Communist literature, as well as with anti-Communist books and periodicals and government publications. At the end of the course, each graduate is urged to bring the anti-Communist message to others by familiarizing them with anti-Communist publications and by converting non-Communists to active anti-Communism.[8]

A constructive step has recently been taken at the high-school level. Concerned about the widespread use of textbooks critical of United States policies and economics while largely uncritical of their Soviet counterparts, the Institute of Fiscal and Political Education has sponsored a textbook called *Democracy versus Communism,* by Professor Kenneth Colegrove, a distinguished retired political scientist. This excellent book, published by Van Nostrand, now provides for the first time a realistic and factual analysis of Communism and democracy for high-school students. Leftists have protested, as usual, that a book which relates in plain terms what Communism has done to the world is not sufficiently "objective." However, many Americans refuse to be disturbed by the idea that a sharp look at the record of tyranny should engender some revulsion against Moscow and some belated enthusiasm for America's achievements under freedom.

It is clear from this brief resumé that a start, however modest, has been made by the anti-Communist forces in our colleges, universities, and high schools. But beyond this, what can be done to strengthen anti-Communism in academic life and the influence of anti-Communist academicians in public life? Here are some suggestions:

1. Anti-Communism can be strengthened by encouraging promising young men and women to join the anti-Communist academic fraternity. Anti-Communist professors should increase their efforts to win over their best students not only to anti-Communism, but also to careers in the movement to defeat the Communist conspiracy. Such students should be encouraged to do graduate work at those universities where consistency in the matter of totalitarianism is at least tolerated and under those professors whose records indicate stability and consistency with respect to the same matter. Young men and women armed with advance degrees are not only in a position to teach, write, and do research, but they are also better equipped to obtain positions in government, where anti-Communist intellectuals today are often in the minority.

2. Students who do not plan to do graduate work and who do not contemplate careers in teaching, writing, research, or government, should be encouraged to make their anti-Communist influence felt in the legal profession, in politics directly, and in industry. Here again, sympathetic professors and parents can play a decisive role.

3. Anti-Communist professors, graduate students, and college seniors should be more aggressive in applying for the numerous grants, fellowships, and scholarships offered by myriad foundations, government agencies, and universities. As it is, the applicants tend to be of other persuasions.

4. Such programs as the Conference on Democratic Theory (Professor Stokes of Wisconsin), the Foreign Policy Research Institute

in Philadelphia (Professor Strausz-Hupé) and the National Military-Industrial Conference (contact Frank Barnett, The Richardson Foundation, New York), should be emulated. Here, those who have not been led astray by the siren song of Moscow can become acquainted, exchange ideas, develop anti-Communist projects and publications, make better contacts with government, and pave the way for united and national anti-Communist action on the academic level. The less well-known foundations have already done much good work, and with the help of industry and certain discerning colleges, much more can be accomplished.

5. Anti-Communist professors should strive to have incorporated into the curricula of their respective colleges courses on the theory and practice of Communism, to be taught by themselves or some other qualified persons. They should also develop anti-Communist leadership training programs for adult groups. Interested readers are invited to contact the author about this.

6. Existing courses in American government should be strengthened and introduced where they are not now compulsory. The Defense Department's Advisory Committee on Prisoners of War reported in 1955: "Many of the POW's knew too little about the United States and its ideals and traditions. The uninformed POW's were up against it. They couldn't answer arguments in favor of Communism with arguments in favor of Americanism. . . . They lacked sufficient patriotism because of their limited knowledge of democracy." Courses should be revised with respect to content and required reading to take this criticism into consideration.

7. These professors should improve their contacts with governmental and private organizations interested in effective counteraction against Communist aggression and subversion. Much good can result from improving such contacts—to all concerned.[9]

8. Anti-Communist professors should support the Communism study project in Washington headed by Charles Lowry and William Yandell Elliott. This group is studying ways and means of introducing critical courses in Communism into our high schools

and colleges. This project and others similar to it give promise of accomplishing much good.

9. Greater use should be made of group letters to the editors of the *New York Times,* to the President, and to the Secretary of State, with appropriate publicity. Professors of other persuasions constantly utilize these stratagems to great effect. Such issues as Hungary, neutralism, nuclear testing, the missiles program, and security require constant attention.

10. Maximum support should be given to such high-level academic journals as *Modern Age, Orbis,* and *Free World Review.*

11. Anti-Communist professors can do more to focus attention on the crucial issues of our day by stressing the urgency of the problem and the need for action now. Since the Communist invasion of Greece in 1944, 800,000,000 human beings have come under Communist control, as have 8,000,000 square miles of territory. If the rate of expansion in the future continues to hold the pattern of the last twelve years, the international Communist movement may control the world by 1980 (assuming no counterattack led by the United States). Soviet advances in earth satellites and missiles make the problem even more urgent. In this connection, a reappraisal of the "let's let them strike first" thesis is called for.

12. These professors should exploit the dramatic events in Hungary to the utmost and inform their audiences of the deception of Communist "peace offensives" and "coexistence." Wide circulation should be given the following government publications: *Communism, U.S.A.* (Senate Internal Security Subcommittee), *Soviet Total War* (House Un-American Activities Committee), and *The Great Pretense* (same committee). Additionally, wide circulation and support of such publications as *Human Events, U.S. News and World Report, National Review, Counterattack,* and other intelligent anti-Communist periodicals should be encouraged.

Such opportunities for anti-Communism as exist in the academic world must be taken advantage of—now. The mistakes, inconsistencies, and, in some cases, the collaboration with Communism of those who think anti-Communism is worse than Communism need to be brought to light by others than legislative committees. If nothing else, the vigor and sustained effort of the "liberal" intellectuals should arouse anti-Communist academicians into launching that counterattack which, if co-ordinated with similar movements elsewhere (including that of Freedom Fighters within the Communist empire), will lead inevitably to the eventual eradication of Communism from the world body politic.

CHAPTER 18

What One Person Can Do: The Christopher Approach

The Christopher movement is a unique and aggressive effort to encourage positive action against Communism. It was started to stir up among millions of Americans a sense of personal responsibility in restoring truth to national and international life. The Christopher Director, Father James Keller, holds that God has put a "bit of the missionary" in every human being. His aim is to encourage as many persons as possible to put that power for good to use, not only in emergencies, but at all times—not from fear of what is wrong, but from love of what is right.

The name "Christophers" is derived from the Greek word "Christophoros," meaning "Christ-bearer." Its meaning sums up the Christopher objective of encouraging individual initiative in carrying into the mainstream of life the truths that can bring lasting peace to America and to the world—truths that have come down to us through 1,900 years of Christianity, as well as those kept alive by the Jews for ages before the birth of Christ.

The chief aim of the Christophers is to encourage each individual "to accentuate the positive"—to improve, rather than merely disapprove, to *do* rather than merely to talk. The entire theme of the movement is: "Better to light one candle than to curse the darkness."

The public reaction to the Christopher approach has been encouraging beyond all expectations. It started in 1945 with a few hundred followers, and by the end of 1953, more then 10,000,000 persons were in the movement. The *Christopher News Notes* reach 1,000,000 persons every month; 2,000,000 Christopher books are in circulation; 4,544 prints of Christopher movies are being shown to uncounted millions in thousands of schools, churches, clubs, and other organizations; three Christopher television programs are seen coast-to-coast by more than 8,000,000 persons; the Christopher radio program is presented by more than 400 stations over the country and is heard by several million people; the Christopher column, appearing in eighteen newspapers, is read daily by more than 1,000,000 persons.

Attention is focused on the individual by the Christopher approach because in Father Keller's view, much of the chaos in the world results from the tendency of the average person to "let George do it." The Christophers emphasize what one person can do to help change the world for the better by playing a positive, constructive part in life. They insist that there can be no lasting peace or freedom without truth. Father Keller points out that anyone can do something—by starting in the home, the office, the farm, and reaching out from there to the world. The housewife, banker, nurse, serviceman, office worker, doctor, farmer, teacher, mechanic, lawyer, student, clerk, bus driver, scientist, or "just plain American"—all can do something constructive in behalf of God and America and against Communism.

Christophers are urged to make their influence felt in those all-important fields which shape the course of history: (1) education; (2) government; (3) the creative side of newspapers, magazines, books, radio, television, and motion pictures; (4) labor relations; (5) social service; (6) library work. None of these fields can be better than the people who staff them. "The player makes the team." It is in these vital fields that the Communists have concentrated. "While most of the good people have been taking care of themselves, the evil-doers have been taking care of everybody else. The Communists and other enemies of truth have swarmed into teaching, government work, writing, labor unions, social service, and library work because they know they can spread their ideas through these media. These fields give the anti-God forces their opportunity to broadcast ideas that can undermine and wreck the home, the Church, the professions, business and similar institutions."[1] Even today, Father Keller points out, most good people take too much for granted. Many assume that someone else—not themselves—will serve up good government, good education, and good everything else for them while they sit on the sidelines, complaining when things go wrong. The Christopher leader insists that each has the right and the duty to raise his voice in support of what is good and in rejection of what is evil, for God and country, and against Communism.

One of the unique features of the Christopher movement is that there are no memberships, no chapters, no meetings, no subscriptions, and no dues. Each person interested in following the Christopher approach decides for himself how, when, and where he will make his voice heard. The kind and amount of his contribution and participation lies entirely between him and his own conscience.

To persons who have complained that one individual can do little good, Father Keller replies that during the wartime blackouts, the flame of a single match on the beach could be seen from several miles out at sea; in the same way, a single candle can make an impression on the whole horizon—the divine spark in each individual can light that candle. To start to change the world for the better requires only the presence of one Christopher in any environment. Even in the worst environment, one Christ-bearer can be a candle to dispel the darkness, a step in the right direction. One human being devoted to the good of others can do much to bring out the best qualities of everyone he meets. Of course, this activity is much more effective if it is undertaken by many rather than few.

Although Father Keller is a Catholic priest, the Christopher movement reaches out and includes individuals of all races, colors, and creeds. Everyone is accordingly invited to become a Christ-bearer to the extent that he can and will. Because there are no members, each individual is left on his own to participate as much or as little as he chooses, according to the dictates of his conscience. Those who choose to follow the Christopher movement are not forced in any way to accept or do any more than each may determine for himself.

The basic truths in which the Christopher movement is rooted are exactly the same truths which the Communists everywhere are working to undermine, ridicule, and eliminate. They are: (1) the existence of a personal Triune God Who has spoken to the world; (2) Jesus Christ, true God and true man; (3) the foundation by Jesus Christ of a Church to teach all men and bring them to eternal salvation; (4) the Ten Commandments; (5) the sacred character of the individual; (6) the sanctity of the lifelong marriage bond; (7) the sanctity of the home as the basic unit of the whole human family; (8) the human rights of every person as coming from God, not from the state; (9) the right, based on human nature, to possess private property, with its consequent obligation to society; (10) due respect for domestic, civil, and religious authority; and (11) judgment after death. Little, however, is accomplished by merely recognizing these truths. They must be integrated or incarnated into everyday living, especially in the great fields of influence which affect the destiny of all men. The apostles of evil are undisturbed if we merely talk our convictions, wring our hands over the breakdown of faith, morals, and Americanism, and confine ourselves to complaining. Their only fear is that someday those who believe in God and country will wake up and start acting their beliefs.

The one special truth accentuated by the Chistophers which is essential to the American form of government is that each and every human being is created by Almighty God in His own image and likeness; that he gets his fundamental rights from God and not the state; and that the chief purpose of the state—as the Founding Fathers stressed in the Declaration of Independence—is to protect these God-given rights. The Christophers consider the Declaration of Independence to be the charter of American freedom. The Founding Fathers made four explicit references to God in this basic document. In the first sentence they wrote: "to which the Laws of Nature and of Nature's God entitle them." In the second sentence: "that all men are created equal, that they are endowed by their Creator with certain inalienable rights." In the next to the last sentence: "appealing to the Supreme Judge of the World." And in the last sentence: "with a firm reliance on the protection of divine providence."

The Christopher approach is made known through every possible channel of communications—talks, the *News Notes*, books, articles, movies, television, radio, etc. The *News Notes* are sent each month free of charge to anyone wishing to receive them. In this way, everyone "votes himself in" by his own consent. The *Notes* provide examples of what average persons have actually done to change the world for the better. The idea is that one candle lights another, and when there are enough lighted candles the darkness will disappear.

Suggestions and patterns are also presented which each individual can carry into practice in his own way. As for the Christopher books, about two million are now in circulation, including translations into German, Spanish, Japanese, Chinese, and Malayan. Royalties (twenty cents on each two-dollar book and one cent on each thirty-five-cent book) are used entirely to donate copies to schools, libraries, and individuals. Two hundred thousand free copies have been given away. These books include *You Can Change the World, Careers That Change the World,* and *Government Is Your Business,* as well as other titles. These books outline specific ways in which each person can strengthen God and country and thus weaken and ultimately help eliminate Communism. They are handbooks, or manuals, on how one person can contribute to the victory of truth and a lasting peace. The motion pictures are all half-hour 16 mm. films suitable for showing in a home, church, school, or club, as well as on television and may be purchased for $30 a print (actual cost to the Christophers) or rented for $5 per showing. A print of each film is donated to every television station in the country. Stars of these films include Jack Benny, Ann Blyth, Bing Crosby, Bob Hope, Irene Dunne, Loretta Young, and William Holden. Fifty-four quarter-hour films for the "Christopher Program" are now presented over eighty-two television stations each week. In addition, one hundred one-minute films with a brief Christopher message have been produced. Television stations have given the Christophers free time for the showing of Christopher films, and stars and personalities also donate their time and talent. The actual cost per week to produce these films is therefore cut to $3,000. As for radio, more than four hundred stations carry the fifteen-minute Christopher radio program throughout the country under the title "You Can Change the World."

Another way in which the Christopher approach is advanced is through the "Do It Now" groups throughout the United States. The idea is for ten or twelve people to get together and discuss ways and means by which each of them can individually do something positive and practical to bring the truths of Christ into the vital spheres. The Christopher headquarters, from time to time, furnishes a booklet containing twelve lessons, with material for discussion and suggestions to apply in a practical way. The "Do It Now" groups are encouraged to spread their work through the Christopher Awards, which are cash prizes offered to hundreds of winners several times a year. These awards dramatize and pinpoint what one person can do to change the world for the better; they focus attention on the tremendous power resting in the hands of those who do creative work in the book, motion-picture, television, radio, theatre, newspaper, and magazine fields.

The headquarters of the Christopher movement are at 18 East 48th Street, near Madison Avenue, in the heart of New York City.

The offices are on the fourteenth floor of the Great Lakes Carbon building, where a staff of thirty cares for the extensive detail connected with the maintenance and expansion of the Christopher program. The movement does not maintain branch organizations because it stresses individual initiative and personal responsibility. The Christopher leadership leaves it to each individual to decide whether he will work alone or through any one of the many excellent organizations already in existence to fight Communism.

Many people have asked Father Keller why the Christophers have a policy of "no dues, no subscriptions, no collections." His answer is that "we wish to highlight the importance of 'doing.'" Many a person who can do valuable Christopher work is not in a position to contribute financially. It is therefore a Christopher belief that the "doers" should be stirred up, leaving to God most of the task of inspiring the "donors." An inscription in the Library of Congress sums up the Christopher attitude here: "For a web begun, God supplies the thread." As to where the money comes from, the answer is that "God provides it through thousands of individuals who, without any urging or solicitation, supply the funds needed to pay the cost of free literature, TV films, and other Christopher projects." This does not mean that the movement has no financial worries. Indeed, such free projects as the *News Notes* are occasionally held up for lack of funds, but Father Keller feels that by keeping the entire movement on a voluntary basis, more good can be done over a sustained period primarily through spontaneous zeal and inner drive.

Father Keller holds that prayer is a powerful means of offsetting the harm of Communism and simultaneously strengthening the ranks of the Christ-bearers. He urges prayer, for instance, that at least one person with a Christ-like purpose may be found to fill one of the 160,000 vacancies in the teaching profession throughout the United States: "The harvest indeed is great, but the laborers are few. Pray we therefore the Lord of the harvest, that he send forth laborers into his harvest." (Matt. 9:38, 39)

The Christopher leader reminds us that those who would enslave the world know how important it is to eliminate all traces of the spiritual from the daily lives of the people. Reports from all over the world constantly show that when the forces of Communism take over any country, the one vital power that they quickly try to eliminate is religion. The reason for this is that religion is forever reminding millions of persons that there exists a Supreme Being Who is the Author of all life and from Whom our every human right is derived. Awareness of this truth is a powerful roadblock to any and all who would set up a slave state. In 1951, the East German Communist regime instructed all public school teachers to spread the word that "Jesus Christ never existed and the Bible is a collection of myths." This Communist government realized that it could never completely subjugate the minds and hearts of the people so long as they put Christ first.

A leader of Communism in the United States told one of his aides: "All our talk about capitalism being the one big enemy of Communism is just for public consumption. Our real struggle is against religion. That is the one big obstacle in our way." Albert Einstein, no special friend of organized religion, stated during World War II: "Only the Church stood squarely across the path of Hitler's campaign for suppressing the truth. I never had any special interest in the Church before, but now I feel a great affection and admiration because the Church alone had the courage and persistence to stand for intellectual truth and moral freedom."

Father Keller argues that if the enemies of civilization work furiously to eliminate God from everything in order to destroy our liberty, that ought to be argument enough for us to work even more zealously to put God back into everything. He reminds us that we in America have a rich heritage stemming from a profound belief in God. More than one hundred years ago, the great de Tocqueville wrote: "The Americans combine the notions of Christianity and liberty so intimately in their minds that it is impossible to make them conceive the one without the other."

William Penn once wrote that "those who are not governed by God will be ruled by tyrants." Father Keller warns us that we are in danger of being hypocritical if we fail to insist that God-given inalienable rights be brought to life in our government, our schools, and in every other phase of life. Those who are devoted followers of the anti-God and anti-America thesis and who insist that man is just a collection of chemicals are very much on the job. They not only talk, they act. They leave nothing to chance. These apostles of godlessness despise the idea of "this nation under God" and are determined to change it to "this nation, without God."

"What we need," President Eisenhower has said, "is a dynamic constructive force to lead the world. . . . Except for moral regeneration, there is no hope for us, and we are going to disappear one day in the dust of an atomic explosion. The answer is in our hands. It is a terrible challenge, but we must face the facts." Professor John H. Hollowell of Duke University put it this way: "Only if we are concerned about the salvation of our souls shall we be of much use in saving the world; only if our eyes are focused on the Kingdom of God will we be enabled by the power of God to make the self-sacrifices which the salvation of the world demands—in short, only by aiming above the world shall we succeed in mastering the world." Father Keller concludes: "If we but strike the spark, that spark in the Providence of God may one day burst into a flame that will sweep over the earth."

Notes

PREFACE

1. House Un-American Activities Committee, *Soviet Total War* (Washington, Government Printing Office, 1956), 1.

2. *New York Times*, July 3, 1956.

3. Statement of the Defense Department's Advisory Commission on Prisoners of War in Korea, July 29, 1955.

CHAPTER 1

1. He was especially concerned over the Russian demand for a sphere of influence in Bulgaria.

2. In his address to the Twentieth Congress of the Russian Communist party on February 14, 1956, Khrushchev reiterated the thesis that wars or revolutions would be necessary to conquer leading capitalist states (like the United States), but pointed out that Communism might gain control of countries like France and Italy via popular fronts with Socialists and "liberals."

3. The so-called downgrading of Stalin by Khrushchev in 1956 was undertaken to persuade citizens of the U.S.S.R. that their past unhappiness was due to a "Stalinism" that was now to be modified. But the June 30, 1956, report of the Central Committee of the U.S.S.R. stressed that not all of Stalinism had been scrapped. Events in Hungary, Poland, and China during 1957 confirm this.

4. See *The Great Pretense* (published by the House Un-American Activities Committee), May 19, 1956, and the works of W. W. Kulski, William Henry Chamberlin, David Dallin, and Eugene

Lyons; see also Harry Schwartz, "Communism: The Promise and the Reality," *New York Times Magazine,* May 2, 1954.

CHAPTER 2

1. See *The Great Pretense.*

2. Anti-Communist uprisings in East Germany, Poland, and Hungary suggest that the colonies are ripe for liberation.

3. Khrushchev had suggested that in some cases Communists could win power peacefully where non-Communists chose not to resist.

4. See *Nazi-Soviet Relations, 1939–1941,* edited by Sontag and Beddie and published by the Department of State (Government Printing Office, 1947).

5. According to former Ambassador Arthur Bliss Lane, this was largely the work of Dean Acheson, then Undersecretary of State.

6. The United States government published a censored version of the Yalta agreements in 1955.

7. Ingenious liberals suggest that if we had not made these concessions at Yalta, Russia would have conquered Manchuria anyway. Yet we had far greater military power in the Far East than they had in 1945, including the atomic bomb. Yalta apologists have ridiculed Neville Chamberlain's argument that Munich was necessary because Hitler was going to take Sudeten anyway.

8. The Soviets subsequently withdrew from East Austria, but only after gaining major economic concessions and extracting a promise from Austria to accept permanent neutrality.

9. The Soviets evacuated their Finnish bases in 1955 after insuring Finland's neutrality in a future conflict.

10. Service was reinstated in 1957 after the Supreme Court held that Secretary of State Acheson had lacked the power to dismiss him.

11. The Subcommittee described Lattimore as "a conscious, articulate instrument of the Soviet conspiracy."

12. Attorney General Brownell went to the unusual length of asking Judge Youngdahl to disqualify himself as "biased." Youngdahl refused.

13. October 7, 1950.

14. See especially C. Turner Joy, *How Communists Negotiate* (Macmillan), and Mark Clark, *From the Danube to the Yalu* (Harper).

15. Ingenious neutralists have suggested that the Nationalists give these islands to the Communists because they are closer to the Communist mainland than to Formosa.

CHAPTER 3

1. This is precisely what Soviet dictator Khrushchev wants them to think. See his speech to the Twentieth Congress of the Russian Communist party, February 14, 1956.

2. Stalin, *Works* (Russian edition, Moscow, 1949), X, 123.

3. Stalin, *Problems of Leninism* (Moscow, 1940), 156.

4. For instance, the Communists obtained at the Panmunjom conference table what they had failed to obtain on the field of battle.

5. See the testimony of Generals Clark and Stratemeyer before the Senate Internal Subcommittee, August 10 and 25, 1954.

6. For an intelligent discussion, see Sidney Hook, *The 5th Amendment* (New York, Macmillan, 1957).

7. *New Leader* (December 6, 1954).

CHAPTER 4

1. Since General Sarnoff wrote his memorandum several years ago, his predictions have indeed come true. The U.S.S.R. has developed a respectable nuclear weapons supply and the means of delivering these weapons, most notably, an intercontinental ballis-

tic missile capability. Among the countermeasures available to us are: (1) to strike first; (2) to make clear our willingness to retaliate immediately with overseas intermediate range ballistic missiles, in-the-air, aircraft-launched missiles, and missiles launched from mobile naval vessels near the Soviet homeland which cannot be destroyed by ICBM's because these require fixed targets.

CHAPTER 10

1. In 1955, international Communism again accepted Tito, with certain reservations, and in 1957, an even closer *rapprochement* was indicated.

2. Security risks include those who drink too much, engage in perversion, are susceptible to Communist or other influences, or maintain affiliation with Communism or associations with Communists. Between May 28, 1953, and July 1, 1954, 2,611 government employees were discharged under the Security Program. Of these, 1,743 were expelled for subversion and 618 for perversion.

3. Subsequently, Secretary of State Dulles retired Vincent because of "mistaken judgment" rather than disloyalty, and the Supreme Court ruled that Secretary of State Acheson lacked the power to discharge Service. The latter was reinstated in 1957.

CHAPTER 12

1. A few travel restrictions were imposed in January, 1955, in protest against comparable restrictions imposed on us by the U.S.S.R.

2. There is some evidence that Burgess, First Secretary of the British Embassy in Washington during the Korean War, leaked information to Moscow and Peiping indicating to the Chinese Communists that the United States would not retaliate against the Manchurian bases if Red China intervened south of the Yalu.

3. For the full transcript of the program see *U.S. News and World Report* (September 14, 1956).

4. Bisson now teaches at a women's college in Oxford, Ohio.

5. See Freda Utley, *The China Story* (Henry Regnery Company, 1957).

6. He now resides in Mexico City.

7. One of the counts was subsequently declared too vaguely worded, and the Justice Department then tried to get it reinstated under different language but failed. Judge Luther Youngdahl, charged by Attorney General Brownell as "biased" in favor of Lattimore, threw out the heart of the indictment. Lattimore then returned to his teaching post at Johns Hopkins University, from which he had been on leave, with pay.

8. The IPR had a tax-exempt status until 1955.

9. Committee on Un-American Activities, *Review of the Scientific and Cultural Conference for World Peace* (Government Printing Office, April 19, 1949), 17–18.

10. *Loc. cit.*

11. *Loc. cit.*

12. See J. B. Matthews, "Communism in the Colleges," *American Mercury* (May, 1953). See also E. Merrill Root, *Collectivism on the Campus* (Devin-Adair).

13. See U.S. Atomic Energy Commission, *In the Matter of J. Robert Oppenheimer* (Government Printing Office, April 12, 1954–May 6, 1954), and Medford Evans, "An Open Letter to Dr. J. Robert Oppenheimer," *National Review* (March 9, 1957).

14. Committee on Un-American Activities, *100 Things You Should Know About Communism* (Government Printing Office, May 14, 1951), 81–82.

15. *Loc. cit.*

16. In the above section on labor, I have borrowed freely from Louis Budenz's *The Techniques of Communism* (Henry Regnery Company, 1954).

17. Excerpts from an address to the National Religion and Labor Foundation, New York City, December 13, 1955.

18. Senate Internal Security Subcommittee, *Activities of U.S.*

Citizens Employed by the United Nations (Government Printing Office, March 22, 1954).

CHAPTER 13

1. *New York Times Magazine*, June 14, 1953.

2. *Loc. cit.*

3. These were, respectively, the French, Indian, British, and Norwegian architects of collaboration with Fascism.

4. Particularly between 1935 and 1939.

5. Sidney Hook, "Six Fallacies of Robert Hutchins," *New Leader* (March 19, 1956).

CHAPTER 14

1. See Committee on Un-American Activities, *Guide to Subversive Activities and Publications* (Government Printing Office, 1957).

2. Both schools temporarily, at least, went out of business at the end of 1956.

3. *New York Times*, May 13, 1957.

4. See *Counterattack* (May 31 and June 21, 1957) and *U.S.A.* (December 6, 1957).

CHAPTER 16

1. An example of this was the publicity carried on in 1954 and 1955 by the "Fighting Homefolks" group of Captain Eugene Guild of Glenwood Springs, Colorado, relative to the 944 Americans still presumably held captive by the Chinese Reds. Captain Guild lost

his son in the Korean War. Another was the protest against Soviet repression in Hungary organized by Leo Cherne and the International Rescue Committee. Dr. Joseph F. Thorning of Frederick, Maryland, has done much to keep the hopes of freedom alive in eastern Europe through his personal contacts in Washington.

2. Goettling was a leading anti-Communist German resistance leader who was kidnapped by the Communists in Berlin and brutally murdered.

3. Such a resolution was unanimously approved by the Senate in 1954.

CHAPTER 17

1. See U.S. Atomic Energy Commission, *In the Matter of J. Robert Oppenheimer,* and Medford Evans, "An Open Letter to Dr. J. Robert Openheimer," *National Review* (March 9, 1957).

2. "The Firing of Herbert Fuchs," *National Review* (January 25, 1956); James Rorty, "The Case of the Fired 'Informer,'" *New Leader* (April 30, 1956); Sidney Hook, "The AAUP and Academic Integrity," *New Leader* (May 21, 1956).

3. Committee on Un-American Activities, *Review of the Scientific and Cultural Conference for World Peace,* 17–18.

4. The Wexley book claims that the Rosenbergs and Morton Sobell were framed by the Truman administration. The book has had the energetic support of the Communist party.

5. William Henry Chamberlin, "Anti-Anti-Communism: A Ford Investment," *National Review* (April 11, 1956).

6. A general discussion of the political activities of certain foundations is found in René Wormser, *Foundations* (New York, Devin-Adair, 1957).

7. A partial list appears in my "Communism and Anti-Communism in Our Colleges," *Human Events* (March 15, 1957).

8. The author has conducted a number of such courses in the Milwaukee area.

9. A list of such organizations is included in the Appendix.

CHAPTER 18

1. James Keller, *Careers That Change The World* (Doubleday).

Appendix

CHECK OF ANTI-COMMUNIST ACTIVITIES

A. KNOW YOUR ENEMY

1. Subscribe to a good newsletter or magazine specializing on Communist exposure which gives facts and suggestions on Communism.

2. Read one or more books on Communism each month.

3. See that books and periodicals exposing Communism are in school and public libraries.

4. Bring good lecturers to your community.

5. Ask opinion-influencing media, such as newspapers, magazines, and radio, to carry useful material on Communism. Praise them when they do so.

6. Be sure that your local bookstores feature good books exposing Communism.

B. STOP, LOOK, AND LISTEN

1. Be on the alert for Communist sympathizers in your community, especially those who can mold youth or public opinion. . . .

2. Be as cautious in sponsoring movements as you would be in signing a business contract. Look before you sign or join.

Reprinted from U.S. Chamber of Commerce, *Communism, Where Do We Stand Today?* (Washington, 1952), pp. 44-46.

3. Find out from reputable sources, such as *Counterattack*, *Alert*, or the American Legion about Communist sympathizers in the entertainment field. When sure of the facts protest to *sponsors* about such employment.

4. Identify public officials and policies displaying softness towards Communism. Demand a more patriotic attitude.

5. Ask questions before you send your children to a college or university. Avoid schools which tolerate pro-Communist professors. Bring this subject up at alumni meetings. Find out what is being taught in schools you support.

6. Urge bookstores not to feature books which aid Communism, even though their authors may not be Party members.

C. BE ACTIVE

1. Support organizations which are fighting Communist infiltration. Suggest that schools give students practice in parliamentary law and practice, so that these students can run their organizations and papers without Communist infiltration.

2. Assist, as your position allows, efforts to free labor unions from Communist control or to prevent such infiltration.

3. Get the habit of writing to newspapers, magazines, and public officials to protest aid to Communism. Praise sound anti-Communist moves. Write at once: delayed letters are rarely written.

4. Demand enforcement of existing laws designed to control Communism.

5. Give and get financial support for competent private groups fighting Communism.

6. Coordinate on a local level the anti-Communist activities of private groups. Urge joint action on higher levels. Favor small but active committees.

7. Report evidence of espionage and sabotage to the F.B.I.

8. Urge that schools and universities teach *facts* about Communism.

9. Take a strong and informed interest in American foreign policy.

10. Publicize activities of Communist fronts in your community. Be sure of your facts. Get advice on libel.

11. Have the courage to act in face of possible smears and slander from Communist sympathizers. Support patriotic ex-Communists who co-operate with the F.B.I.

12. Be alert regarding Communist efforts to promote racial or religious bigotry or to infiltrate minority groups. . . .

13. Check "peace" groups. Do they take the stand that Russia is always right and we are always wrong? . . . Communists are also promoting appeasement in the guise of peace.

14. Never use the term "Communist" loosely or inaccurately. Misuse of the term only gains friends for Communism.

15. Consider anti-Communist action as your personal responsibility. What is everybody's business is often never done. But organized efforts can be more effective and efficient.

EXCERPTS FROM AN ADDRESS BY J. EDGAR HOOVER TO CATHOLIC UNIVERSITY ALUMNI

Unfortunately, there are many seemingly well educated and intelligent people in our own country who have not yet awakened to the realization of the world-wide perils which are a potential threat to our own peace and security. . . . There are still too many citizens who are prone to scoff and underestimate the Communist menace.

Recently, I had occasion to observe a simple truth which has been well-documented in the public record, namely, that the Com-

The address from which these passages are taken was delivered at the homecoming banquet of the Catholic University of America on November 13, 1954, at which time Mr. Hoover received the Cardinal Gibbons Award for 1954. The excerpts are reprinted here by permission of Mr. Hoover.

munist Party is "exerting power and influence in almost every field of thought" and that the Communists "wield an influence far greater than their numbers suggest." . . .

Some very articulate people have been preaching for years that national security is incompatible with personal freedom. This ostrich-like attitude fails to recognize that security and freedom, to be realized, must complement each other. A nation without freedom is a nation dead and soulless. A nation without security cannot exist. Security and freedom are the essential ingredients interwoven in the ever-growing process which created and which maintains a democratic society.

This nation is a reality today because it was founded by people dedicated to win and hold their freedom. It will remain a fact only if there is adequate security to maintain the freedoms won by blood and toil. There can be no compromise with the forces that have as their aim the plowing under of our free way of living. Those forces are the debauchers of the American mind, the corrupters of our youth, the poisoners of the wells of the education of our children. . . .

But there is a vast difference between free inquiry and academic license. . . . All too often academic license has contributed to the spread of Communism. . . .

Some professors have aided the Communist cause by tearing down respect for agencies of government, belittling traditional and moral custom and by creating doubts in the validity of the American way of life. . . .

Pseudo liberals, who seek to conceal themselves behind the cloak of liberalism, have been beguiled, captivated, and perverted because they have not been conscious of the horror, duplicity, and godlessness of atheistic Communism. The eager readiness of some in this group to attack everyone and everything related to the efforts to expose the Communist conspiracy in this country is hardly the mark of a true "liberal." Indeed, the true liberal is opposed to everything Communism represents, for the very nature of Communism is the antithesis of liberalism.

EXCERPTS FROM THE REPORT OF THE DEFENSE DEPARTMENT'S ADVISORY COMMITTEE ON PRISONERS OF WAR

When plunged into a Communist indoctrination mill, the average American POW was under a serious handicap. Enemy political officers forced him to read Marxian literature. He was compelled to participate in debates. He had to tell what he knew about American politics and American history. And many times the Chinese or Korean instructors knew more about these subjects than he did. This brainstorming caught many American prisoners off guard. To most of them it came as a complete surprise and they were unprepared. Lectures—study groups—discussion groups—a blizzard of propaganda and hurricanes of violent oratory were all a part of the enemy technique.

A large number of American POWs did not know what the Communist program was all about. Some were confused by it. Self-seekers accepted it as an easy out. A few may have believed the business. They signed peace petitions and peddled Communist literature. It was not an inspiring spectacle. It set loyal groups against cooperative groups and broke up camp organization and discipline. It made fools of some men and tools of others. And it provided the enemy with stooges for propaganda shows. . . .

The Committee heard evidence which revealed that many of the POWs knew too little about the United States and its ideals and traditions. So the Chinese indoctrinators had the advantage.

These excerpts from the Report of the Secretary of Defense's Advisory Committee on Prisoners of War are reprinted from pages 12, 13, and 31 of *The U.S. Fighting Man's Code* (Washington, November, 1955), a publication of the Office of Armed Forces Information and Education, Department of Defense. Reprinted by permission of the Department of Defense.

The uninformed POWs were up against it. They couldn't answer arguments in favor of Communism with arguments in favor of Americanism, because they knew very little about their America. The Committee heard a number of ex-POWs who stated that a knowledge of Communism would have enabled them to expose its fallacies to their camp-mates. . . .

. . . the inability of many to speak up for Democracy distressed loyal POWs. Active collaborators aside, there were other passive prisoners that "went along." They lacked sufficient patriotism because of their limited knowledge of American Democracy. . . .

The responsibility for the maintenance and preservation of the United States and all it stands for is one which must be shared by every citizen. Every American is in the front line in the war for the minds of men.

The battlefield of modern warfare is all inclusive. Today there are no distant front lines, remote no man's lands, far-off rear areas. The home front is but an extension of the fighting front. In the dreaded event of another all-out war—a thermonuclear war—the doorstep may become the Nation's first line of defense.

EXCERPTS FROM AN ADDRESS BY SECRETARY OF STATE JOHN FOSTER DULLES, MARCH 8, 1955

I come back from Asia greatly impressed by the spirit and the purpose of the governments and peoples with whom I had contact. They want to preserve their freedom and independence. However, patriotism alone is not enough. Small nations cannot easily be self-confident when they are next door to Communist China. Its almost unlimited manpower would easily dominate, and could quickly engulf, the entire area were it not restrained by the mutual security structure which has been erected. But that struc-

The address from which these excerpts are taken was delivered by Mr. Dulles on March 8, 1955.

ture will not hold if it be words alone. Essential ingredients are the deterrent power of the United States and our willingness to use that power in response to a military challenge.

The Chinese Communists seem determined to make such a challenge. At the same time they are persistently trying to belittle our power and to throw doubt on our resolution. They boast that in 1950, in Korea, they drove the United States forces back from the Yalu and gained a great victory. They boast of their victory over the French Union forces in Indochina and they misrepresent our non-participation as due to our weaknesses of will. When we recently helped the Chinese Nationalists to evacuate the Tachens and other coastal islands, the Chinese Communists claimed that this represented great "victories" for them. They continue wrongfully to hold our fliers and other citizens.

In such ways Chinese Communist propaganda portrays the United States as being merely a "paper tiger." It suggests to the small peoples whom they threaten that the United States will always find reasons to fall back when faced by brutal and uncompromising force, and that Communist China is sure to win.

The United States, in the interest of peace, has made great sacrifices and has shown great self-restraint. That is nothing for which we should feel ashamed. Indeed, it is something in which we can take pride. But we must always remember that the free nations of the Western Pacific and Southeast Asia will quickly lose their freedom if they think that our love of peace means peace at any price. We must, if occasion offers, make it clear that we are prepared to stand firm and, if necessary, meet hostile force with the greater force that we possess.

A big step in the right direction was taken by the Congress when, at the President's request, it passed the Joint Resolution which authorized the President actually to *use* the armed forces of the United States for the defense of Formosa and, to the extent the President judges appropriate for that defense, to protect related areas in friendly hands. That non-partisan action, taken with virtual unanimity, did more than any other recent act to inspire our Asian friends with confidence in us. I believe that their confidence is not misplaced.

We have power that is great. We have a cause that is just. I do not doubt that we have the fortitude to use that power in defense of that just cause.

EXCERPTS FROM THE 1956 CHRISTMAS ADDRESS OF POPE PIUS XII

For our part We, as head of the Church, have up to now avoided, just as we did in previous cases, calling Christendom to a crusade. We can, however, call for full understanding of the fact that, where religion is a vital living heritage, men do look upon the struggle unjustly forced upon them by their enemy as a crusade.

We must with deepest sadness mourn the help given by some Catholics, both ecclesiastical and lay, to the tactics of obfuscation, calculated to bring about a result that they themselves did not intend.

How can they fail to see that such is the aim of all that insincere activity which hides under the name of "talks" and "meetings"?

Why *enter* a discussion, for that matter, without a common language?

How is it possible to meet if the paths are divergent; that is, if one party rejects or denies the common absolute values, thereby making all "co-existence in truth" unattainable?

Out of respect for the name of Christian, compliance with such tactics should cease; for, as the Apostle warns, "it is inconsistent to wish to sit at the table of God and at that of His enemies." (I Corinthians X, 21)

And if there still be any vacillating spirits, notwithstanding the black testimony of ten years of cruelty, the blood just shed and the immolation of many lives sacrificed by a martyred people should finally convince them.

We are convinced that today, too, in face of an enemy determined to impose on all peoples, in one way or another, a special and intolerable way of life, only the unanimous and courageous behavior of all who love the truth and the good can preserve peace, and will preserve it.

It would be a fatal error to repeat what, in similar circumstances, happened during the years preceding the Second World War, when all the threatened nations, and not merely the smallest, sought their safety at the expense of others, using them as shields, so to speak, and even seeking very questionable economic and political advantages from their neighbors' suffering. In the end all together were overwhelmed in the holocaust.

Present day conditions, which find no counterparts in the past, should be made clear to everyone. There is no longer room for doubt concerning the aims and methods which rely on tanks, when these latter noisily crash over borders, sowing death in order to force civilian peoples into a pattern of life they explicitly detest. . . .

It is clear that in the present circumstances there can be verified in a nation the situation wherein, every effort to avoid war being expended in vain, war—for effective self-defense and with the hope of a favorable outcome against unjust attack—could not be considered unlawful.

If, therefore, a body representative of the people and a government—both having been chosen by free elections—in a moment of extreme danger decide, by legitimate instruments of internal and external policy, on defensive precautions, and carry out the plans which they consider necessary, they do not act immorally; so that a Catholic citizen cannot invoke his own conscience in order to refuse to serve and fulfill those duties the law imposes. On this matter We feel that we are in perfect harmony with Our predecessors.

There are, then, occasions and times in the life of nations in which only recourse to higher principles can establish clearly the boundaries between right and wrong, between what is lawful and what is immoral, and bring peace to consciences faced with grave decisions. It is therefore consoling that in some countries, amid today's debates, men are talking about conscience and its demands.

Although the program which is at the foundation of the United Nations aims at the realization of absolute values in the coexistence of peoples, the recent past has, however, shown that the false realism is succeeding in prevailing in not a few of its members, even when it is a question of restoring respect for these same values of human society, openly trampled upon.

No one expects or demands the impossible, not even from the United Nations; but one should have a right to expect that their authority should have had its weight, at least through observers, in the places in which the essential values of man are in extreme danger.

Although the United Nations' condemnation of the grave violations of the rights of men and of entire nations is worthy of recognition, one can nevertheless wish that, in similar cases, the exercise of their rights, as members of this organization, be denied to states which refuse even the admission of observers—thus showing that their concept of state sovereignty threatens the very foundations of the United Nations.

This organization ought also to have the right and the power of forestalling all military intervention of one state in another, whatever be the pretext under which it is effected, and also the right and power of assuming, by means of a sufficient police force, the safeguarding of order in the state which is threatened.

EXCERPTS FROM AN ADDRESS BY GEORGE MEANY

Too many in the Free World are still prisoners of the illusion that Communism is, historically speaking, a progressive system—extreme liberalism temporarily making bad mistakes.

Actually, Communism represents darkest reaction. . . . Too many

These passages are quoted from George Meany's address to the National Religion and Labor Foundation on December 13, 1955, in New York City. Reprinted by permission of Mr. Meany.

in the Free World seem to have lost their capacity for moral indignation against the most brutal inhumanities when they are perpetrated by Communists. . . . They never find the time to utter a word of condemnation against the Communist-imperialist destruction of the national independence and democratic rights of hundreds of millions of people in Europe and Asia. . . . Many people in our country who call themselves liberals are stone silent about the Soviet concentration camps. . . . Communism is the very opposite of liberalism. Communism is the deadliest enemy of liberalism. . . . Liberals must be on guard against developing a certain type of McCarthyism of their own. They must shun like the plague the role of being anti-anti-Communist. Only by refusing to be thus entrapped can liberals shed every vestige of subconscious and conscious regard for Communism as a movement with which they have something in common. . . . Not until we of the Free World can give rebirth to a vibrant moral attitude, to a burning indignation against such frightful bestialities, can the freedom-loving peoples be sufficiently stirred to gather the moral strength for resisting and defeating the totally antimoral dogmas and deeds of Communism at home and abroad. Yes, this means above all a moral struggle against Communism. . . . No country, no people, no movement can stand aloof and be neutral in this struggle. Nehru and Tito are not neutral. They are aides and allies in fact and in effect, if not in diplomatic verbiage. . . .

In conclusion, I cannot emphasize too strongly to you: The conflict between Communism and freedom is the problem of our time. It overshadows all other problems. This conflict mirrors our age, its toils, its tensions, its troubles and its tasks. On the outcome of this conflict depends the future of all mankind.

ANTI-COMMUNIST ORGANIZATIONS

Abraham Lincoln National Republican Club, 116 S. Michigan Blvd., Chicago 3, Illinois. Edgar C. Bundy.

American Anti-Communist League, P.O. Box 365, Park Ridge, Illinois. John Crippen.

American China Policy Association, 1 West 37th Street, New York 18, New York.

American Coalition of New York, 15 Pine Street, New York 5, New York.

American Coalition of Patriotic Societies, 301 Washington Bldg., Washington 5, D. C.

American Federation of Labor Free Trade Union Committee, Box 65, Radio City Station, New York, New York.

American Friends of Russian Freedom, 270 Park Avenue, New York 7, New York.

American Friends of Vietnam, 62 West 45th Street, New York, New York.

American Jewish League Against Communism, 220 West 42nd Street, New York 36, New York. Rabbi Benjamin Schultz, Executive Director.

American Legion, 700 North Pennsylvania Street, Indianapolis, Indiana.

American Patriots Association, 15 Williams Street, New York 5, New York. Godfrey Schmidt.

Americans for Constitutional Action, c/o Admiral Ben Moreell, 3 Gateway Center, Pittsburgh 22, Pennsylvania.

Asian Peoples Anti-Communist League, Republic of China. 101 South Yen Ping Rd., Taipei, Taiwan, China.

Aware, Inc., P.O. Box 1401, Grand Central Station, New York, New York.

Catholic Information Society, 214 West 31st Street, New York, New York.

China Institute in America, 125 East 65th Street, New York, New York. A. C. Wedemeyer.

Christian Anti-Communist Crusade, P.O. Box 890, Long Beach 1, California. Dr. Fred E. Schwarz, Executive Director.

Christian Crusade, 302 N. Rosedale, Tulsa, Oklahoma.

Christophers, 18 East 48th Street, New York 17, New York. The Reverend James Keller, M.M.

Church League of America, 1407 Hill Avenue, Wheaton, Illinois.

Circuit Riders, 308 West Court Street, Cincinnati 2, Ohio. M. G. Lowman.

Citizens Foreign Policy Committee, 1 West 37th Street, New York, New York. Alfred Kohlberg.

Committee of One Million Against Admission of Communist China to the U.N., 17 Park Ave., New York 16, New York.

Committee of Patriots, 112 East 36th Street, New York, New York.

Congress of Freedom, 1330 Turner Boulevard, Omaha 5, Nebraska. George Thomas, Executive Director.

Congress of the European Center of Documentation and Information, Madrid, Spain.

Fighting Homefolks of Fighting Men, Glenwood Springs, Colorado. Captain Eugene R. Guild, National Director.

For America, 208 La Salle Street, Chicago 4, Illinois.

Foreign Policy Research Institute, c/o Dr. Robert Strausz-Hupé, Department of Political Science, University of Pennsylvania, Philadelphia, Pennsylvania.

Foundation for Economic Education, Inc., Irvington-on-Hudson, New York.

Foundation for Foreign Affairs, Inc., 64 East Jackson Boulevard, Chicago 4, Illinois.

Foundation for Religious Action, 1112 Dupont Circle Building, Washington 6, D.C. Dr. Charles Lowry.

Foundation for Social Research, 1521 Wilshire Blvd., Los Angeles, California.

Freedom Clubs, Inc., 5218 Melrose Avenue, Los Angeles, California. Dr. James Fifield, President.

Institute of Applied Citizenship, 550 Fifth Avenue, New York 36, New York. Norman Lombard, President.

Institute of Contemporary Russian Studies, Fordham University, New York, 58, New York.

Institute of Far Eastern Studies, Seton Hall University, Newark 2, New Jersey.

Institute of Foreign Trade, New York, New York. J. Anthony Marcus.

International Rescue Committee, 62 West 45th Street, New York 19, New York. Carl Spaatz.

Joint Committee Against Communism, 220 West 42nd Street, New York 36, New York. Rabbi Benjamin Schultz.

Keep America Free Council, P.O. Box 281, Canton, Ohio. Charles O'Hare.

Manion Forum, South Bend, Indiana.

National Military-Industrial Conference, 140 S. Dearborn Street, Chicago 3, Illinois.

Ohio Coalition of Patriotic Societies, Inc., Box 3111, University Station, Columbus 10, Ohio.

Pro-America, 2511 Baker Street, San Francisco, California.

Public Action, Inc., 951 Madison Avenue, New York 21, New York.

Self-Help of Emigrés from Central Europe, 147 West 42nd Street, Room 519, New York 18, New York.

Spiritual Mobilization, 1521 Wilshire Boulevard, Los Angeles, California.

Students for America, P.O. Box 2124, Hollywood 28, California.

The Alliance, Inc., 200 E. 66th Street, New York 21, New York. Colonel Archibald B. Roosevelt, President.

The Christianform, 2200 R Street, N.W., Washington, D.C. Nicholas T. Nonnenmacher, President.

The Protect America League, Inc., Box 8, Oakley Station, Cincinnati 9, Ohio. Neil E. Wetterman, President.

Tolstoy Foundation, 300 West 58th Street, New York 19, New York. Alexandra Tolstoy.

Universal Research and Consultants, Inc., Suite 221, Dupont Circle Building, Washington 6, D.C.

We the People, 111 North Wabash Avenue, Chicago 2, Illinois.

Bibliography

BOOKS

Barmine, Alexander. *One Who Survived.* Putnam.
Bentley, Elizabeth. *Out of Bondage.* Devin-Adair.
Biagoluski, Michael. *The Case of Colonel Petrov.* McGraw-Hill.
Blair, C., and J. Shepley. *The Hydrogen Bomb.* McKay.
Borkenau, Franz. *European Communism.* Praeger.
Bouscaren, Anthony T. *Imperial Communism.* Public Affairs Press.
———. *America Faces World Communism.* Vantage.
Brown, Elizabeth C. *The Enemy at His Back.* Bookmailer.
Brzezinski, Zbigniew K. *The Permanent Purge.* Harvard University Press.
Buckley, William F. *God and Man at Yale.* Regnery.
———, and Brent Bozell. *McCarthy and His Enemies.* Regnery.
Budenz, Louis F. *The Cry Is Peace.* Regnery.
———. *Men Without Faces.* Harper Brothers.
———. *Techniques of Communism.* Regnery.
Bundy, Edgar. *Collectivism in the Churches.* Devin-Adair.
Burnham, James. *Containment or Liberation.* John Day.
———. *The Web of Subversion.* John Day.
Caldwell, John. *South of Tokyo.* Regnery.
———. *Still the Rice Grows Green.* Regnery.
Calomiris, Angela. *Red Masquerade.* Lippincott.
Chamberlin, John. *National Review Reader.* Bookmailer.
Chamberlin, William H. *America's Second Crusade.* Regnery.
———. *Beyond Containment.* Regnery.
———. *The Russian Revolution.* Macmillan.
Chambers, Whittaker. *Witness.* Random House.
Ciechonowski, Jan. *Defeat in Victory.* Doubleday.

Clark, Mark. *From the Danube to the Yalu.* Harper.

Colegrove, Kenneth. *Democracy versus Communism.* Van Nostrand.

Cookridge, E. H. *The Net That Covers the World.* Henry Holt and Company.

Creel, George. *Russia's Race for Asia.* Bobbs-Merrill.

Dallin, David. *The New Soviet Empire.* Yale University Press.

———. *Slave Labor in Russia.* Yale University Press.

———. *Soviet Espionage.* Yale University Press.

D'Arcy, Martin. *Communism and Christianity.* Penguin, London.

Darke, Bob. *Cockney Communist.* John Day.

De Jaegher, Raymond J., and Irene Corbally Kuhn. *The Enemy Within.* Doubleday.

De Toledano, Ralph, and Victor Lasky. *Seeds of Treason.* Funk & Wagnalls.

De Toledano, Ralph. *Spies, Dupes, and Diplomats.* Duell, Sloan & Pearce. Little, Brown.

Dodd, Bella V. *School for Darkness.* Kenedy.

Draskovich, Slobodan M. *Tito, Moscow's Trojan Horse.* Regnery.

Ebon, Martin. *World Communism Today.* McGraw-Hill.

Einaudi, Mario. *Communism in Western Europe.* Cornell University Press.

Einsiedel, Heinrich von. *I Joined the Russians.* Yale University Press.

Evans, F. Bowen. *Worldwide Communist Propaganda Activity.* Macmillan.

Evans, Medford. *Secret War for the A-Bomb.* Regnery.

Fischer, Ruth. *Stalin and German Communism.* Harvard University Press.

Fitch, Geraldine. *Formosa Beachhead.* Regnery.

Flynn, John T. *The Road Ahead.* Devin-Adair.

———. *While You Slept.* Devin-Adair.

———. *The Lattimore Story.* Devin-Adair.

Garrett, Garet. *The People's Pottage.* The Caxton Printers.

Gitlow, Benjamin. *The Whole of Their Lives*. Scribner's.
Gliksman, Jerzy. *Tell the West*. Gresham.
Gouzenko, Igor. *Fall of a Titan*. Norton.
———. *Iron Curtain*. Dutton.
Gsovski, Vladimir. *Church and State Behind the Iron Curtain*. Praeger.
Hazlitt, Henry. *The Great Idea*. Appleton-Century-Crofts.
Hellor, Andor. *No More Comrades*. Regnery.
Herling, A. K. *Soviet Slave Empire*. Wilfred Funk.
Hildebrandt, Rainer. *The Explosion: The Uprising Behind the Iron Curtain*. Duell, Sloan & Pearce.
Hobbs, A. H. *The Claims of Sociology*. Stackpole.
Hodgkinson, Harry. *The Language of Communism*. Pitman.
Hook, Sidney. *Common Sense and the Fifth Amendment*. Macmillan.
Hoover, J. Edgar. *Master of Deceit*. Henry Holt and Company.
Huddleston, Sisley. *France: The Tragic Years, 1939–1947*. Devin-Adair.
Hughes, Frank. *Prejudice and the Press*. Devin-Adair.
Hunt, R. N. Carew. *Theory and Practice of Communism*. Macmillan.
Hunter, Edward. *Brain-washing in Red China*. Vanguard.
———. *The Story of Mary Liu*. Farrar, Straus and Cudahy.
Huszar, George. *Soviet Power and Policy*. Crowell.
Hyde, Douglas. *I Believed*. Putnam.
James, Daniel. *Red Designs for the Americas: Guatemalan Prelude*. John Day.
Joy, Admiral C. Turner. *How Communists Negotiate*. Macmillan.
Kasenkina, Oksana. *Leap to Freedom*. Lippincott.
Keller, James. *Careers That Change The World*. Doubleday.
Ketchum, Richard M. *What Is Communism?* Dutton.
Kieffer, John E. *Realities of World Power*. David McKay.
Kintner, William. *The Front Is Everywhere!* University of Oklahoma Press.

Kirkpatrick, Evron M. *Target: The World.* Macmillan.
———. *Year of Crisis.* Macmillan.
Kravchenko, Victor. *I Chose Freedom.* Scribner's.
———. *I Chose Justice.* Scribner's.
Kulski, W. W. *The Soviet Regime.* Syracuse University Press.
Lane, Arthur B. *I Saw Poland Betrayed.* Bobbs-Merrill.
Lipper, Elinor. *Eleven Years in Soviet Prison Camps.* Regnery.
Lowry, Charles. *Communism and Christ.* Morehouse-Gorham.
Lyons, Eugene. *Our Secret Allies.* Little, Brown and Company.
McCarthy, Joseph. *McCarthyism, The Fight for America.* Devin-Adair.
MacEóin, Gary, and Akos Zombory. *Communist War on Religion.* Devin-Adair.
Manly, Chesly. *The Twenty-Year Revolution.* Regnery.
———. *The UN Record.* Regnery.
Mather, John S., and Donald Seaman. *The Great Spy Scandal. Daily Express,* London.
Mikolajczyk, Stanislaw. *Rape of Poland.* McGraw-Hill.
Miller, Harry. *The Communist Menace in Malaya.* Praeger.
Mises, Ludwig von. *The Anti-Capitalistic Mentality.* Van Nostrand.
Monsterleet, Jean. *Martyrs in China.* Regnery.
———. *Red Book of the Persecuted Church.*
Moorehead, Alan. *The Traitors.* Scribner's.
Morris, Robert. *No Wonder We Are Losing.* Bookmailer.
Muhlen, Norbert. *The Return of Germany.* Regnery.
Niemeyer, Gerhart, and John S. Resheter, Jr. *An Inquiry into Soviet Mentality.* Praeger.
Noble, John. *I Was a Slave in Russia.* Devin-Adair.
Nolan, William. *Communism versus the Negro.* Regnery.
Oliver, Robert T. *Verdict in Korea.* Bald Eagle Press.
———. *Syngman Rhee.* Dodd, Mead.
Orwell, George. *Animal Farm.* Harcourt, Brace.
Palmer, Edward. *The Communist Problem in America.* Crowell.
Pasley, Virginia. *Twenty-one Stayed.* Farrar, Straus and Cudahy.

Pattee, Richard. *This Is Spain.* Bruce.
Petrov, Vladimir. *Soviet Gold.* Farrar, Straus and Cudahy.
Philbrick, Herbert. *I Led Three Lives.* Grosset and Dunlap.
Possony, Stefan. *A Century of Conflict.* Regnery.
Rawicz, Slavomir. *The Long Walk.* Harper's.
Record, Wilson. *The Negro and the Communist Party.* University of North Carolina Press.
Reinhardt, Guenther. *Crime Without Punishment.* Hermitage.
Root, E. Merrill. *Collectivism on the Campus.* Devin-Adair.
Schwartz, Harry. *Russia's Soviet Economy.* Prentice-Hall.
Sethe, Paul. *A Short History of Russia.* Regnery.
Sheed, F. J. *Communism and Man.* Sheed and Ward.
Sheen, Fulton J. *Communism and the Conscience of the West.* Bobbs-Merrill.
Smal-Stocki, Roman. *The Nationality Problem in the USSR.* Bruce.
Soloviev, Mikhail. *When the Gods Are Silent.* David McKay.
Spolansky, Jacob. *Communist Trail in America.* Macmillan.
Sternberg, Fritz. *The End of a Revolution.* John Day.
Strausz-Hupé, Robert, Cottrell, Alvin J., and James E. Dougherty. *American-Asian Tensions.*
Stripling, Robert, and Bob Considine. *Red Plot Against America.* Drexel Hill, Pennsylvania.
Thorin, Duane. *A Ride to Panmunjom.* Regnery.
Utley, Freda. *The China Story.* Regnery.
———. *Will the Middle East Go West?* Regnery.
Van der Vlugt, Ebed. *Asia Aflame: Communism in the East.* Devin-Adair.
Walker, Richard. *China Under Communism.* Yale University Press.
Walsh, Edmund. *Total Empire.* Bruce.
Weyl, Nathaniel. *The Battle Against Disloyalty.* Crowell.
White, William L. *The Captives of Korea.* Scribner's.
Whitney, Courtney. *MacArthur, His Rendezvous with History.* Knopf.

Willoughby, General. *Shanghai Conspiracy.* Dutton.
Wittmer, Felix. *The Yalta Betrayal.* The Caxton Printers.
Wormser, René. *Foundations.* Devin-Adair.

GOVERNMENT PUBLICATIONS

Department of State. *Nazi-Soviet Relations, 1939–1941.* 1947.
House Un-American Activities Committee. *Report on the Scientific and Cultural Conference for World Peace.* April 19, 1949.
———. *Guide to Subversive Organizations and Publications.* April 12, 1951.
———. *Organized Communism in the U.S.* Revised, May, 1958.
———. *Report on the Communist Peace Offensive.* April 1, 1951.
———. *Soviet Total War.* September 30, 1956. 2 vols.
———. *100 Things You Should Know About Communism.* May 14, 1951.
———. *The Great Pretense.* May 19, 1956.
———. *Cumulative Index, 1938–1954.* January 20, 1955.
———. *Consultation with Dr. Fred Schwarz on Communism.* May 29, 1957.
———. *Annual Reports.*
Report of the Commission on Government Security. June 21, 1957.
Senate Committee on Government Operations. *Congressional Investigations of Communism, Cumulative Index, 1918–1956.* July 23, 1956.
———. *Korean War Atrocities.* January 11, 1954.
Senate Internal Security Subcommittee. *Report on the Institute of Pacific Relations.* July 2, 1952.
———. *The Communist Party, USA, A Handbook for Americans.* December 21, 1955.
———. *Report on the Korean War and Related Matters.* January 21, 1955.
———. *Scope of Soviet Activity in the United States, 1956–1958.*

———. *Interlocking Subversions in Government Departments.*

———. *Soviet Political Treaties and Violations.* August 1, 1955.

———. *Annual Reports.*

———. *Activities of U.S. Citizens Employed by the United Nations.* March 22, 1954.

———. *Subversive Influence in the Educational Process.* July 17, 1953.

U.S. Atomic Energy Commission. *In the Matter of J. Robert Openheimer,* April 12, 1954–May 6, 1954.

PERIODICALS

American Legion Magazine, 720 Fifth Avenue, New York, New York.

American Mercury, 250 West 57th Street, New York 19, New York.

American Opinion, Belmont 78, Massachusetts.

Bookmailer News, Box 101, Murray Hill Station, New York 16, New York.

Communist Line Bulletin, 108 East 78th Street, New York 21, New York.

Counterattack, 42 Broadway, New York 4, New York.

Dan Smoot Report, P.O. Box 305, Dallas, Texas.

Eastern Europe, Committee for Free Europe, New York, New York.

Faith and Freedom, 1521 Wilshire Boulevard, Los Angeles, California.

Firing Line, Americanism Commission, American Legion, 1608 K Street, N.W., Washington 6, D.C.

Free Front, American-Asian Educational Exchange, Inc., 17 Park Avenue, New York 16, New York.

Free World Review, P.O. Box 1254, New York 8, New York.

Guardpost, Veterans of Foreign Wars, Wire Bldg., Washington, D.C.

Human Events, 408 First Street, S.E., Washington 3, D.C.
National Republic, 511 Eleventh Street, N.W., Washington, D.C.
National Review, 211 East 37th Street, New York 16, New York.
News and Views, 1407 Hill Avenue, Wheaton, Illinois.
New Leader, 7 East 15th Street, New York 3, New York.
Orbis, c/o Prof. Strausz-Hupe, Department of Political Science, University of Pennsylvania, Philadelphia, Pennsylvania.
The Freeman, The Foundation for Economic Education, Inc., Irvington-on-Hudson, New York.
The Tablet, 1 Hanson Place, Brooklyn, New York.
Taw, The American Way, 2501 South 43rd Street, Milwaukee 15, Wisconsin.
U.S.A., P.O. Box 134, Lenox Hill Station, New York 21, New York.
U.S. News & World Report, 435 Parker Avenue, Dayton 1, Ohio.
Wanderer, 128 East 10th Street, St. Paul 1, Minnesota.

NEWSPAPER COLUMNISTS AND COMMENTATORS

Hanson Baldwin
Constantine Brown
George Rothwell Brown
William H. Chamberlin
Bob Considine
Willard Edwards
John T. Flynn
Richard Harkness
Paul Harvey
Robert F. Hurleigh
Arthur Krock
David Lawrence
Fulton Lewis, Jr.
Raymond Moley
Herbert Philbrick
Daniel Poling
Victor Riesel
Harvy Schwartz
Robert Siegrist
George Sokolsky
Walter Trohan